Ludwig Wittgenstein:
Cambridge Letters

B

Ludwig Wittgenstein: Cambridge Letters

Correspondence with Russell, Keynes, Moore, Ramsey and Sraffa

Edited by Brian McGuinness
and G. H. von Wright

BLACKWELL
Oxford UK & Cambridge USA

Copyright © Blackwell Publishers 1995

Some material used in this book appeared previously in *Letters to Russell, Keynes and Moore* (Blackwell Publishers 1974, second impression 1977)

First published 1995
Reprinted 1996

Blackwell Publishers Ltd
108 Cowley Road
Oxford OX4 1JF
UK

Blackwell Publishers Inc.
238 Main Street
Cambridge, Massachusetts 02142
USA

British Library Cataloguing in Publication Data

A CIP catalogue record for this book is available from the British Library.

Library of Congress Cataloging-in-Publication Data

Wittgenstein, Ludwig, 1889–1951.
[Cambridge letters]
Ludwig Wittgenstein, Cambridge letters: correspondence with Russell, Keynes, Moore, Ramsey, and Sraffa / edited by Brian McGuinness and G.H. von Wright.
p. cm.
ISBN 0–631–19015–5 (alk. paper)
1. Wittgenstein, Ludwig, 1889–1951—Correspondence. 2. Philosophers, Modern—England—Cambridge—Correspondence. 3. Cambridge (England)—Intellectual life—20th century.
I. McGuinness, Brian.   II. Wright, G. H. von (Georg Henrik), 1916–.
III. Title.   IV. Title: Cambridge letters.
B3376.W564A4   1995
192—dc20   94–40727
[B]   CIP
Typeset in 11 on 13pt Bembo
by Pure Tech Corporation, Pondicherry, India.
Printed in Great Britain by Hartnolls Ltd, Bodmin, Cornwall
This book is printed on acid-free paper.

Contents

Acknowledgements

For permission to use copyright material in text and notes the editors are indebted to: the Wittgenstein Trustees; the Bertrand Russell Archives of McMaster University, Hamilton, Ontario; the Library of King's College Cambridge, for all Keynes material; Mr Timothy Moore; Mrs Jane Burch and the University of Pittsburgh Library (Special Collections) for Ramsey material; Professor Pierangelo Garegnani for the letter of Piero Sraffa.

The letters from Russell to Lady Ottoline Morrell are in the Humanities Research Center of the University of Texas at Austin. For access to material, for wise advice, and for useful information the editors are much indebted to Dr Kenneth Blackwell of the Bertrand Russell Archives, Miss Jackie Cox, Keeper of Modern Archives at King's College, Cambridge, and Miss Kathleen Cann of the Cambridge University Library. Dr David McKitterick, the Librarian of Trinity College, Cambridge, helped them on many college points and, on general matters they also consulted Dr Joachim Schulte, a colleague for many years in these studies. In which indeed their own involvement has been so long that they are aware, not without some melancholy, of the cloud of witnesses, thanked at best in some previous publication but now no longer living, to whom they largely owe such knowledge as they can here deploy.

The newly discovered letters to Wittgenstein were generously communicated to them by Frau Charlotte Eder of Vienna and Professor Walther Methlagl of the Brenner Archive at the University of Innsbruck where the letters, including those from Keynes to Wittgenstein, are deposited. For copies of previously known letters to Wittgenstein from Keynes and Ramsey they thank, as in earlier volumes, Professor Hermann Hänsel of Vienna. In the preparation of the material for the press they have been much assisted by Miss Miriam Grottanelli de Santi of Siena. Also invaluable was the collaboration in Helsinki of Mr Heikki Nyman.

Brian McGuinness
G. H. von Wright

Introduction

The present volume contains the correspondence, or the bulk of what is known to have survived of it, between Wittgenstein and the chief of his Cambridge friends, by which we mean those who can fairly be regarded as his equals or even mentors rather than his disciples – Bertrand Russell, G. E. Moore, J. M. Keynes, and later Frank Ramsey and (represented by a single but important letter) Piero Sraffa.

The volume differs considerably from our previous Blackwell volume, *Letters to Russell, Keynes and Moore* (1974, second impression 1977) though nearly everything in that volume occurs also here. In the first place there is the inclusion of Ramsey, whose importance for Wittgenstein's development is increasingly being recognized. Then there are a number of hitherto unknown letters from Wittgenstein discovered in each of the main collections (the Bertrand Russell Archives at McMaster University, the Keynes papers in the Modern Archive Room of King's College, Cambridge, and the Moore Collection in the Cambridge University Library). Furthermore (fulfilling a hope expressed by G.H.v.W. in the previous volume) there has been the discovery of a good number of letters to Wittgenstein, principally from the years 1914–23, which have enabled us to make this more truly a volume of correspondence. The reactions of the others are often as interesting

as Wittgenstein's own. The arrangement is now a single chronological one, which we hope makes for more natural reading and
consultation. Finally the passage of time has altered our attitude
towards footnotes. We have found it both necessary and possible to
explain more points in the letters as their temporal context recedes
and as archival material relevant to them becomes more accessible.

No more than the previous one is this book meant as an introduction to Wittgenstein and his circle. Some general acquaintance
and interest is presupposed. But its publication will be justified if it
conveys a picture of an important side of Wittgenstein's development. He appears here in turn shy and affectionate, fierce and
censorious, happy to collaborate and sure of his own judgement.
Four quarrels and four reconciliations are documented. His
struggles to publish the *Tractatus* can be followed, his retreat from
the world, his being wooed back to philosophy by Keynes and
Ramsey, later plans of his too to leave philosophy, all in the end
reversed. A constant theme, despite ambivalence, is the pull of the
Cambridge that these friends represented. It was as important to
him as his solitudes. *Hinc lucem et pocula sacra* is the university's
motto, and he indeed managed to draw from it light and draughts
of inspiration.

Wittgenstein first came to see Russell at Cambridge on 18
October 1911[1] and seems to have stayed until Christmas, though he
was still registered as studying at the University of Manchester for
that autumn. He was admitted as a member of Cambridge University and of Trinity College on 1 February 1912. His status was at
first that of an undergraduate. At the beginning of June the Degree
Committee of the Special Board for Moral Science admitted him as
an Advanced Student to a Course of Research and 'asked Mr.
Bertrand Russell to be kind enough to act as the Director and
Supervisor of the Student.'[2]

---

[1] Letter from Russell to Lady Ottoline Morrell of that date.
[2] Letter of 5 June 1912 from J. N. Keynes (father of J. M. Keynes and University
Registrary) to Dr W. M. Fletcher, Tutor at Trinity College.

Wittgenstein was in residence during all three terms in the year 1912 and during the Lent and Easter Terms of 1913. The greater part of the academic year 1913–14 he spent in Norway, thinking and writing on his own. In April G. E. Moore visited him there. Wittgenstein had returned to Austria for the summer and in August 1914, immediately after the outbreak of the war, he volunteered for the Austro-Hungarian Army. After its surrender in November 1918 he was made a prisoner of war in Italy, spending most of his captivity at Cassino, between Rome and Naples, where he remained until August 1919. He had with him a completed typescript of his early work, the *Tractatus*. He was able to send this to Russell from the prison camp through the intermediacy of another of his friends from Cambridge, John Maynard Keynes.

In December 1919, and thus not long after his release from captivity, Wittgenstein was able to meet Russell at The Hague (it was evidently still necessary to go to a neutral country) where the two friends had an impassioned discussion of the work (letters nos 70–81). On his return to England, Russell wrote an introduction to it (of which Wittgenstein did not approve) and was in other ways instrumental in ensuring its publication both in Germany and in England (letters nos 89–101). The two met again at Innsbruck in 1922 (no. 102 and notes). It turned out to be a somewhat sour encounter, after which their friendship was never restored to what it had been before, though there are at first a couple of amiable letters (nos 103 and 104).

These were the years in which Wittgenstein relinquished his whole fortune to his family and withdrew from philosophy to become a teacher in elementary schools in more or less remote villages in Lower Austria (1920–26), but this did not mean a complete break in his relations with Cambridge. Early in 1923 he wrote to Keynes seeking renewed contact (no. 105). The letter remained unanswered for a whole year, but in the meantime (in September 1923) a young friend of Keynes's from Cambridge, the brilliant mathematician and philosopher, Frank Ramsey, who had translated the *Tractatus* for C. K. Ogden, came to see Wittgenstein at Puchberg am Schneeberg. He seems to have stayed there for at least two weeks and to have had long discussions daily with Wittgenstein, who explained the *Tractatus* to him. One result of these talks was a number of corrections made both to the German text and to the English version,[3] most of which were incorporated in the second impression of 1933. No doubt Ramsey's reports were what stirred Keynes to generous efforts to secure Wittgenstein's return to Cambridge (see nos 111, 112 and 115). There is evidence that in the autumn of 1923 Wittgenstein himself was contemplating the possibility of giving up his job as a teacher and coming to Cambridge to complete his work for a degree. But a year later he declined Keynes's invitation, explaining his reasons both to Keynes himself and to Ramsey, who was once again on a visit to Austria. In August 1925, however, Wittgenstein did visit England, stayed with Keynes and met Ramsey and other friends. Keynes helped him to pay for this trip (nos 120–121).

In the years 1926 to 1928 Wittgenstein was principally engaged on the construction of a house for his sister in Vienna, but at the same time, courted by Moritz Schlick and some of the philosophers round him, he slowly renewed his contact with philosophy.[4] When the house was complete, he went to Cambridge at the beginning of 1929, ostensibly for a holiday, but in fact (as when he left Manchester for Cambridge in 1911) he soon decided to stay. It seems likely that he had once again been gripped by the fascination of philosophy.

It is a coincidence worth recording that on the occasion of this return to Cambridge Wittgenstein found himself on the same train from London as G. E. Moore. The friendship of the two had gone through a crisis soon after Moore's visit to Norway in 1914 (nos 45 and 47) and there had apparently been no direct contact between them for fifteen years. From the time of Wittgenstein's return their friendship was resumed and it remained unbroken until

---

[3] See C. Lewy, "A Note on the Text of the *Tractatus*", *Mind* N.S. 76, 1967 and letters 107 and 116 below.

[4] Cf. the account by the late Herbert Feigl, "The Wiener Kreis in America", in *Perspectives in American History*, vol. II, Harvard University Press, 1968, p. 639.

Wittgenstein's death. Wittgenstein's letters bear witness to the deep affection and respect he had for Moore in spite of the fundamental dissimilarity of the two men's personalities and thinking.

On his arrival in Cambridge Wittgenstein at first stayed in King's College as the guest of Keynes. From there he moved to the house of Frank and Lettice Ramsey. With Ramsey (as with Moore) he evidently quickly overcame an estrangement which had suspended all personal correspondence since 1925. Wittgenstein's notebooks from this period (like his later introduction to *Philosophical Investigations*) testify to the pleasure he took in philosophical discussion with Ramsey and the value he attached to it. Ramsey was to die at the beginning of 1930 at the age of twenty-eight.

Wittgenstein was readmitted to Trinity and the university on 18 January 1929. He kept residence during the Lent and Easter Terms, proceeding to the Ph.D. degree on 18 June, the *Tractatus* being accepted as a thesis. Ramsey was formally his supervisor and Moore and Russell his examiners. (For most of this period he lodged with the economist and Marxist, Maurice Dobb.) He also resided (now in the house of Mrs Quiggin in Grantchester Road) for the three terms of 1929–30 and the Michaelmas Term 1930. During the academic year 1929–30 he was paid a small sum in respect of lectures on philosophical logic given at the invitation of the Moral Sciences Faculty Board. This was converted into a Faculty Lecturership in October 1930, and continued on the same basis in the following years. He was elected a Fellow of Trinity College under Title B on 5 December 1930, and returned to his old rooms in college. After a prolongation the fellowship eventually expired at the end of the academic year 1935–6, when his Faculty Lecturership also came to an end.

About this time (see letter no. 154 and notes) it seems to have been Wittgenstein's general plan, often modified by circumstances, to publish his results if possible and to leave academic life, at any rate as far as England was concerned. In September 1935 he visited the Soviet Union with the idea of starting a new life there and in early 1938 he thought of taking up the study of medicine, perhaps in Ireland. In between, with no post, he spent the remainder of 1936 (after the expiry of his fellowship) and much of 1937 in his cabin in Norway, preparing his book for publication and meditating on what he saw as his own shortcomings. One upshot of the latter preoccupation was a series of confessions which he made to family and friends (including Keynes and Moore) at the beginning of 1937, while the former activity did eventually lead to his offering an early version of *Philosophical Investigations* to the Cambridge University Press, though it is not clear that it was complete and he had difficulty finding a good translator. He had not always been whole-hearted about publication, since, for a period at the beginning of 1938, he appears (see letter no. 173) to have contemplated placing his papers in Trinity College Library for possible publication after his death (which is more or less what did in the end happen).

The annexation of Austria in March 1938 altered Wittgenstein's preoccupations, perhaps decisively. He had to consider his own situation, whether to change his nationality and if so what new nationality to seek, and, a related problem, what to do to help his family, threatened with racial persecution. He had also to find an occupation. The letters show how he resolved these problems with the help and advice of Keynes and Sraffa. In fact he set in train an application for British naturalization, which took almost exactly a year in coming. Also he resumed his previous teaching activities, to a select group on some occasions in Lent Term 1938, more regularly, though still gratis, in the Easter Term. No position as Faculty Lecturer was now available and, though some payment was made for the academic year 1938–9, he was told that such payments could not be guaranteed beyond that period.

In early 1939 Wittgenstein applied for the Professorship of Philosophy (to be vacated by Moore in October) and was elected, again having sought the help and advice of Keynes, though in truth little assistance was needed. In October he took up the chair and was re-elected at Trinity, this time to a Professorial Fellowship. He remained in office, with leave, at first for war work then for writing, during 1943 and 1944. He resumed his professorial duties in January 1945 and continued to discharge them until the summer of 1947: Michaelmas Term of that year was a period of sabbatical leave and he formally resigned his Fellowship and Professorship at the end of the calendar year.

During most of his time at Cambridge (for the qualification, see letter no. 160) Wittgenstein was much interested in the activities of the philosophical discussion society there, the Moral Sciences Club, and it is frequently referred to in the letters. He it was who first proposed, in 1912, the election of a standing Chairman to guide the discussions. For a long period this was Moore, but at the end Wittgenstein largely succeeded him in this role as well as in the chair of philosophy. Wittgenstein followed the proceedings of the Club with almost as much intensity as he devoted to the organization of his own lectures or classes.[5]

After resigning as professor, Wittgenstein continued to work on philosophy in Ireland and during visits to the United States or even Vienna. He also moved between Oxford and Cambridge. His fatal illness pronounced itself in the course of 1949 and he died at Cambridge in April 1951. Keynes, like Ramsey, had pre-deceased him, dying in 1946; Russell he had long lost contact with; and of the friends represented here only Moore attended his burial.

Such was the life revolving round Cambridge that these letters illustrate. We now have sixty of them from Wittgenstein to Bertrand Russell and twenty-one in the opposite direction, twenty-nine letters to Keynes and nine from him, and sixty-five letters or other communications worthy of note to Moore with two replies. Only one personal letter from Wittgenstein to Ramsey is known, but we have the beginning of a draft of a letter evidently written in 1923 and part of a letter from 1927. This is in fact a short essay on the concept of identity in answer to some points in Ramsey's paper 'The Foundations of Mathematics'. Nine letters or brief communications from Ramsey to Wittgenstein, and two longer drafts of letters, are preserved. Possibly they are all that existed.

Wittgenstein usually observed the practice of keeping letters of any importance or interest. This was probably true even before the

---

[5] For examples of this see Theodore Redpath, *Ludwig Wittgenstein, A Student's Memoir*, London: Duckworth, 1990, pp. 77 ff.

First World War, for it is hard to imagine Wittgenstein destroying Russell's letters, for example. But anything from that period is probably irremediably lost. We have already mentioned the collection of letters from the period of the war and the early 1920s recently rediscovered. They were kept in one of his family's houses, but knew strange fates, and were saved owing to the quick perceptions of Frau Charlotte Eder of Vienna. For a later part of the 1920s, while he was still living in Austria, he made the house of his friend, Ludwig Hänsel, his centre and left a number of letters there for safe keeping. Finally a considerable collection, now somewhat dispersed, of letters that he had received in Cambridge in the 1930s and 1940s was among his papers at the time of his death. In the case of some friends and perhaps all family members he kept every letter, but in other cases only a letter or two, perhaps a particularly characteristic one as a kind of memento.[6] This was natural in the case of Cambridge friends and colleagues, where the correspondence mostly served to make arrangements to meet, while the relationship was essentially conducted face to face. The two letters from Moore printed here are probably all of his that Wittgenstein kept, and we could include as many as nine from Keynes only because the latter often kept carbon copies of letters despatched. Sraffa's important letter was a singleton in Wittgenstein's bundles.

On the other side, Russell and Keynes kept nearly all papers of any interest. Sraffa's collection suffered in his last years, and all letters from Wittgenstein are still missing. Of Moore it may fairly be said that he hoarded every scrap. Thus as well as all the letters and brief communications printed here, there are a mass of Christmas and Easter cards from Wittgenstein. It is of some interest to note that while from Vienna Wittgenstein would send chaste cards with Biedermaier views of the Josefsplatz or the like – the sort of thing his sisters would order from a Kohlmarkt stationer in boxes – his English cards were chosen especially for the banality of the illustrations and of the accompanying verses, as for example:

---

[6] So, for example, a longish letter full of news and plans from Miss Ambrose, his keeping which helps to put letters 151.–153. in perspective.

If wishes count, you'll surely have
Life's blessings rich and true
For I am wishing from my heart
Such good things all for you.

These were not the cards usually exchanged at Cambridge, but (it is legitimate to suppose) the clumsy sincerity of a different level of English life was more acceptable to him; and, as for taste, he was chiefly concerned to avoid the half and half.[7]

Some of the letters to Russell (also one from him) and fragments from letters to Keynes and Ramsey are in German. They are so printed but an English version is provided. B.McG. is responsible for these and for occasional other translations, including that of the poem referred to in letter no. 190.

Wittgenstein's English of the earlier years was not always idiomatic, and his spelling, whether in English or in German, was never entirely sure. The editors' policy has been not to interfere with grammar and idiom at all. The English orthography and occasionally also the punctuation has usually been corrected without indication. German orthography too has been corrected where it was obviously erroneous. Words or parts of words in square brackets are the editors' insertions.

A characteristic of Wittgenstein's style is his use of underlinings to give emphasis to words and phrases. Words once underlined are here printed in italics; words twice underlined in small capitals; words thrice underlined in normal capitals; and words four times underlined in normal capitals underlined.

The letters are numbered in what is taken to be their chronological order. For letters that have been printed previously the number then assigned is indicated or a page reference is given. The previous publications referred to are *Letters to Russell, Keynes and Moore*, mentioned above; *Briefe* (Suhrkamp: Frankfurt am Main, 1980); *Letters to C. K. Ogden* (London: Routledge and Kegan Paul

---

[7] Redpath, *Ludwig Wittgenstein, A Student's Memoir*, pp. 94–5, in the course of making a similar observation, says that Wittgenstein was avoiding "the aesthetic".

and Basil Blackwell (jointly), Oxford, London, and Boston, 1973) – for all of the above Wittgenstein is given as the author; and "Unpublished correspondence between Russell and Wittgenstein" (credited to the present editors) in *russell*, N.S. vol. 10, no. 2, 1990–1.

Letters

1 .   **LW – BR**

4 Rose Cr[escent, Cambridge]
Tuesday 1 *a*:m
[Probably June 1912]

DEAR MR RUSSELL,

I feel very much tempted to write to you although I have very
little to say. I have just been reading a part of Moore's Principia
Ethica: (now please don't be shocked) I do not like it at all. (Mind
you, quite *apart* from disagreeing with most of it.) I don't believe –
or rather I am sure – that it cannot dream of comparing with Frege's
or your own works (except perhaps some of the Phil[osophical]
Essays). Moore repeats himself dozens of times, what he says in 3
pages could – I believe – easily be expressed in half a page. *Unclear
statements don't get a bit clearer by being repeated!!* – The concert
of the 7th of June was most gorgeous! I wish you had heard it. I
need not say that I miss you awfully and that I wish I knew how
you are and that I am

Yours most, etc.

LUDWIG WITTGENSTEIN

P.S. My logic is all in the melting-pot.

R.1   Briefe 1

Philosophical Essays.—In its first edition (1910) this collection of Russell's contained
a number of papers "concerned with ethical subjects" ("The Elements of Ethics",
"The Free Man's Worship" etc.), which are probably referred to here.
concert of the 7th of June. – That of the Cambridge University Musical Society. A Miss
Harrison performed in Beethoven's Violin Concerto.

2.   **LW – BR**

Cambridge 22.6.12.

DEAR RUSSELL,

There are yet some nice events happening in one's life e.g.
getting a letter from you (thanks *very* much for it). Much less nice
is the following event: I had a discussion with Myers about the
relations between Logic and Psychology. I was very candid and I
am sure he thinks that I am the most arrogant devil who ever lived.
Poor Mrs Myers who was also present got – I think – quite wild
about me. However, I think he was a bit less confused after the
discussion than before. – Whenever I have time I now read James's
"Varieties of religious exp[erience]". This book does me a *lot* of
good. I don't mean to say that I will be a saint soon, but I am not
sure that it does not improve me a little in a way in which I would
like to improve *very much*: namely I think that it helps me to get rid
of the *Sorge* (in the sense in which Goethe used the word in the 2ⁿᵈ
part of Faust). Logic is still in the melting-pot but one thing gets
more and more obvious to me: The prop[osition]s of Logic contain
ONLY APPARENT variables and whatever may turn out to be
the proper explanation of apparent variables, its consequence *must*
be that there are NO *logical* constants.

Myers. – Charles Samuel Myers (1873–1946) taught psychology at Cambridge and
founded the psychological laboratory there in 1912. One of Myers' special interests
was the psychology of music, a topic on which Wittgenstein made some
experimental research during his studies at Cambridge. In a letter to Lady Ottoline
Morrell, Russell tells that Wittgenstein, at the opening of the laboratory in May
1913, had exhibited an apparatus for psychological investigation of rhythm. Cf. also
3. and 41., and *A Portrait of Wittgenstein as a Young Man, From the Diary of David
Hume Pinsent 1912–1914*, ed. G. H. von Wright, with an introduction by Anne
Pinsent Keynes, p. 3 and passim.

Logic must turn out to be of a TOTALLY different kind than any other science.

The piece of poetry which you sent me is *most* splendid! DO come to Cambridge soon.

Yours most, etc.

LUDWIG WITTGENSTEIN

I am staying here till about the 20th of July.

R.2   Briefe 2

poetry. – Perhaps by Russell, who had in April and May 1912 written several poems and showed them to Lady Ottoline.

3.   **LW – BR**

1.7.12.

DEAR RUSSELL,

Thank you very much for your kind letter.

Will you think that I have gone mad if I make the following suggestion?: The sign $(x).\varphi x$ is not a complete symbol but has meaning only in an inference of the kind: from $\vdash \varphi x \supset_x \psi x.\varphi(a)$ follows ψa. Or more generally: from $\vdash(x).\varphi x.\varepsilon_0(a)$ follows $\varphi(a)$. I am – of course – most uncertain about the matter but something of the sort might really be true. I am sorry I cannot spend as much time on thinking about this stuff as I would like to because I have to write a *most* absurd paper on rhythms for the psychological meeting on the 13th. – I hear just now that a sister of mine is going to visit me here on the 6th. Would you mind me introducing her to you? She ought to see everything worth seeing!

Yours most, etc.

LUDWIG WITTGENSTEIN

R.3   Briefe 3

---

paper on rhythms. – Probably on the difference between perceived and real rhythms, see B. McG., *Young Ludwig*, pp. 125–8.

a sister of mine. – This was Wittgenstein's eldest sister, Hermine, who records a meeting with Russell in her memoirs of the family (see R. Rhees, *L. Wittgenstein, Personal Recollections*, pp. 3 and 15).

4.　　　　　　LW – BR

Hochreit
Post Hohenberg
N[ieder]-Ö[sterreich]
[Summer 1912]

DEAR RUSSELL,

The above address and this perfectly earthly writing paper will show you that I am not in hell. In fact I am quite well again and philosophizing for all I am worth. What troubles me most at present, is not the apparent-variable-business, but rather the meaning of "∨", ".", "⊃" etc. This latter problem is – I think – still more fundamental and, if possible, still less recognized as a problem. *If* "p ∨ q" means a complex at all – which is quite doubtful – *then*, as far as I can see, one must treat "∨" as *part* of a copula, in the way we have talked over before. I have – I believe – tried all possible ways of solution *under that hypothesis* and found that if any one will do it *must* be something like this: Let us write the prop[osition]

The dating of the letter is by Russell.

Hochreit. – The estate Hochreit in Lower Austria had belonged to Wittgenstein's father since 1894. The family used to live there during the summer. Later in life too, when he had again settled at Cambridge, Wittgenstein often visited the Hochreit and worked there. A considerable part of his literary Nachlass was stored at the Hochreit and discovered after his death.

this perfectly earthly writing paper . . . not in hell. – The allusion seems to be lost, thought it may be connected with Russell's exclamation to Wittgenstein, 'Logic is hell!', recounted to and then by Norman Malcolm, *Memoir*, p. 57.

"from ⊢p and ⊢q follows ⊢r" that way: "i[p; q; r]". Here "i" is a copula (we may call it inference) which copulates *complexes*. Then "$\varepsilon_1(x, y) .v.\varepsilon_1(u, z)$" is to mean:

" ⊢$(\varepsilon_1(x, y), \varepsilon_1(z, u), \beta(x, y, z, u))$. $i[\varepsilon_1(x, y); \varepsilon_1(z, u); \beta(x, y, z, u)]$
⊢$(\varepsilon_1(x, y), \varepsilon_1(z, u), \beta(x, y, z, u))$. $i[\sim\varepsilon_1 (x, y); \varepsilon_1(z, u); \beta(x, y, z, u)]$
⊢$(\varepsilon_1(x, y), \varepsilon_1(z, u), \beta(x, y, z, u))$. $i[\varepsilon_1 (x, y); \sim\varepsilon_1(z, u); \beta(x, y, z, u)]$
⊢$(\varepsilon_1(x, y), \varepsilon_1(z, u), \beta(x, y, z, u))$. $i[\sim\varepsilon_1 (x, y); \sim\varepsilon_1 (z, u); \beta(x, y, z, u)]$
⊢ $\beta(x, y, z, u)$".

If "p ∨ q" does not mean a complex, then heaven knows what it means!! –

Now I would like to know how you are and *all* about you! If you are so good to write to me, please write to the following address:

> L. W. *junior* (please don't forget this)
> bei Paul Wittgenstein
> Oberalm bei Hallein
> Salzburg Austria

We have excellent weather here, such that one can do most thinking in the open air. There is nothing more wonderful in the world than the *true* problems of Philosophy.

Always yours most, etc.

LUDWIG WITTGENSTEIN

R.4 *Briefe 4*

"p ∨ q".—There seems to be an error in the symbolic expression for a disjunction above. The fourth inference should be '$i[\sim\varepsilon_1(x, y); \sim\varepsilon_1(z, u); \sim\beta(x, y, z, u)]$'. Also the order of the variables in the definiendum should be '$\varepsilon_1 (z, u)$'.

L. W. junior. – An uncle of Wittgenstein's was also called Ludwig (or Louis).

Paul Wittgenstein. – Another uncle of Ludwig Wittgenstein's. He seems to have been the only one in the family circle who encouraged Ludwig's work in philosophy. In an early version of the Preface to the *Tractatus* Wittgenstein acknowledges his gratitude to his uncle for this.

5.   **LW – BR**

Oberalm bei Hallein
Salzburg
16.8.12.

DEAR RUSSELL,

Thanks for your letter. I am glad you read the lives of Mozart and Beethoven. These are the actual sons of God. Now as to "p ∨ q", etc.: I have thought that possibility – namely that all our troubles could be overcome by assuming different sorts of Relations of signs to things – over and over and over again! for the last 8 weeks!!! But I have come to the conclusion that this assumption does *not* help us a bit. In fact if you work out ANY such theory – I believe you will see that *it does not even touch our problem*. I have lately seen a new way out (or perhaps not out) of the difficulty. It is too long to be explained here, but I tell you so much that it is based on new forms of propositions. For instance: ∼(p. q), which is to mean "the complex p has the opposite form of q's form". That means that ∼(p. q) holds for instance when p is $\varepsilon_1(a, b)$ and q is $\sim\varepsilon_1(c, d)$. Another instance of the new forms is ψ(p, q, r) which means something like: "The form of the comp[lex] r is composed of the forms of p and q in the way 'or'." That means that ψ(p, q, r) holds for instance when p is $\varepsilon_1(a, b)$, q is $\varepsilon_1(c, d)$ and r is $\varepsilon_1 (e, f) \vee \varepsilon_1(g, h)$ etc. The rest I leave to your imagination. All this however seems to me *not half* as important as the fact (if it is one) that the whole problem has become very much clearer to me now than it has ever been before. I wish you were here and I could tell you the whole matter for I cannot write it down; it is MUCH too long! Also the app[arent] var[iable]-business has become by far clearer.

Do write again SOON!

Yours most, etc.

LUDWIG WITTGENSTEIN
I feel like mad.

R.5   Briefe 5

6.   **LW – BR**

[Summer 1912]

DEAR RUSSELL,

I believe that our problems can be traced down to the *atomic* prop[osition]s. This you will see if you try to explain precisely in what way the Copula in such a prop[osition] has meaning.

I cannot explain it and I think that as soon as an exact answer to this question is given the problems of "∨" and of the app[arent] var[iable] will be brought *very* near their solution if not solved. I therefore now think about "Socrates is human". (Good old Socrates!). My Iceland boat leaves Leith on the 7th and I am going to be in Cambridge and London from the 3rd to the 6th. I wonder if I can see you anywhere in that time? I have just read "Chadschi-Murat" by Tolstoy! Have you ever read it? If not, you ought to for it is *wonderful*. I am awfully sorry you have such beastly weather in England! Come with me to Iceland!

Yours most, etc., etc.

L. WITTGENSTEIN

R.6   Briefe 7

My Iceland boat. – Wittgenstein and his friend David Pinsent left Leith, the port of Edinburgh, on 7th September 1912 for a journey to Iceland which lasted four weeks. For details of their journey, see *A Portrait*, pp. 9–32.

7.   **LW – BR**

IV. Alleegasse 16
Wien
26.12.12.

DEAR RUSSELL,

On arriving here I found my father *very* ill. There is no hope that
he may recover. These circumstances have – I am afraid – rather
lamed my thoughts and I am muddled although I struggle against it.

I had a long discussion with Frege about our Theory of Symbolism of which, I think, he roughly understood the general outline.
He said he would think the matter over. The complex problem is
now clearer to me and I hope very much that I may solve it. I wish
I knew how you are and what sort of time you are having, and all
about you!

Yours ever most, etc.

LUDWIG WITTGENSTEIN

R.7   Briefe 8

Alleegasse. – The street in which the house belonging to Wittgenstein's parents
stood, a pompous building in nineteenth-century baroque style. The name of the
street was later changed to Argentinierstrasse. It was in this house that Wittgenstein
stored the manuscript writings from the time of the germination of the *Tractatus*
which, on his last visit to Vienna round the New Year 1950, he ordered to be
burnt. (See Editor's Preface to *Notebooks 1914–1916*).

8.   **LW – JMK**

IV. Alleegasse 16
3.1.13.

DEAR KEYNES,

Thanks for your very kind letter. I thought of writing to you just before I got it to tell you that I will not be able to come over to England until or after the beginning of term, there being all sorts of troubles at home. – I excuse your slanging Philosophy as you were just coming from McTaggart and just thinking of me when you did it. I am very glad to hear that you had a good time.

Yours, etc., etc.

LUDWIG WITTGENSTEIN

K. 1   *Briefe 9*

troubles at home. – Wittgenstein is evidently referring to the serious illness of his father mentioned in 7.

McTaggart. – J. McT. E. McTaggart (1866–1925), Fellow and Lecturer of Trinity College, Cambridge, an Hegelian, one of Cambridge's leading philosophers.

just thinking of me. – Presumably a miswriting, by dittography, for "not thinking of me".

9.   **LW – BR**

IV. Alleegasse 16
Wien
6.1.13.

DEAR RUSSELL,

I am very sorry not yet to have had a line from you!!! Not that there was anything in my last letter to you, that wanted answering; but you might have guessed that I feel von allen guten Geistern verlassen and that therefore I want a letter from you very necessarily. However – I may not be able to come back to Cambridge at the beginning of Term, as the illness of my poor father is growing very rapidly.

The Complex Problem is getting clearer to me every day and I wish I could write clear enough to let you know what I think of it. Logic is a very good Invention.

Immer der Ihrige

LUDWIG WITTGENSTEIN

R. 8   Briefe 10

---

von allen guten Geistern verlassen / *abandoned by all good spirits* (colloquially used to mean: "beside myself", "out of my mind").

Immer der Ihrige. – yours ever.

10.　　　　　　　　　　**LW – BR**

IV. Alleegasse 16
Jan[uary] 1913

DEAR RUSSELL,

Thanks *very* much for both your kind letters! I cannot yet tell
when I shall be able to come back to Cambridge, as the doctors are
still quite uncertain about the duration of my father's illness. He has
not yet any pains but feels on the whole *very* bad having constantly
high fever. This makes him so apathetic that one cannot do him any
good by sitting at his bed, etc. And as this was the only thing that I
could ever do for him, I am now perfectly useless here. So the time
of my staying here depends entirely upon whether the illness will
take so rapid a course that I could not risk to leave Vienna; or not.
I hope I shall be able to decide this in a week's time and I have told
Fletcher so. – I have changed my views on "atomic" complexes: I
now think that Qualities, Relations (like Love), etc. are all copulae!
That means I for instance analyse a subject-predicate prop[osition],
say, "Socrates is human" into "Socrates" and "Something is
human" (which I think is not complex). The reason for this, is a
very fundamental one: I think that there cannot be different Types
of things! In other words whatever can be symbolized by a simple
proper name must belong to one type. And further: every theory of
types must be rendered superfluous by a proper theory of the
symbolism: For instance if I analyse the prop[osition] Socrates is
mortal into Socrates, Mortality and $(\exists x, y) \varepsilon_1(x, y)$ I want a theory
of types to tell me that "Mortality is Socrates" is nonsensical,
because if I treat "Mortality" as a proper name (as I did) there is

Letter dated by Russell

Fletcher. – W. M. Fletcher (1873–1933), later Sir Walter, physiologist and adminis-
trator, was a Fellow of Trinity College, where he was at this time Wittgenstein's
Tutor.

nothing to prevent me to make the substitution the wrong way round. *But* if I analyse [it] (as I do now) into Socrates and (∃x)x is mortal or generally into x and (∃x)φ(x)* it becomes impossible to substitute the wrong way round, because the two symbols are now of a different *kind* themselves. What I am *most* certain of is not however the correctness of my present way of analysis, but of the fact that all theory of types must be done away with by a theory of symbolism showing that what seem to be *different kinds of things* are symbolised by different kinds of symbols which *cannot* possibly be substituted in one another's places. I hope I have made this fairly clear!

I was *very* interested to hear your views about matter, although I cannot imagine your way of working from sense-data forward. Mach writes such a horrid style that it makes me nearly sick to read him; however, I am very glad that you think so much of a countryman of mine.

Yours most, etc.

LUDWIG WITTGENSTEIN

* Prop[osition]s which I formerly wrote $\varepsilon_2(a, R, b)$ I now write $R(a, b)$ and analyse them into a, b, and $\underbrace{(\exists\, x, y)\, R\, (x, y)}_{\text{not complex}}$.

R. 9   *Briefe 11*

Mach. – Ernst Mach (1838–1976) was born in Moravia and hence in Austria-Hungary.

11.   **LW – BR**

IV. Alleegasse 16
21.1.13.

DEAR RUSSELL,

My dear father died yesterday in the afternoon. He had the most beautiful death that I can imagine; without the slightest pains and falling asleep like a child! I did not feel sad for a single moment during all the last hours, but most joyful and I think that this death was worth a whole life.

I will leave Vienna on Saturday the 25th and will be in Cambridge either on Sunday night or Monday morning. I long very much to see you again.

Yours ever

LUDWIG WITTGENSTEIN

R.10   Briefe 12

12.   **LW – JMK**

[1913]

DEAR KEYNES,

Would you mind having tea with me tomorrow? If you can come please don't trouble to reply.

Y[ou]rs

LUDWIG WITTGENSTEIN

Briefe 13

13.   **LW – BR**

> IV. Alleegasse 16
> Wien
> 25.3.13.

DEAR RUSSELL,

I can't refrain from writing to you, although I have nothing to tell you. I am as perfectly sterile as I never was, and I doubt whether I shall ever again get ideas. Whenever I try to think about Logic, my thoughts are so vague that nothing ever can crystallize out. What I feel is the curse of all those who have only half a talent; it is like a man who leads you along a dark corridor with a light and just when you are in the middle of it the light goes out and you are left alone. –

I suppose you are staying with the Whiteheads at present and hope you are having a good time. If once you have nothing better to do, do send me a line letting me know how you are, etc., etc.

L. WITTGENSTEIN

R.11   Briefe 14

14.   **LW – BR**

[June 1913]

DEAR RUSSELL,

My mother will stay at the Savoy Hotel. So we shall expect you there on Wednesday about 1–15. By the by, please remember that my mother must not know that I was operated last July (if by any chance the conversation should turn on such topics).

I can now express my objection to your theory of judgment exactly: I believe it is obvious that, from the prop[osition] "A judges that (say) a is in the Rel[ation] R to b", if correctly analysed, the prop[osition] "aRb.∨.~aRb' must follow directly *without the use of any other premiss*. This condition is not fulfilled by your theory.

Yours ever

L.W.

R. 12   *Briefe 15*

Letter dated by Russell. According to Russell's Appointments Diary for 1912–1913, the lunch was going to be on Wednesday, 18 June.

operated. – An operation for a rupture. Wittgenstein had been exempted from military service because of a rupture. He volunteered, however, for the Austrian army immediately after the outbreak of the war in 1914, and was accepted.

your theory of judgment. – The reference evidently is to a projected work on the theory of knowledge which Russell was then writing. Only the first six chapters were published during Russell's lifetime (in *The Monist*, January 1914–April 1915). The whole manuscript was published posthumously as vol. 7 of *Russell's Collected Papers: Theory of Knowledge*, ed. Elizabeth Ramsden Eames and Kenneth Blackwell. See also comment on 18.

15.   **LW – GEM**

Savoy Hotel, London
18.6.1913.

DEAR MOORE,

My Mother stays in the Savoy Hotel. So we shall expect you there on Friday at about 1 p.m.

yours etc.

L. WITTGENSTEIN

Briefe 16

16.   **LW – JMK**

Midland Hotel
Manchester
22.6.13.

DEAR KEYNES,

You will perhaps remember that I once told you I wished to give some money to the research fund – or whatever you call it – of King's Coll[ege] in order to let Johnson have it. I was then not decided as to whether I would give a capital sum once for all, or two hundred pounds every year. The latter way has turned out to be by far the most convenient to me. Now I do not know when and to whom to send the money, etc., etc. and as you are the only person who knows about the matter and I do not wish to tell any one else of my acquaintances I cannot help asking your advice about it. You would oblige me very much if you kindly wrote to me about it, unless there is time for your advice till October, when of course I shall be up at Cambridge. My address till the middle of August will be: L. W. *jun*. IV. Alleegasse 16, Austria, Wien.

Yours truly

LUDWIG WITTGENSTEIN

K.3   Briefe 17

Johnson. – W. E. Johnson (1858–1931), Fellow of King's College and Lecturer in the University of Cambridge, subsequently author of a treatise on *Logic* in three volumes (1921–4), had been appointed as Wittgenstein's supervisor. The two men found it difficult to talk about logic (see notes on no. 121 below) but formed a warm friendship none the less. Wittgenstein gave a grant of £200 a year in order to enable W. E. Johnson to cut down his teaching commitments and have more time for research. Cf. R. F. Harrod, *The Life of John Maynard Keynes*, p. 162.

17.   **LW – JMK**

Hochreit
Post Hohenberg
N[ieder]-Ö[sterreich]
16.7.13.

DEAR KEYNES,

Thanks very much for the trouble you take over my business. –
My reason for not seeing you oftener last term was, that I did not
wish our intercourse to continue without any sign that *you* wished
to continue it.

Yours sincerely

LUDWIG WITTGENSTEIN

K.4   *Briefe 18*

18.   **LW – BR**

Hochreit
Post Hohenberg
N[ieder]-Ö[sterreich]
22.7.13.

DEAR RUSSELL,

Thanks for your kind letter. My work goes on well; every day my problems get clearer now and I feel rather hopeful. All my progress comes out of the idea that the *indefinables* of Logic are of the general kind (in the same way as the so called *Definitions* of Logic are general) and this again comes from the abolition of the real variable. Perhaps you laugh at me for feeling so sanguine at present; but although I have not solved *one* of my problems I feel very, very much nearer to the solution of them all than I ever felt before.

The weather here is constantly rotten, we have not yet had two fine days in succession. I am very sorry to hear that my objection to your theory of judgment paralyses you. I think it can only be removed by a correct theory of propositions. Let me hear from you soon.

Yours ever, etc.

L.W.

R.13   Briefe 19

---

paralyses you. – In a 1916 letter to Lady Ottoline Morrell, quoted in his *Auto-biography*, vol. II, p. 57, Russell wrote: "Do you remember that at the time . . . I wrote a lot of stuff about Theory of Knowledge, which Wittgenstein criticized with the greatest severity? His criticism . . . was an event of first-rate importance in my life, and affected everything I have done since. I saw he was right, and I saw that I could not hope ever again to do fundamental work in philosophy. My impulse was shattered, like a wave dashed to pieces against a breakwater."

19.   **LW – BR**

> Hochreit
> Post Hohenberg
> Nieder–Österreich
> Austria
> [Probably Summer 1913]

DEAR RUSSELL,

Would you be so kind as to forward the enclosed letter to Mrs W., I have forgotten her address. I am afraid there are no logical news today. The weather here is most abominable, it rains all the day like mad. Just now a crash of thunder came down and I said "Hell!", which shews that English swear-words are well in my bones. I hope I can send you some logical news soon. If you have nothing better to do *please* let me know how you are, etc.

> Yours ever most, etc.

> L.W.

R.14   *Briefe 20*

Mrs W .- Presumably Mrs Alfred North Whitehead.

20.   **LW – BR**

DEAR RUSSELL,

   Your axiom of reducibility is $\vdash:(\exists f): \varphi x \equiv_x f!x$; now is this not all nonsense as this prop[osition] has only then a meaning if we can turn the φ into an *apparent* variable. For if we cannot do so no general laws can ever follow from your axiom. The whole axiom seems to me at present a mere juggling trick. Do let me know if there is more in it. The axiom as you have put it is only a schema and the real *Pp* ought to be $\vdash: . (\varphi): (\exists f): \varphi(x) \equiv_x f!x$, and where would be the use of that?!

   Thanks for your letter. I am working very hard. I look forward VERY much to see you in one of the last days of August because I have lots and lots of things to tell you.

                               Yours ever, etc.

                                    L.W.

R.15   *Briefe 21*

Pp. - Primitive proposition.

21.   **LW – BR**

[Probably 1913]

DEAR RUSSELL

   This is a secondhand copy of Lichtenberg but I couldn't get another one. I hope you'll enjoy some of it at least. Let me hear from you again.

                                    Yours ever

                                    LUDWIG WITTGENSTIN

Briefe 22

Lichtenberg. – This "letter" is in fact the dedication that Wittgenstein wrote in a copy of the Reclam edition of Georg Christoph Lichtenberg's *Ausgewählte Schriften* (the selection by Eugen Reichel), which Russell kept to the end of his life and which is now in the McMaster University Library. There are nine or ten side-linings and underlinings, presumably by Wittgenstein (at any rate it was his practice to steer friends' reading in this way), so, for example, at the epigram: 'The question 'Should one philosophize for oneself?' is like the question, 'Should one shave oneself?' the answer is, Yes, if one can do it well."

22.　　　　　　　**LW – BR**

5.9.13.

DEAR RUSSELL,

I am sitting here in a little place inside a beautiful fiord and thinking about the beastly theory of types. There are still some *very* difficult problems (and very fundamental ones too) to be solved and I won't begin to write until I have got some sort of a solution for them. However I don't think that will in any way affect the Bipolarity business which still seems to me to be absolutely untangible. Pinsent is an enormous comfort to me here. We have hired a little sailing boat and go about with it on the fiord, or rather Pinsent is doing all the sailing and I sit in the boat and work. Shall I get anything out??! It would be awful if I did not and all my work would be lost. However I am not losing courage and go on thinking. Pray for me!

If you see the Whiteheads please remember me to them. My address for the next 3 weeks shall be: Hotel Öistensjö, Öistensjö, Norway.

If you've nothing better to do, *do* write to me how you are, etc.

Öistensjö. – We know from the diary which Wittgenstein's friend David Pinsent kept of their journey to Norway that the place was situated on the Hardangerfjord. (The two travellers had reached it by boat from Bergen.) The place, in all probability is that whose name is (nowadays) spelt *Öystese.* It is likely that the name in 1913 was quite commonly spelt *Öistesö,* but Wittgenstein's own spelling here appears to be in error. The spelling Östensö used in the next letter appears on some maps of the time. We are indebted to the late Mr Olav Flo, Bergen, for information concerning this.

About Wittgenstein's time in Norway together with Pinsent, see *A Portrait,* pp. 59–86.

I very often now have the indescribable feeling as though my work was all sure to be lost entirely in some way or other. But I still hope that this won't come true. Whatever happens don't forget me!

Yours ever most, etc.

L.W.

R.16   Briefe 23

23. **LW – BR**

Östensö
Norway
20.9.13.

DEAR RUSSELL,

Types are not yet solved but I have had all sorts of ideas which seem to me very fundamental. Now the feeling that I shall have to die before being able to publish them is growing stronger and stronger in me every day and my greatest wish would therefore be to communicate *everything* I have done so far to you, *as soon as possible*. Don't think that I believe that my ideas are very important but I cannot help feeling that they might help people to avoid *some* errors. Or am I mistaken? If so don't take *any notice* of this letter. I have of course no judgment at all as to whether my ideas are worth preserving after my death or not. And perhaps it is ridiculous of me even to consider this question at all. But if this is ridiculous please try to excuse this foolishness of mine because it is not a superficial foolishness but the deepest of which I am capable. I see that the further I get on with this letter the less I dare to come to my Point. But my point is this: I want to ask you to let me meet you *as soon as possible* and give me time enough to give you a survey of the whole field of what I have done up to now and if possible to let me make notes for you *in your presence*. I shall arrive in London on the 1st of Oct[ober] and shall have to be in London again on Oct[ober]

notes. – See comments to next letter.

Russell noted on the typescript he had made of this letter: "This letter is endorsed in my handwriting "Oct. 4, 1 p.m.", so I responded to his appeal." From a letter to Lady Ottoline we know that Wittgenstein came to see Russell at Cambridge as early as 2 October.

3rd (evening). Otherwise I am not fixed in any way and can meet you wherever you like. My address will be the Grand Hotel. – I know that it may be both arrogant and silly to ask you what I have asked you. But such I am and think of me what you like. I will *always* be yours

L.W.

R. 17   Briefe 24

24.   **LW – BR**

Nordre Bergenhus Amts Dampskibe, Bergen
Dampskibet Kommandör d. 17.10.1913

DEAR RUSSELL,

My address is going to be: L.W. c/o Halvard Draegni, Skjolden,
Sogn, Norway. I am not yet there. – *Identity is the very Devil!* Types
have got a good deal clearer to me on the journey. Hope you have
got typewritten business all right. I saw Whitehead before going
and he was charming as usual. Let me hear from you *as soon as
possible* ; J want it badly! Give my love to everybody who wants it.

The letter is actually dated 17.9. This must be a slip of the pen for 17.10 (see 26.).

In this and the next three letters there is reference to the 'Notes on Logic',
published posthumously as an appendix to the *Notebooks 1914–1916*. The composition and history of these notes once puzzled students of Wittgenstein's work and
the editors (Anscombe and G.H.v.W) of the *Notebooks*. Thanks to the subsequent
accessibility of new material in the Bertrand Russell Archives it is hoped that we
now have a coherent and convincing picture of the whole matter. See B. Mc.G.'s
study "Bertrand Russell and Ludwig Wittgenstein's 'Notes on Logic' " in no. 102
(1972) of *Revue Internationale de Philosophie* devoted to Russell's philosophy. The
basic facts needed for understanding the references to the Notes in the letters are as
follows:

Yours as long as there is such a thing as

L.W.

P.S. I am not as far north as I thought I would be as the Inn I intended to stay at is closed during the winter.

R. 18   *Briefe* 25

In the course of 2–9 October 1913 Wittgenstein saw Russell at Cambridge and tried to explain his ideas. Russell, finding it difficult to grasp and remember what Wittgenstein told him, procured a shorthand writer to whom Wittgenstein dictated a "summary" of his thoughts on logic. Of these dictations, some at least of which were in English, 'Russell evidently had a typescript prepared. This is the typescript to which Wittgenstein refers in this letter 24, as "[the] typewritten business" and in letter 28. as "the typed stuff". This typescript, with corrections by Wittgenstein and Russell, is now in the Bertrand Russell Archives and it contains the misprint ("polarity" for "bi-polarity") referred to in 28. In 27. and 28., however, Wittgenstein also speaks of a manuscript and in 29. he comments on questions put to him by Russell which evidently relate to that manuscript and also quotes from it – *in German*. No such German manuscript is preserved. But there exists an English manuscript in Russell's hand entitled "Wittgenstein" and bearing the sub-headings "First MS", "2nd MS", "3rd MS", and "4th MS". It is evidently Russell's translation into English of a German manuscript (in four parts) which Wittgenstein had sent to Russell after their meeting at Cambridge (see 27.). Since he (in 27.) refers to it as a "copy", it must have been taken (dictated or excerpted) from an original. Later the same winter Russell made a re-arrangement of all this material, providing headings for its main sections. This re-arrangement is the so-called Costello version of the "Notes on Logic", later published in the first edition (1961) of *Notebooks 1914–1916*, while the second edition (1979) reverts to the original form of the material, "Summary", "First MS" etc (Readers should be warned that the index printed in the second edition is in fact based on the first edition).

far north – Wittgenstein's original intention seems to have been to go to Molde in the far north after his return to Norway from England in October 1913. Instead he went to Skjolden near the innermost part of Sognefjord north of Bergen.

25.   **LW – GEM**

[Picture-postcard of Skjolden with
"My rooms" indicated by Wittgenstein]

[Postmark 23 October 1913]

DEAR MOORE,

My address is: L. W. c/o H. Draegni, Skjolden, Sogn, Norway.
The place is very nice and I have got plenty of time to work.
Identity plays hell with me! Please ask Russell whether he has got
my letter because I am not certain if it has been posted. Let me
know EXACTLY how you are.

Yours etc. etc.

L. WITTGEN.

Picture postcard of Skjolden with "My rooms" indicated by Wittgenstein.

Identity. – For the problem see 28. and subsequent letters to Russell.

26.   **LW – JMK**

[Postcard]   23.10.13.

DEAR KEYNES,

My address is: L. W. c/o Halvard Draegni Skiolden, Sogn,
Norway. I did not go as far north as I thought I would. This is a
splendid place.

Yours ever

L. WITTGENSTEIN

Briefe 26

27.   **LW – BR**

> c/o H. Draegni, Skjolden
> Sogn, Norway
> 29.10.13.

DEAR RUSSELL,

I hope you have got my letter which I wrote on the 16th. I left it in the Dining room of the boat and afterwards telephoned that it should be posted but I don't know with what effect. This is an ideal place to work in. – Soon after I arrived here I got a violent influenza which prevented me from doing any work until quite recently. Identity is the very Devil and *immensely important*; *very* much more so than I thought. It hangs – like everything else – directly together with the most fundamental questions, especially with the questions concerning the occurrence of the SAME argument in different places of a function. I have all sorts of ideas for a solution of the problem but could not yet arrive at anything definite. However I don't lose courage and go on thinking. – I have got two nice rooms here in the Postmaster's house and am looked after very well indeed. By the way – would you be so good and send me *two* copies of Moore's paper: "The Nature and Reality of Objects of Perception" which he read to the Aristotelian Soc[iety] in 1906. I am afraid I can't yet tell you the reason why I want *two* copies but you shall know it some day. If you kindly send the bill with them I will send the money immediately after receiving the Pamphlets. – As I hardly meet a soul in this place, the progress of my Norwegian is exceed-

copy of my manuscript. – See comment to 24.

ingly slow; so much so that I have not yet learned a single swear-word. Please remember me to Dr and Mrs Whitehead and Erik if you see them. Write to me <u>SOON</u>.

Yours as long as E! L.W.

P.S. How are your conversation-classes going on? Did you get the copy of my manuscript? I enclose a roseleaf as sample of the flora in this place.

30.10.

I wrote this letter yesterday. Since then quite new ideas have come into my head; new problems have arisen in the theory of molecular prop[osition]s and the theory of inference has received a new and very important aspect. One of the consequences of my new ideas will – I think – be that the whole of Logic follows from one P.p. only!! I cannot say more about it at present.

L.W.

R19   *Briefe 27*

Erik. – A son of the Whiteheads, subsequently killed in the Great War.

28.   **LW – BR**

[Skjolden, Sogn, Norway]
[November 1913]

DEAR RUSSELL,

Thanks for your letter and the typed stuff! I will begin by answering your questions as well as I can:

(1) Your question was – I think – due to the misprint (polarity instead of *bi*polarity). What I mean to say is that we *only* then understand a prop[osition] if we know *both* what would be the case if it was *false and* what if it was *true*.

(2) The symbol for ~p is a—b—p—a—b. The prop[osition] *p* has two poles and it does not matter a hang where they stand you might just as well write ~p like this:

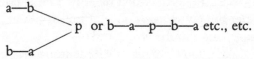

all that *is* important is that the new *a*-pole should be correlated to the old *b*-pole and vice versa WHEREVER THESE OLD POLES MAY STAND. If you had only remembered the WF scheme of ~p you

---

Your questions.— See 29.

the typed stuff. – See comment on 24. Wittgenstein evidently now sent this back to Russell with some corrections and additions (see answers (1) and (6) below). It is printed, under the title "Summary" in *Notebooks 1914–1916*,[2] See especially p. 94 for the points raised here.

the WF scheme of ~ p. – This system (a derivative of truth-tables) is explained in proposition 4.442 of the *Tractatus*. It had been expounded to Russell by Wittgenstein in the last months of 1912 (see *Young Ludwig* pp. 160–2). Thus it antedates the ab-notation, though perhaps its use in a decision procedure does not.

would never have asked this question (I think). In fact all rules of the ab symbolism follow directly from the essence of the WF scheme.

(3) Whether ab-f [unctio]ns and your truth-f [unctio]ns are the same cannot yet be decided.

(4) "The correlation of new poles is to be transitive" means that by correlating one pole in the symbolizing way to another and the other to a third we have *thereby* correlated the first in the symbolizing way to the third, etc. For instance in

$$\underset{\equiv}{a}-\underset{\equiv}{b}-\underset{\equiv}{a}-\underset{-}{b}\,p\,\underset{-}{a}-\underset{\equiv}{b}-\underset{\equiv}{a}-\underset{\equiv}{b}$$

$\underset{\equiv}{a}$ and $\underset{\equiv}{b}$ are correlated to $\underset{-}{b}$ and $\underset{-}{a}$ respectively and this means that our symbol is the same as a—bpa—b.

(5) (p) p∨~p *is* derived from *the function* p∨~q but the point will only become quite clear when identity is clear (as you said). I will some other time write to you about this matter at length.

(6) Explanation in the typed stuff.

(7) You say, you thought that Bedeutung was the "fact", this is quite true, but remember that there are no such Things as facts and that therefore this prop[osition] itself wants analysing! If we speak of "die Bedeutung" we seem to be speaking of a Thing with a proper name. Of course the symbol for "a fact" is a prop[osition] and this is *no* incomplete symbol.

(8) The exact ab-indefinable is given in the manuscript.

(9) An account of general indefinables? Oh Lord! It is *too* boring!!! Some other time! – Honestly – I *will* write to you about it some time, if by that time you have not found out all about it. (Because it is all quite clear in the manuscript, I think). But just now

---

Bedeutung. – "Meaning", nowadays often translated "reference".

the manuscript. – See comment on 24. Questions (7), (8), and (9) evidently refer to it. For the "ab-indefinable" see perhaps *Notebooks 1914–1916²*, p. 102 l.l.12–21 (from the "Third MS").

I am SO troubled with Identity that I really cannot write any long jaw. All sorts of new logical stuff seems to be growing in me, but I can't yet write about it.

Would you do me a great favour: I have promised last year to book *two* serial tickets for the C.U.M.S. Chamber Concerts. Would you kindly book them for me, keep one of them for yourself, give the other to somebody else and charge me for both. If you let me know the price I shall send you the money *at once*.

Pray for me and God bless you! (If there is such a thing).

Yours as long as

$$(\exists x).x = L.W.*$$

* This prop[osition] will probably turn out to have no meaning. *Write again soon.*

R.20   *Briefe 28*

C.U.M.S. – Cambridge University Musical Society.

29.   **LW – BR**

[Skjolden, Sogn, Norway]
[November 1913]

DEAR RUSSELL,

There is the Cheque for 42 Kroner. Thanks very much for having bought the tickets. You haven't yet sent me Miss Harwood's bill! – The following is a list of the questions you asked me in your letter of the 25th.10.:

(1) "What is the point of 'p. ≡ .'p' is true'? I mean why is it worth saying[?]"

(2) "If 'apb' is the symbol for p, is 'bpa' the symbol for ~p and if not, what is?["]

(3) "What you call ab-functions are what the Principia calls 'truth-f [unctio]ns'. I don't see why you shouldn't stick to the name 'truth-f [unctio]ns'."

(4) "I don't understand your rules about *a*'s and *b*'s, i.e. 'the correlation of new poles is to be transitive'."

(5) (Is obvious from my letter.) So is (6).

(7) "You say 'Weder der Sinn noch die Bedeutung eines Satzes ist ein Ding. Jene Worte sind unvollständige Zeichen'. I understand neither being a *thing*, but I thought the Bedeutung was the *fact*, which is surely not indicated by an incomplete symbol?"

I don't know whether I have answered the question (7) clearly.

Weder der Sinn . . . Zeichen. – "Neither the sense nor the meaning of a proposition is a thing. These words are incomplete symbols."
This remark occur in the "3rd MS". It is printed in *Notebooks* 1914–1916², p.102, ll. 29–30. That the meaning of a proposition is the fact which actually corresponds to it is stated in the "summary" (ibid., p.94 ll. 19–20).

The answer is *of course* this: The Bedeutung of a prop[osition] is symbolized by the proposition – which is *of course* not an incomplete symbol, *but the word "Bedeutung"* is an incomplete symbol.

(8) and (9) are obvious.

Write soon!

Yours

L.W.

R.21   Briefe 29

30.   **LW – BR**

[Skjolden, Sogn, Norway]
[November 1913]

LIEBER RUSSELL,

I intended to write this letter in German, but it struck me that I did not know whether to call you "Sie" or "Du" and so I am reduced to my beastly English jargon! –

I will begin by explaining why there must be a prop[osition] from which all Logic follows:

I beg you to notice that, although I shall make use in what follows of my ab-Notation, the Meaning of this Notation is not needed; that is to say, even if this Notation should turn out not to be the final correct Notation what I am going to say is valid if you only admit – as I believe you must do – that it is a *possible* Notation. Now listen: I will first talk about those logical prop[osition]s which are or might be contained in the first 8 Chapters of Princ[ipia] Math[ematica]. That they all follow from *one* Pp is clear enough because ONE *symbolic rule* is sufficient to recognize each of them as true or false. And this is the *one* symbolic rule: write the prop[osition]

Letter dated by Russell.

In this and the next letter Wittgenstein explains the essentials of his decision procedure for the propositional calculus. The invention was evidently made roughly at the time at which Wittgenstein wrote this letter. The method is the one explained in *Tractatus* 6.1203. It is not the same as the now familiar truth-table method. The remark 6.1203, interestingly enough, does not occur in the *Prototractatus* manuscript or in the typescripts for the book. It was, we know, added only after the completion of the work when Wittgenstein was a prisoner of war at Cassino. (See *Prototractatus*, ed. B. F. McGuinness, T. Nyberg and G. H. von Wright, with an historical introduction by G. H. von Wright, p. 11.) It is interesting that Wittgenstein should have been working on the problem of applying the ab-Notation to formulas involving identity with a view to inventing a decision procedure for them, too. He never solved the problem. It is also interesting that he was looking for a decision method for the whole realm of logical truth. This problem, as we now know, cannot be solved.

down in the ab-Notation, trace all Connections (of Poles) from the outside to the inside Poles: Then if the b-Pole is connected to such *groups of inside Poles* ONLY *as contain opposite poles of* ONE *prop[osition]*, then the whole prop[osition] is a true, logical prop[osition]. If on the other hand this is the case with the a-Pole the prop[osition] is false and logical. If finally neither is the case the prop[osition] may be true or false but is in no case logical. Such for instance (p).~p - p limited to a suitable type of course – is not a logical prop[osition] at all and its truth can neither be proved nor disproved from logical prop[osition]s alone. The same is the case – by the way – with your axiom of reducibility – *it is not a logical Prop[osition] at all* and the same applies to the axioms of infinity and the mult[iplicative] ax[iom]. IF *these are true prop[osition]s* they are *what I shall call "accidentally" true and not "essentially" true.* Whether a prop[osition] is accidentally or essentially true can be seen by writing it down in the ab-Notation and applying the above rule. What I – in stating this rule – called "logical" prop[osition] is a prop[osition] which is either essentially true or essentially false. This distinction of accid[entally] and essent[ially] true prop[osition]s explains – by the way – the feeling one always had about the infin[ity] ax[iom] and the axiom of reducibility, the feeling that if they were true they would be so only by a lucky accident.

Of course the rule I have given applies first of all only for what you called elementary prop[osition]s. But it is easy to see that it must also apply to all others. For consider your two Pps in the Theory of app[arent] var[iable]s *9.1 and *9.11. Put there instead of φx, (∃y).φy.y = x and it becomes obvious that the special cases of

---

elementary propositions. – "A proposition which contains no apparent variables is called "elementary"." *Principia Mathematica*, vol. I, p. 127.

your two Pps in the theory of app[arent] var[iable]s. – The two primitive propositions are:

$$* \, 9.1 \quad \vdash : \varphi x . \supset . (\exists z) \qquad \qquad \text{Pp}$$
$$* \, 9.11 \quad \vdash : \varphi x \lor \varphi y. \supset .\varphi z \; (\exists z p) \; \varphi z \; \text{Pp}$$

these two Pps like those of all the previous ones becomes tautologous if you apply the ab-Notation. The ab-Notation for Identity is not yet clear enough to show this clearly but it is obvious that such a Notation can be made up. I can sum up by saying that a logical prop[osition] is one the special cases of which are either tautologous – and then the prop[osition] is true – or "self-contradictory" (as I shall call it) and then it is false. And the ab-Notation simply shows directly which of those two it is (if any). That means that there is *one* Method of proving or disproving all logical prop[osition]s and this is: writing them down in the ab-Notation and looking at the connections and applying the above rule. But if *one* symbolic rule will do, there must also be *one* P.p. that will do. There is much that follows from all this and much that I could only explain vaguely but if you really think it over you will find that I am right. – I am glad that your classes are a success. As to Wiener I can only say that, if he is good at Math[ematics], Math[ematics] isn't much good. However –

Write again soon! And think always well of your

L.W.

P.S. Please remember me to Hardy. Every letter of yours gives me infinite pleasure!

R.22   Briefe 30

Wiener. – The reference is evidently to Norbert Wiener (1894–1964), the cyberneticist and polymath, who had received his Ph.D. from Harvard in June 1913 and was now continuing his studies under Russell at Cambridge, England. Wittgenstein presumably met Wiener during his visit to Cambridge earlier in the autumn.

Hardy. – G. H. Hardy, 1877–1947, generally thought the leading English mathematician of his time, was a friend and later a sponsor of Wittgenstein's.

31.   **LW – GEM**

c/o H. Draegni
Skjolden, Sogn, Norway
19.11.13.

DEAR MOORE,

Many thanks for your P. C. I am very sorry that you feel so miserable at times about your work. I think, the cause of it is, that you don't regularly discuss your stuff with anybody who is not yet stale and is *really* interested in the subject. And I believe that at present there is no such person up at Cambridge. Even Russell – who is of course most extraordinarily fresh for his age – is no more pliable enough for *this* purpose. Don't you think it would be a good thing if we had regular discussions when you come to me at Easter? Not – of course – that I am any good at the subject! But I am not yet stale and care for it very much. I can't help thinking that this would make you lose your feeling of sterility. I think you ought to think about your problems with the view to discussing them with me at Easter. Now don't you think that I am arrogant in saying this! I don't for a moment believe that I could get as clear about your questions as you can, but – as I said before – I am not yet wasted and am very interested in the stuff. *Do* think this over. – Let me hear from you soon.

Yours most, etc.

L. WITTGENSTEIN

M.2   Briefe 31

32.   **LW – BR**

[Skjolden, Sogn, Norway]
[November or December 1913]

LIEBER RUSSELL!
Vielen Dank für Deinen lieben Brief. Ich will dasjenige, was ich
in meinem letzten Brief über Logik schrieb, noch einmal in anderer
Weise wiederholen: Alle Sätze der Logik sind Verallgemeinerungen
von Tautologien und alle Verallgemeinerungen von Tautologien
sind Sätze der Logik. Andere logische Sätze gibt es nicht. (Dies halte
ich für definitiv.) Ein Satz wie „($\exists$x) . x = x" z.B. ist eigentlich ein
Satz der *Physik*. Der Satz

$$\text{„}(x) : x = x \; . \; \supset \; . \; (\exists y) \; . y = y \text{ "}$$

ist ein Satz der Logik; es ist nun Sache der *Physik* zu sagen, *ob es ein
Ding gibt*. Dasselbe gilt vom infin[ity] ax[iom]; ob es $\aleph_0$ Dinge gibt,
das zu bestimmen ist Sache der Erfahrung (und die kann es nicht
entscheiden). Nun aber zu Deinem Reductions-Axiom: Stell' Dir
vor, wir lebten in einer Welt, worin es nichts als $\aleph_0$ *Dinge* gäbe und
außerdem NUR *noch eine* Relation, welche zwischen unendlich
vielen dieser Dinge bestehe und zwar so, daß sie nicht zwischen
jedem Ding und jedem anderen besteht, und daß sie ferners auch
nie zwischen einer endlichen Anzahl von Dingen besteht. Es ist
klar, daß das ax[iom] of Red[ucibility] in einer solchen Welt sicher
nicht bestünde. Es ist mir aber auch klar, daß es nicht die Sache der
Logik ist darüber zu entscheiden, ob die Welt worin wir leben nun
wirklich so ist, oder nicht. Was aber Tautologien eigentlich sind,
das kann ich selber noch nicht ganz klar sagen, will aber trachten es
ungefähr zu erklären. Es ist das eigentümliche (und *höchst* wichtige)
Merkmal der *nicht*-logischen Sätze, daß man ihre Wahrheit *nicht* am
Satzzeichen selbst erkennen kann. Wenn ich z.B. sage „Meier ist
dumm", so kannst Du dadurch, daß Du diesen Satz anschaust, nicht
sagen ob er wahr oder falsch ist. Die Sätze der Logik aber – und sie

allein – haben die Eigenschaft, daß sich ihre Wahrheit bezw. Falschheit schon in ihrem Zeichen ausdrückt. Es ist mir noch nicht gelungen, für die Identität eine Bezeichnung zu finden, die dieser Bedingung genügt; aber *ich zweifle* NICHT, daß sich eine solche Bezeichnungsweise finden lassen muß. Für zusammengesetzte Sätze (elem[entary] prop[ositions]) genügt die ab-Bezeichnungsw[eise]. Es ist mir unangenehm, daß Du die Zeichenregel aus meinem letzten Brief nicht verstanden hast, denn es langweilt mich - UNSAGBAR sie zu erklären!! Du könntest sie auch durch ein bißchen Nachdenken selber finden!

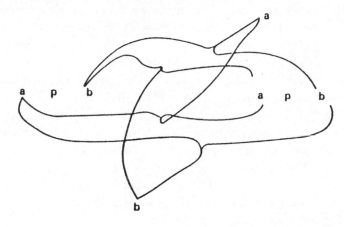

Dies ist das Zeichen für p ≡ p; es ist tautologisch weil *b* nur mit solchen Pol-paaren verbunden ist, welche aus den entgegengesetzten Polen eines Satzes (nämlich p) bestehen; wenn Du dies auf Sätze anwendest, die mehr als 2 Argumente haben so erhältst Du die allgemeine Regel, wonach Tautologien gebildet werden. Ich bitte Dich denke selbst über die Sachen nach, es ist mir SCHRECKLICH eine schriftliche Erklärung zu wiederholen, die ich schon zum ersten Mal mit dem *allergrößten Widerstreben* gegeben habe. Die Identität ist mir – wie gesagt – noch gar nicht klar. Also hierüber ein andermal! Wenn Dein Ax[iom] of Red[ucibility] fällt, so wird wahrscheinlich

(elem[entary] prop[ositions]). – See notes to 30.

57

manches geändert werden müssen. Warum gebrauchst Du als Definition der Klassen nicht diese:

$$F [\hat{x}\ \varphi(x)]. = :\varphi z \equiv_z \psi z. \supset_\psi\ .\ F(\ \psi\ )\ \ Def?$$

– Zu Weihnachten werde ich LEIDER nach Wien fahren müssen.

Meine Mutter nämlich wünscht es sich so sehr, daß sie schwer gekränkt wäre, wenn ich nicht käme; und sie hat vom vorigen Jahr gerade an diese Zeit so böse Erinnerungen, daß ich es nicht über's Herz bringen kann wegzubleiben. Ich werde aber sehr bald wieder hierher zurückkehren. Meine Stimmung ist mittelmäßig, weil meine Arbeit nicht rasch vorwärts geht und weil mir der Gedanke an meine Heimfahrt entsetzlich ist. Die Einsamkeit hier tut mir unendlich wohl und ich glaube, daß ich das Leben unter Menschen jetzt nicht vertrüge. In mir gärt alles! Die große Frage ist jetzt: Wie muß ein Zeichensystem beschaffen sein, damit es jede Tautologie AUF EINE UND DIESELBE WEISE als Tautologie erkennen läßt? Dies ist das Grundproblem der Logik! – Ich bin überzeugt, ich werde in meinem Leben nie etwas veröffentlichen. Aber nach meinem Tod mußt Du den Band meines Tagebuchs, worin die ganze Geschichte steht, drucken lassen. *Schreib bald hierher* und versuche aus meinen verwirrten Erklärungen klar zu werden.

Immer Dein

L.W.

böse Erinnerungen/bad memories. – Refers to the illness and death of Wittgenstein's father in January 1913. See 7–11.

Band meines Tagebuchs/volume of my journal. – This is probably the manuscript, or part of the manuscript, which Wittgenstein in a later letter (46.) says that he showed to Moore, when Moore visited him in Norway in April 1914. It was in all likelihood a notebook of the same character as those which he wrote during the war-years, three of which have been preserved and published. Cf. G. H. v. W's essay in his *Wittgenstein*.

P.S. Deine Briefe sind mir eine große Wohltat; laß es Dich nicht reuen, mir so oft zu schreiben. Ich will nur noch sagen, daß Deine Theorie der "Descriptions" *ganz* ZWEIFELLOS richtig ist, selbst wenn die einzelnen Urzeichen darin ganz andere sind als Du glaubtest.

– Ich glaube oft daß ich verrückt werde.

R.23 *Briefe 32*

English Translation

DEAR RUSSELL,

Many thanks for your kind letter. I want to repeat again, in a different form, what I wrote about logic in my last letter. All the propositions of logic are generalizations of tautologies and all generalizations of tautologies are propositions of logic. There are no other logical propositions. (I regard this as definitive.) A proposition such as "$(\exists x) . x = x$", for example, is really a proposition of *physics*. The proposition

$$ \text{"}(x) : x = x . \supset . (\exists y) . y = y \text{"} $$

is a proposition of logic and it is then for *physics* to say *whether any thing exists*. The same holds for the axiom of infinity: whether there exist $\aleph_0$ things is a matter for experience to determine (and one which experience cannot decide). But now, as to your Axiom of Reducibility: imagine we lived in a world in which nothing existed except $\aleph_0$ *things* and, over and above them, ONLY a *single* relation holding between infinitely many of the things and in such a way that it did not hold between each thing and every other thing and further never held between a finite number of things. It is clear that the axiom of reducibility would certainly *not* hold good in such a world. But it is also clear to me that whether or not the world in which we live is really of this kind is not a matter for logic to decide. As to what tautologies really are, however, I myself am not yet able to say quite clearly but I will try to give a rough explanation. It is the peculiar (and *most* important) mark of *non*-logical propositions that one is *not* able to recognize their truth from the propositional sign alone. If I say, for example, 'Meier is stupid', you cannot tell by looking at this proposition whether it is true or false. But the propositions of logic – and only they – have the property that their truth or falsity, as the case may be, finds its expression in the very sign for the proposition. I have not yet succeeded in finding a notation for identity that satisfies this condition; but *I have* NO *doubt* that it must be possible to find such a notation. For compound propositions ("elementary propositions") the ab-notation is sufficient. It distresses me that you did not understand the rule dealing with signs in my last letter because it bores me BEYOND WORDS to explain it. If you thought about it for a bit you could discover it for yourself!

The diagram [see the German text on previous pages] is the sign for $p \equiv p$; it is tautological because b is connected only with those pairs of poles that consist of opposite poles of a single proposition (namely p). Apply this to propositions with more than two arguments and you will obtain the general rule for the construction of tautologies. I beg you to think about these matters for yourself: it is INTOLERABLE for me, to repeat a written explanation which even the first time I gave only with the *utmost repugnance*. I find identity, as I say, still far from clear. So I will deal with that another time. If your axiom of reducibility fails, then probably a lot of things will have to be changed. Why do not you use the following as the definition of a class

$$F[\hat{x} \ (\varphi x)] .= : \varphi z \equiv_z \psi z . \supset_\psi .F(\psi) \quad Def?$$

– At Christmas I must UNFORTUNATELY go to Vienna.

The fact is, my mother very much wants me to, so much so that she would be grievously offended if I did not come; and she has such bad memories of just this time last year that I have not the heart to stay away. But I shall return here very early. I am in mediocre spirits because my work is not progressing rapidly and because the thought of going back home appals me. Being alone here does me no end of good and I do not think I could now bear life among people. Inside me, everything is in a state of ferment. The big question now is, how must a system of signs be constituted in order to make every tautology recognizable as such IN ONE AND THE SAME WAY? This is the fundamental problem of logic! – I am convinced I shall never publish anything in my lifetime. But after my death you must see to the printing of the volume of my journal with the whole story in it. *Write here soon* and try to understand my muddled explanations.

Yours ever,

L.W.

P.S. Your letters are a great boon to me. Do not feel sorry for writing to me so often. I only want to add that your "Theory of Descriptions" is *quite* CERTAINLY correct, even though the individual primitive signs in it are not at all the ones you thought.

– I often think I am going mad.

33.   **LW – GEM**

[Postcard of Skjolden]

[December 1913]

DEAR MOORE,

Many thanks for your letter. I am glad that you will have regular
discussions with me when you come up and *I can't see for my life*
why you shouldn't be able to! That Johnson at last gives a paper to
the Club interests me enormously! What was it like?? And what was
it *really* about? To say the truth I don't like the title. However –
Identity still plays hell with me. We had already heavy snowfalls but
it isn't cold. Write soon and a lot about Johnson's paper.

Yours etc

LUDWIG WITTGENSTEIN

Is Muscio still alive? And, if so, what's he doing?

The minutes of the Moral Sciences Club for 5 December 1913 show that "the
President" (i.e. Johnson) read a paper entitled "Possibility". Roughly, for there
was evidently some dispute over the minutes, his idea was that a strict definition
could be given of possibility relative to a given set of propositions and that
counter-factual possibility (as it came to be called) was relative to the Laws of
Nature (which were not mere universals). The minutes also show that Moore was
in the chair. Moore himself in his diary records, "can't say much, walk home with
R[ussell]". Russell also comments on the occasion of this talk (a rare one as
Wittgenstein's remark implies) in a letter to Lady Ottoline of 6 December 1913,
saying "W. E. Johnson is a terrible example of waste. He has a *very* fine intellect and
all the makings of a great philosopher except vitality." To be sure, Johnson's health
was not good and he was much oppressed by teaching. The completion and
publication of his *Logic* (see notes on 16. above) is known to have owed much to
the assistance and energy of pupils and of Miss Naomi Bentwich in particular.
Letter 16. itself is some evidence of Wittgenstein's efforts in the same direction.

Muscio. – Bernard Muscio (1887–1928), University Demonstrator in Experimental
Psychology at Cambridge, later Professor of Philosophy, University of Sydney. He
had collaborated with Wittgenstein in psychological experiments in 1912–13, see
Young Ludwig, pp. 125 ff. As is clear from 41., Muscio must have failed Wittgenstein in some minor obligation, perhaps connected with these.

34. **LW – BR**

Skjolden, Sogn
15.12.13.

LIEBER RUSSELL!

Ich schicke heute 720 Kroner an Messrs Child & Co. für Deine Rechnung. Die Frage nach dem Wesen der Identität läßt sich nicht beantworten, ehe das Wesen der Tautologie erklärt ist. Die Frage nach diesem aber, ist die Grundfrage *aller* Logik. – Mein Tag vergeht zwischen Logik, Pfeifen, Spazierengehen und Niedergeschlagensein. Ich wollte zu Gott, ich hätte mehr Verstand und es würde mir nun endlich alles klar; oder ich müßte nicht mehr lange leben! –

Du hast die Eroika gehört! Was hast Du zu dem zweiten Satz gesagt? ist er nicht unglaublich? –

Ist es nicht höchst merkwürdig, was für eine große und unendlich eigenartige Wissenschaft die Logik ist; ich glaube, weder Du noch ich haben das vor 1 ½ Jahren gewußt.

Immer Dien

L.W.

R.24   *Briefe 33*

English Translation

DEAR RUSSELL,

I am sending Messrs Child & Co. 720 Kroner today for credit to your account. The question as to the nature of identity cannot be answered until the nature of tautology has been explained. But that question is fundamental to the *whole* of logic. – My day passes between logic, whistling, going for walks, and being depressed. I wish to God that I were more intelligent and everything would finally become clear to me – or else that I needn't live much longer! –

You heard the Eroica! What did you think of the second movement? Isn't it incredible? –

It's extraordinary, isn't it, what a huge and infinitely strange science logic is? Neither you nor I knew that, I think, a year and a half ago.

Yours ever

L.W.

35.   **LW – BR**

IV. Alleegasse 16
[Probably Christmas 1913]

LIEBER RUSSELL!

Vielen Dank für Deinen Brief! Ich bin wie Du siehst zu Hause, und LEIDER wieder einmal ganz unfruchtbar. Ich hoffe nur die Ideen werden wiederkommen, wenn ich in meine Einsamkeit zurückkehre. (Ich bleibe noch etwa 8–10 Tage hier.) Was Deine amerikanischen Vorlesungen anbelangt, so brauchtest Du mich – von *mir* aus – natürlich gar nicht zu nennen; aber – wie Du willst –. Hier geht es mir jeden Tag anders: Einmal glaube ich, ich werde verrückt, so stark gärt alles in mir; den nächsten Tag bin ich wieder ganz und gar phlegmatisch. Am Grunde meiner Seele aber kocht es

This letter, undated by its writer, was assigned to "Spring 1914" by Russell, but that dating seems improbable since no visit to Vienna at Easter is known of and Moore's visit to Norway (29 March to 4 April) and Wittgenstein's remarks in 46. about the progress of his work almost exclude one. Summer 1914 seems ruled out by the town address (compare 47. written from Neuwaldegg on the outskirts of Vienna) nor did Wittgenstein then mean to go back immediately from Austria to Norway, as we know from plans made with both David Pinsent and W. Eccles(engineer, a friend of Wittgenstein's from his days in the University of Manchester. Wittgenstein's letters to him are included in *Briefe*). We conclude that it must have been written around Christmas 1913 and it does indeed seem to be echoed in 36. below.

Deine amerikanischen Vorlesungen/your American lecture- course. – Russell was due to give the Lowell Lectures at Harvard University in March and April 1914. He composed them between September and late November 1913, as is clear from his correspondence with Lady Ottoline Morrell. (The account, in his autobiography, that he began dictating them, from scratch, on 1 January 1914 must be the result of some confusion. The issue is discussed by K. Blackwell in *Russell* 12 (1973): 11–13.) They were published in 1914 as *Our Knowledge of the External World* (in America the spine but not the title-page bore the title *Scientific Method in Philosophy*, which, prefixed by "On", was the subtitle of the English edition). In the preface to these (and also in the notes to Lecture VII, first edition p. 208, later editions p. 213) there is an acknowledgement of the importance of Wittgenstein's work. No doubt Russell had announced this acknowledgement in a letter.

fort und fort wie am Grunde eines Geisirs. Und ich hoffe immer noch es werde endlich einmal ein endgültiger Ausbruch erfolgen, und ich kann ein anderer Mensch werden. Über Logik kann ich Dir heute nichts schreiben. Vielleicht glaubst Du daß es Zeitverschwendung ist über mich selbst zu denken; aber wie kann ich Logiker sein, wenn ich noch nicht Mensch bin! *Vor allem* muß ich mit mir selbst in's Reine kommen!

Immer Dein

L.W.

R.29   *Briefe 34*

English Translation

DEAR RUSSELL,

Many thanks for your letter. As you see, I am at home and UNFORTUNATELY once again quite unproductive. I only hope the ideas will start to flow again when I go back into isolation. (I am staying here for about another eight or ten days.) As regards your American lecture-course, there was naturally no need at all, as far as I'm concerned, to mention my name. But – as you wish –. Here I feel different every day. Sometimes things inside me are in such a ferment that I think I'm going mad: then the next day I am totally apathetic again. But deep inside me there's a perpetual seething, like the bottom of a geyser, and I keep on hoping that things will come to an eruption once and for all, so that I can turn into a different person. I can't write you anything about logic today. Perhaps you regard this thinking about myself as a waste of time – but how can I be a logician before I'm a human being! *Far* the most important thing is to settle accounts with myself !

Yours ever

L.W.

36.   **LW – BR**

Lᴇɪʙᴇʀ Rᴜssᴇʟʟ!

Vielen Dank für Deinen lieben Brief! ʟᴇɪᴅᴇʀ kann ich Dir auch diesmal wieder keine logischen Neuigkeiten berichten: denn es ist mir in den letzten Wochen fürchterlich schlecht gegangen. (Eine Folge meiner Wiener ,,Ferien".) Ich war jeden Tag abwechselnd von schrecklicher Angst und Depression gequält und selbst wenn diese aussetzten so erschöpft, daß ich an ein Arbeiten gar nicht denken konnte. Die Möglichkeiten der geistigen Qual sind unsagbar entsetzlich! Erst seit zwei Tagen kann ich wieder die Stimme der Vernunft durch den Lärm der Gespenster hören und habe wieder angefangen zu arbeiten. Und *vielleicht* werde ich jetzt genesen und etwas anständiges hervorbringen können. Aber ich habe *nie* gewußt, was es heißt, sich nur noch *einen* Schritt vom Wahnsinn zu fühlen. – Hoffen wir das Beste! –

Ja, Mörike ist freilich ein *großer* Dichter und seine Gedichte gehören zum besten was wir haben. Aber ich bin neugierig, ob Du ihn wirklich genießen wirst, weil Du doch Goethe nicht genießest. Und Mörikes Schönheit ist ganz nahe verwandt mit Goethes. Aber *wenn* Du Mörike *wirklich* genoßen hast, dann versuch' einmal die Iphigenie von Goethe: vielleicht geht Dir dann ein Licht auf. –

Jetzt noch eine Frage: Sagt der ,,Satz vom zureichenden Grunde" (Law of causality) nicht einfach, daß Raum und Zeit relativ sind? Dies scheint mir jetzt ganz klar zu sein; denn alle die Ereignisse von denen dieser Satz behaupten soll, daß sie nicht eintreten können, könnten überhaupt nur in einer absoluten Zeit und einem ab-

---

Mörike – In a letter to Lady Ottoline, dated from Rome, 30 December 1913 (on holiday), Russell recounts how a Frau Liese von Hattenberg (her true name, though he says "Hattingberg") "read poems by a man named Mörike whom Wittgenstein has always raved about – he even left a volume of him in my rooms, hoping I should read him, but I never did. However I liked the poems she read." For further details see Ronald Clark, *Life of Bertrand Russell*, pp. 211, 219–22.

soluten Raum eintreten. (Dies wäre freilich noch kein unbedingter Grund zu meiner Behauptung.) Aber denke an den Fall des Massenteilchens, das, allein in der Welt existierend, und seit aller Ewigkeit in Ruhe, plötzlich im Zeitpunkt A anfängt sich zu bewegen; und denke an ähnliche Fälle, so wirst Du – glaube ich – sehen daß KEINE Einsicht a priori uns solche Ereignisse als unmöglich erscheinen läßt, *außer eben in dem Fall* daß Raum und Zeit relativ sind. Bitte schreibe mir Deine Meinung in diesem Punkte.

Ich wünsche Dir alles Beste zu Deinen Vorlesungen in Amerika. Vielleicht geben sie Dir doch Gelegenheit mehr als sonst Deine *Gedanken* und nicht *nur* fertig formulierte Resultate auszusprechen. Und DAS gerade wäre von dem denkbar größten Wert für Deine Hörer, wenn sie den Wert des *Gedankens*, nicht den des fertigen Resultats, kennen lernten. Schreib' mir bald und denk' an mich, wenn Du im Mörike liesest.

Immer Dein

L.W.

P.S. Noch eine Bitte! Ich schicke Dir beiliegend meine College-Rechnung und einen Check für 80 Kroner; ich bitte Dich hiervon die Rechnung zu zahlen, da ich nicht weiß, ob Barclay & Co. Norwegisches Geld annimmt.

I[mmer] D[ein]

L.W.

R.25   *Briefe 35*

Vorlesungen in Amerika / lecture-course in America – Here the reference is probably not so much to the Lowell Lectures (see note to 33.) but to either or both of the courses, on Theory of Knowledge and Advanced Logic, which Russell was to give in the Department of Philosophy of Harvard University in the same period and which he was now engaged in preparing.

English Translation

DEAR RUSSELL,

Many thanks for your kind letter. It's VERY sad but I've once again no logical news for you. The reason is that things have gone terribly badly for me in the last weeks. (A result of my "holidays" in Vienna.) Every day I was tormented by a frightful *Angst* and by depression in turns and even in the intervals I was so exhausted that I wasn't able to think of doing a bit of work. It's terrifying beyond all description the kinds of mental torment that there can be! It wasn't until two days ago that I could hear the voice of reason over the howls of the damned and I began to work again. And *perhaps* I'll get better now and be able to produce something decent. But I *never* knew what it meant to feel only *one* step away from madness. – Let's hope for the best! –

Yes: Mörike really is a *great* poet and his poems are among the best things we have. But I am curious to know whether you will really enjoy him. After all, you don't enjoy Goethe and the beauty of Mörike's work is very closely related to that of Goethe's. But *if* you have *really* enjoyed Mörike, then just try Goethe's *Iphigenie*. Then perhaps you'll see the light.

Now for a question: isn't what the "principle of sufficient reason" (law of causality) says simply that space and time are relative? I now think this is quite obvious, because all the events which, according to this assertion, are not meant to be possible could only occur, if at all, in an absolute time and space. (Admittedly this wouldn't in itself be an adequate reason for my assertion.) But think of the case of a particle that is the only thing existing in the world and that has been at rest for all eternity and that suddenly, at time A, begins to move. Think of this and similar cases and you will see, I believe, that it is NOT an a priori insight that makes such events seem impossible to us *unless it is the case* that space and time are relative. Please write and tell me your opinion on this point.

All best wishes for your lecture-course in America! Perhaps it will give you at any rate a more favourable opportunity than usual to tell them your *thoughts* and not *just* cut and dried results. THAT is what would be of the greatest imaginable value for your audience – to get to know the value of *thought* and not that of a cut and dried result. Write to me soon and think of me when you read Mörike.

Yours ever

L.W.

P.S. Another request! I enclose my College bill and a cheque for 80 Kroner. Please pay the bill out of this, because I don't know whether Barclay & Co. will accept Norwegian money.

Yours ever

L.W.

37.   **LW – GEM**

[Postcard stamped at Sogn 30.1.14.]

About 2 months ago I wrote to you asking you to write to me about Johnson's lecture, and I haven't got an answer yet. Isn't that a shame? Also I should like to know how you are and when the Easter vac's begin. Have you ever thought about the nature of a tautology? That's what I am now bothered with.

Now *do* write to me soon and much!

Yours, etc., etc.

LUDWIG WITTGENSTEIN

P.S. I am now learning to ski and find it great fun.

M.3   Briefe 36

Johnson's lecture. – See 33. above and 39.

38. LW – BR

[Skjolden, Sogn, Norway]
[February 1914]

LIEBER RUSSELL!

Ich danke Dir für Deinen freundlichen Brief. Es war sehr schön von Dir, daß Du mir auf diese Weise geantwortet hast! Deine Forderung aber, ich solle so tun als sei nichts vorgefallen, kann ich Dir unmöglich erfüllen, da dies ganz gegen meine Natur ginge. VERZEIH *mir daher diesen langen Brief* und bedenke daß ich meiner Natur ebenso folgen *muß*, wie Du der Deinen. Ich habe in der letzten Woche viel über unser Verhältnis nachgedacht und bin zu dem Schluß gekommen, daß wir eigentlich nicht zu einander passen. DIES MEINE ICH NICHT ALS TADEL! weder für Dich noch für

In this letter, and in 40., there is reference to a quarrel (*Streit*) between Russell and Wittgenstein. Russell refers to the matter in a letter to Lady Ottoline Morrell, dated 19 February 1914, as follows: "Since I began writing this, I have had a letter from Wittgenstein saying he and I are so dissimilar that it is useless to attempt friendship, and he will never write to me or see me again. I dare say his mood will change after a while. I find I don't care on his account, but only for the sake of Logic. And yet I believe I do really care too much to look at it. It is my fault – I have been too sharp with him." On 23 February he wrote, "I wrote to Wittgenstein and I hope he relents." Probably the present letter is that received by Russell on 19 February. Perhaps a letter of Wittgenstein's between 36 and 38 has been lost, since two intermediate letters from Russell (one sharp and one emollient) seem to be attested. Russell's letters to Lady Ottoline in this period alternately describe the stimulus of Wittgenstein and the fatigue of his company, the folly of his going to Norway and the relief it provided, the supreme value of his work for the future of logic and the difficulty that his criticisms created for Russell's own work. There was material for a quarrel here: the occasion may have been a sharp reaction of Russell's to Wittgenstein's well-meant advice in 36.

mich. Aber es ist eine Tatsache. Wir hatten ja schon so oft unge-
mütliche Gespräche mit einander, wenn wir auf gewisse Themen
kamen. Und die Ungemütlichkeit war nicht eine Folge von
schlechter Laune auf seiten eines von uns beiden, sondern sie war
die Folge enormer Unterschiede in unserem Wesen. Ich bitte Dich
inständigst nicht zu glauben, ich wolle Dich irgendwie tadeln, oder
Dir eine Predigt halten; sondern ich will nur unser Verhältnis
klarlegen *weil ich daraus einen Schluß ziehen werde.* – Auch unser
letzter Streit war bestimmt nicht bloß die Folge Deiner Empfind-
lichkeit oder meiner Rücksichtslosigkeit, sondern der tiefere
Grund lag darin, daß Dir jener Brief von mir zeigen mußte, wie
grundverschieden unsere Auffassungen z.b. des Wertes eines wis-
senschaftlichen Werkes sind. Es war natürlich dumm von mir, Dir
damals so lang über jene Sache geschrieben zu haben, denn ich
hätte mir ja sagen müßen, daß sich solche wesentliche Unterschiede
nicht durch einen Brief ausgleichen lassen. Und dies ist ja nur EIN
Fall unter *vielen*. Ich sehe jetzt, wo ich dies in aller Ruhe schreibe,
vollkommen ein, daß Deine Werturteile ebenso gut sind und
ebenso tief in Dir begründet sind wie meine in mir, und daß ich
kein Recht habe Dich zu katechisieren; aber ebenso klar sehe ich
jetzt, daß wir eben darum kein rechtes Freundschaftsverhältnis zu
einander haben können. *Ich werde Dir so lange ich lebe vom* GANZEM
HERZEN *dankbar und zugetan sein, aber ich werde Dir nicht mehr schreiben
und Du wirst mich auch nicht mehr sehen.* Jetzt wo ich mich mit Dir
wieder versöhnt habe, will ich *in Frieden* von Dir scheiden, damit
wir nicht irgend einmal wieder gegen einander gereizt werden und
dann vielleicht in Feindschaft auseinander gehen. Ich wünsche Dir
alles Beste und bitte Dich mich nicht zu vergessen und oft *freundlich*
an mich zu denken. Leb wohl!

Immer Dein

LUDWIG WITTGENSTEIN

R.26   *Briefe 37*

English Translation

DEAR RUSSELL,

Thank you for your friendly letter. It was very good of you to answer me in such a way. But I can't possibly carry out your request to behave as if nothing had happened: that would go clean contrary to my nature. *So* FORGIVE *me for this long letter* and remember that I *have* to follow my nature just as much as you. During the last week I have thought a lot about our relationship and I have come to the conclusion that we really don't suit one another. THIS IS NOT MEANT AS A REPROACH! either for you or for me. But it is a fact. We've often had uncomfortable conversations with one another when certain subjects came up. And the uncomfortableness was not a consequence of ill humour on one side or the other but of enormous differences in our natures. I beg you most earnestly not to think I want to reproach you in any way or to preach you a sermon. I only want to put our relationship in clear terms *in order to draw a conclusion.* – Our latest quarrel, too, was certainly not simply a result of your sensitiveness or my inconsiderateness. It came from deeper – from the fact that my letter must have shown you how totally different our ideas are, E.G. of the value of a scientific work. It was, of course, stupid of me to have written to you at such length about this matter: I ought to have told myself that such fundamental differences cannot be resolved by a letter. And this is just ONE instance out of *many*. Now, as I'm writing this in complete calm, I can see perfectly well that your value-judgments are just as good and just as deep-seated in you as mine in me, and that I have no right to catechize you. But I see equally clearly, now, that for that very reason there cannot be any real relation of friendship between us. *I shall be grateful to you and devoted to you* WITH ALL MY HEART *for the whole of my life, but I shall not write to you again and you will not see me again either.* Now that I am once again reconciled with you I want to part from you *in peace* so that we shan't sometime get annoyed with one another again and then perhaps part as enemies. I wish you everything of the best and I beg

you not to forget me and to think of me often *with friendly feelings.*
Goodbye!

Yours *ever*

LUDWIG WITTGENSTEIN

39.   LW – GEM

Skjolden
18.2.14.

DEAR MOORE,

Thanks so much for your letter. I'm sorry I caused you horrid troubles. I didn't really expect such a long account of the meeting. But all you wrote to me interested me enormously because I think I know exactly what Johnson was at. It – of course – all turns on the question as to the nature of deduction. And – I think – the clue to it all lies in the fact that $\varphi x \supset_x \psi x$ only then expresses the deductive relation when this prop[osition] is the generalization of a tautology.

You must come as soon as Term ends and I shall meet you in Bergen. I am looking forward to your coming more than I can say! I am

the meeting. – That referred to in 33. and 37. above.

Logik. – Either the discipline of logic or the work referred to in 43. and 45. below. Russell's letter to Lady Ottoline quoted in the notes on 38. may also be taken to indicate (note the capital letter for "Logic") that Wittgenstein was writing a work with this as title.

Sedgwick. – Presumably R. R. Sedgwick, 1894–1972, historian and public servant, who was at the time an undergraduate at, and later a fellow of, Trinity.

Hardy. – See note on 30.

the Society. – The semi-secret, ancient discussion club at Cambridge also known as "The Apostles". Russell, Moore, and Keynes were members of the Society. Russell had in 1912 proposed Wittgenstein for membership. For an account of the activities of the Society in the years before the First World War see Russell's *Autobiography*, vol. I, pp. 68–70 and passim, also Paul Levy, *Moore*, passim, from which it appears (p. 311) that Sedgwick was not elected. For Wittgenstein's own connexions with the Society see *Young Ludwig*, pp. 146–51.

bothered to death with Logik and other things. But I hope I shan't die before you come for in that case we couldn't discuss *much*.

Yours, etc..

L.W.

P.S. Boats run from Newcastle to Bergen 3 times a week. I shall expect you in Bergen about the 20th of March, What has happened with young Sedgwick whom Hardy [tried] to run? Has he become a member of the Society?

M.4   Briefe 38

40. **LW – BR**

Skjolden
3.3.14.

LIEBER RUSSELL!

Dein Brief war *so* voll von Güte und Freundschaft, daß ich nicht glaube, auf ihn schweigen zu *dürfen*. Ich muß also mein Vorhaben brechen: was ich Dir aber sagen muß, kann ich leider nicht kurz fassen und ich habe kaum irgendwelche Hoffnung, daß Du mich wirklich verstehen wirst. Vor allem muß ich nocheinmal sagen: Unsere Streitigkeiten kommen nicht *nur* aus äußerlichen Gründen (Nervosität, Übermüdung u. dgl.) sondern sind—jedenfalls in *mir* – *sehr* tief begründet. Du magst darin recht haben, daß *wir selbst* vielleicht nicht einmal *so sehr* verschieden sind: aber *unsere Ideale* sind es ganz und gar. Und darum konnten und können wir *nie* über Dinge, worin unsere Werturteile in Betracht kamen, mit einander reden, ohne zu heucheln, oder zu zanken. *Ich glaube dies läßt sich nicht leugnen* und war mir schon seit langer Zeit aufgefallen; und war mir schrecklich, denn unser Verkehr bekam dadurch etwas vom Beisammensitzen in einem Sumpfe. Denn wir beide haben Schwächen, besonders aber *ich* und mein Leben ist VOLL von den häßlichsten und kleinlichsten Gedanken und Taten (dies ist *keine* Übertreibung). Wenn aber ein Verkehr nicht beide Teile herabziehen soll, dann dürfen die *Schwächen* der beiden *nicht* mit einander verkehren. Sondern zwei Leute sollen nur dort mit einander verkehren, wo sie beide *rein* sind; d.i. dort wo sie gegen einander *ganz* offen sein können, ohne einander zu verletzen. Und *das* können wir beide NUR, wenn wir unseren Verkehr auf die Mitteilung objectiv feststellbarer Tatsachen beschränken und etwa noch auf die Mitteilung unserer freundschaftlichen Gefühle. Alle anderen Themen aber führen bei uns zur Heuchelei oder zum Zank. Du sagst vielleicht: es ist ja bisher so ziemlich gegangen, warum sollte es nicht so weitergehen. Aber ich bin des ewigen schmutzigen und halben ZU müde! Mein Leben war bisher *eine* große Schweinerei – aber soll es immer so weitergehen? – Ich schlage Dir nun dies vor: Machen wir einander Mitteilungen über unsere Arbeiten, unser Befinden und dergleichen, aber unterlassen wir gegen einander jedwedes Werturteil – worüber immer –, in dem vollen Bewußtsein, daß wir hierin gegen einander nicht *ganz* ehrlich sein könnten, ohne den anderen zu verletzen (zum mindesten gilt dies bestimmt von *mir*). Meiner tiefen Zuneigung brauche ich Dich nicht erst zu versichern, *aber sie wäre in großer Gefahr, wenn wir mit einem Verkehr fortführen, der Heuchelei zur Grundlage hat und deshalb für uns beide beschämend ist.* Aber ich glaube, es wäre ehrenvoll für uns beide, wenn wir ihn auf einer reineren Grundlage fortsetzten. – Ich bitte Dich, Dir dies alles zu überlegen, mir aber *nur dann* zu antworten, wenn Du es im Guten tun kannst. In jedem Fall sei meiner Liebe und Treue versichert. Möchtest Du diesen Brief so verstehen wie er gemeint ist!

Immer Dein

L.W.

R.27   Briefe 39

English Translation

DEAR RUSSELL,

Your letter was *so* full of kindness and friendship that I don't think I have the *right* to leave it unanswered. So I have to break my resolution. Unfortunately, however, I can't put what I have to say to you in a few words and I have scarcely any hope that you'll really understand me. The chief thing, I must tell you again, is that our quarrels don't arise *just* from external reasons such as nervousness or over-tiredness but are – at any rate on *my* side – *very* deep-rooted. You may be right in saying that *we ourselves* are not *so very* different, but *our ideals* could not be more so. And that's why we haven't been able and we shan't *ever* be able to talk about anything involving our value-judgements without either becoming hypocritical or falling out. *I think this is incontestable*; I had noticed it a long time ago; and it was frightful for me, because it tainted our relations with one another: we seemed to be sitting side by side in a marsh. The fact is, we both of us have weaknesses, but especially *I* have, and my life is <u>FULL</u> of the ugliest and pettiest thoughts and actions imaginable (this is *not* an exaggeration). But if a relationship is not to be degrading for both sides then it should *not* be a relationship between the weaknesses on either side. No: a relationship should be confined to areas where both people involved have clean hands, i.e. where each can be completely frank without hurting the other. And that's something *we* can do ONLY by restricting our relationship to the communication of facts capable of being established object- ively, with perhaps also some mention of our friendly feelings for one another. But any other subject will lead, in our case, to hypocrisy or to falling out. Now perhaps, you'll say, "Things have more or less worked, up to the present. Why not go on in the same way?" But I'm *too* tired of this constant sordid compromise. My life has been one nasty mess so far – but need that go on indefinitely? – Now, I'll make a proposal to you. Let's write to each other about our work, our health, and the like, but let's avoid in our communica- tions any kind of value-judgment, on any subject whatsoever, and let's recognize clearly that in such judgments neither of us could be *completely* honest without hurting the other (this is certainly true in *my* case, at any rate). I don't need to assure you of my deep affection for you, *but that affection would be in great danger if we were to continue with a relationship based on hypocrisy and for that reason a source of shame to us both*. No, I think the honourable thing for both of us would be if we continued it on a more genuine basis. – I beg you to think this over and to send me an answer *only when* you can do it without bitterness. Feel assured in any case of my love and loyalty. I only hope you may understand this letter as it is meant to be understood.

Yours ever

L.W.

41.   **LW – GEM**

Skjolden
5.3.14.

DEAR MOORE,

   Only a few lines because I'm just now in the right mood. First of all: *write* soon when exactly you're going to come to Bergen. Secondly: *come* soon. Thirdly: I've got out LOTS of new logical stuff. (I don't dare to say more.) Fourthly: If you see Johnson please give him my kindest regards. Fifthly: if you see Muscio *please* tell him that he's a *beast* (he'll know why). Sixthly: once more – come soon. That's all.

Yours, etc., etc.

L.W.

M.6   Briefe 40

in the right mood. – For work, is meant.

42. **LW – GEM**

[Telegram]

10.3.14

MOORE TRINITY COLLEGE CAMBRIDGE ENGLAND
DO YOUR PAPER HERE YOU SHALL GET YOUR
OWN SITTINGROOM WRITING

WITTGENSTEIN

Briefe 41

43.　　　　　　　**LW – GEM**

[Skjolden, Sogn, Norway]
[March 1914]

Dear Moore,

Why on earth won't you do your paper *here*? You shall have *a
sitting-room* with a splendid view ALL BY YOURSELF and I shall leave
you alone as much as you like (*in fact the whole day, if necessary*). On
the other hand we *could* see one another whenever both of us
should like to. And we *could* even talk over your business (which
might be fun). Or do you want *so* many books? You see – I've
PLENTY to do myself, so I shan't disturb you a bit. *Do* take the Boat
that leaves Newcastle on the 17th arriving in Bergen on the 19th and
do your work here (I might even have a good influence upon it by
preventing too many repetitions). I *think*, now, that Logic must be
very nearly done if it is not already. – So, DO think over what I've
said!!

Yours, etc., etc.

L.W.

P.S. Oh – *Do* buy the "Schicksalslied" by Brahms in an arrangement for 4 hands and bring it with you. And, please, send a telegram
if you come on the 19th. I *hope* you will.

M.7　　Briefe 42

Presumably of the same date as 42., which refers to it.

Logic. – Evidently a piece of writing by Wittgenstein, perhaps already referred to
in 39. See comment in 45. below.

44. **LW & GEM – JMK**

[Postcard]   14, April 1914
                                   Bergen

J. M. Keynes Esq.
38 Brunswick Square
London W. C
England

                     G. E. MOORE
                  LUDWIG WITTGENSTEIN

Briefe 43

45.   **LW – GEM**

DEAR MOORE,

Your letter annoyed me. *When I wrote Logik I didn't consult the Regulations,* and therefore I think it would only be fair if you gave me my degree without consulting them so much either! As to a Preface and Notes; I think my examiners will easily see how much I have cribbed from Bosanquet. – If I'm not worth your making an exception for me *even in some* STUPID *details* then I may as well go to

---

my degree. – This letter seems to indicate that Wittgenstein meant to submit an essay entitled "Logic" (hardly "Logik") for the BA degree, which Research Students (as Advanced Students, see Introduction, were now called) would normally be expected to take. According to the regulations for Advanced Students, such a dissertation was expected to contain a preface and notes in which the students had to state the sources on which he had relied and "the extent to which he had availed himself of the work of others". There is a diary entry by Moore which would indicate that Moore had shown the stuff to W. M. Fletcher, tutor at Trinity College (see 10.), and been told that it could not possibly pass for a dissertation. Thereupon he had written to Wittgenstein about this, provoking his angry and probably unjustified reaction. It is of some interest to note that Wittgenstein is referring to the writing under the German title Logik. This may be taken as an indication that the dissertation was originally written in German, though Wittgenstein's spelling is not seldom erratic. The essay cannot be identical with "Notes on Logic" (see 24. above), given that Wittgenstein was working on it in February and March 1914 (see 39. and 43.). Presumably its original and German form was the manuscript shown to Moore in April (see 48.). The content of this is surely at least summarized in the so-called "Notes dictated to G. E. Moore in Norway" (published as Appendix II to *Notebooks 1914–16*), which Moore himself entitled "Wittgenstein on Logic, April 1914". Much speaks for the supposition that it was these notes that Moore showed to Fletcher and that Wittgenstein meant to submit. Fletcher's role is not entirely clear: perhaps Moore approached him for an impartial opinion from an outsider, for, in fact, Moore himself was Secretary of the Degrees Committee of the Special Board for Moral Sciences and, on the two occasions that year when applications were made, was one of the two referees. Both those applications were in the event rejected. All of these facts will have been known to Moore and enough of them to Wittgenstein: this perhaps explains the awkwardness of the situation. Something like it was to occur again in the small world of the Cambridge faculty, see 129.

Hell directly; and if I *am* worth it and you don't do it then – by God – *you* might go there.

The whole business is too stupid and too beastly to go on writing about it so –

L.W.

M.8 / *Briefe 44*

Bosanquet. – Bernard Bosanquet (1848–1923, and hence an almost exact contemporary of Frege's) was an Hegelian philosopher. The second edition of his *Logic* appeared in 1911. The reference is no doubt intended ironically.

46.   **LW – BR**

[Skjolden, Sogn, Norway]
[Probably June 1914]

LIEBER RUSSELL!

Nur ein paar Zeilen um Dir zu sagen daß ich Deinen l[ieben] Brief erhalten habe und daß meine Arbeit in den letzten 4–5 Monaten große Fortschritte gemacht hat. Jetzt aber bin ich wieder in einem Zustand der Ermüdung und kann weder arbeiten noch meine Arbeit erklären. Ich habe sie aber Moore als er bei mir war *ausführlich* erklärt und er hat sich verschiedenes aufgeschrieben. Du wirst also alles am besten von ihm erfahren können. Es ist viel Neues. – Am besten wirst Du alles verstehen wenn Du Moores Aufzeichnungen selber liesest. Es wird jetzt wohl wieder einige Zeit dauern bis ich wieder etwas hervorbringe. Bis dahin,

Dein

L.W.

Russell arrived back from the United States on 14 June. Wittgenstein may have known from Russell's letters to him, when Russell was supposed to return to England. If this is so, then the use of the past tense in "Hoffentlich war Deine Reise erfolgreich" (I hope your journey was a success), would indicate that the letter was written in the middle or second half of June.

Moore's visit was from 29 March to 14 April. Wittgenstein seems to have returned to Austria from Norway about the turn of the months June–July. We know from 47. that he was in Vienna in the beginning of July. Later in July he was on the Hochreit and on the eve of the outbreak of the war again in Vienna. (See Ludwig Wittgenstein, *Briefe an Ludwig von Ficker*, ed. by G. H. von Wright in co-operation with W. Methlagl.)

Before the war Wittgenstein did not live in the hut he was building. After the war, in 1921, he visited the place in the company of his friend Arvid Sjögren and that was the first time he lived in the hut. Apart from shorter visit he lived there again for the greater part of the academic year 1936–7. (See 165., 166., and 167.). It was then that he started work on the *Investigations*. His last visit to Skjolden was towards the end of 1950 in the company of his friend, Dr Ben Richards.

P.S. Ich baue mir jetzt hier ein kleines Haus in der Einsamkeit. Hoffentlich war Deine Reise erfolgreich.

R.28   *Briefe45*

English Translation

DEAR RUSSELL,

Just a few lines to tell you that I received your kind letter and that my work has made considerable progress in the last four or five months. But I have now relapsed into a state of exhaustion and can neither do any work nor explain what I did earlier. However I explained it *in detail* to Moore when he was with me and he made various notes. So you can best find it all out from him. Many things in it are new. – The best way to understand it all would be if you read Moore's notes for yourself. It will probably be some time now before I produce anything further. Till then –

Yours

L.W.

P.S. I am now building myself a small house here miles from anyone. I hope your journey was a success.

47.   LW – GEM

Wien XVII
Neuwaldeggerstraße 38
July 3rd, '14

DEAR MOORE,

Upon clearing up some papers before leaving Skjolden I popped upon your letter which had made me so wild. And upon reading it over again I found that I had probably no sufficient reason to write to you as I did. (Not that I like your letter a bit *now*.) But at any rate my wrath has cooled down and I'd rather be friends with you again

---

Neuwaldeggerstraße. – the address of a big house which the Wittgenstein family had on the outskirts of Vienna.

Moore had every reason to be offended by Wittgenstein's previous letter (45.). He did not reply to 45. or to 47. In an autobiographical annotation Moore says that after the 'violent letter of abuse' (45.) he had no contact with Wittgenstein until Wittgenstein's return to Cambridge in January 1929. Moore did however hear, indirectly, from Wittgenstein, since on 15 January 1915 (misdated 1914 by a common slip of the pen) Wittgenstein's friend David Pinsent wrote to him as follows:

> Dear Mr Moore,
> I have heard from Wittgenstein several times since the beginning of the War (he is serving in the Austrian Army) and in his last letter he asks me to send a message to you. He writes:
>> If you get to Cambridge next time please go and see Moore with whom I had a quarrel – give him my love and say that I'm sorry I offended him, in short make my peace with him. As it is unlikely that I shall be in Cambridge in the near future [This was perhaps the meaning of "next time". *Ed.*] I thought it would be best if I wrote to you instead. . . . [The rest of the letter consists of directions for writing to Wittgenstein via the Red Cross, information which Moore doubtless already had from Russell. *Ed.*]

Moore continued to worry over the quarrel – his diaries show that he told Desmond McCarthy "all about Wittgenstein" the week-end after receiving Pinsent's letter – but made no outward response to this overture. From Pinsent's letters to Wittgenstein, printed in *A Portrait*, pp. 100 f., it is obvious that Wittgenstein returned to the topic of his amende. On 6 April 1915 Pinsent eventually said, "I am so sorry if Moore won't behave like a Christian: as a matter of fact he never acknowledged my letter."

than otherwise. I consider I have strained myself enough now for I would *not* have written this to many people and if you don't answer this I shan't write to you again.

Yours, etc., etc.

L.W.

M.9   *Briefe 46*

48.   **LW – BR**

[Probably Christmas 1914]

LIEBER RUSSELL!

Erst heute erhielt ich Deinen lieben Brief, den Du am 28. Juli an mich geschrieben hast. Daß Moore meine Ideen Dir nicht hat erklären können, ist mir unbegreiflich. Hast Du aus seinen Notizen irgend etwas entnehmen können?? Ich fürchte, Nein! Sollte ich in diesem Krieg umkommen, so wird Dir mein Manuskript, welches ich damals Moore zeigte, zugeschickt werden; nebst einem, welches ich jetzt während des Krieges geschrieben habe. Im Falle ich am Leben bleibe, so möchte ich nach dem Kriege nach England kommen und Dir meine Arbeit – wenn es Dir recht ist – mündlich erklären. Ich bin auch im ersten Fall davon überzeugt, daß sie früher oder später von jemandem verstanden werden wird! Besten

Moore – Russell showed this letter to Moore (or read to him from it) on 20 January, according to Moore's diary. Moore comments, 'Russell must have told him that I couldn't [explain his ideas] but he had no right to say this because he has never tried to get me to explain them.'

Subsequently, on 10 February, Russell did ask to see Moore's notes.

Notizen/Notes – Refers to the Notes dictated by Wittgenstein to Moore in Norway, published as an appendix to *Notebooks 1914–1916*.

Manuskript/Manuscript. – The manuscript which Wittgenstein had shown to Moore in Norway is apparently lost; the manuscript written during the war must be the first of the posthumously published *1914–1916* notebooks.

Letters

Dank für die Zusendung Deiner Schrift über Sense-Data. Ich habe sie noch nicht gelesen. Möge der Himmel mir bald wieder gute Ideen schenken!!! –

Dein

LUDWIG WITTGENSTEIN

Bitte grüße Johnson herzlichst!

Meine Adresse ist   :   Art[illerie] Autodetachement
„Oblt Gürth"
Feldpost No 186

R.30   *Briefe 61*

English Translation

DEAR RUSSELL,

It was only today that I got your kind letter which you wrote me on 28th July. I find it inconceivable that Moore wasn't able to explain my ideas to you. Were you able to get anything at all out of his notes? I'm afraid the answer is, No. If I should not survive the present war, the manuscript of mine that I showed to Moore at the

Schrift über Sense-Data/piece about Sense Data. – This must be "The Relation of Sense-Data to Physics", *Scientia*, 16 July 1914 (reprinted in *Mysticism and Logic*.)

Oblt. – Oberleutnant.

For Wittgenstein's military career during the First World War see the Editor's Appendix to Paul Engelmann, *Letters from Ludwig Wittgenstein with a Memoir*, ed. B. F. McGuinness, pp. 140–2 and *Young Ludwig*, pp. 211–68.

time will be sent to you, along with another one which I have written now, during the war. In the case that I am still alive, I should like to come to England after the war and explain my work to you orally, if you've no objection. Even in the former case, I'm convinced that it will be understood by somebody sooner or later. Thank you very much for sending your piece about sense-data. I haven't read it yet. Heaven send I'll have some good ideas again soon!!!

Yours

LUDWIG WITTGENSTEIN

Please remember me very kindly to Johnson.

My address is: Artillerie Autodetachment
                   "Oblt Gürth"
                   Feldpost No 186.

49.   **LW – JMK**

K.u.k. Art. Autodetachment
Feldpost No 186
[Jan 4, 1915]

DEAR KEYNES,

I've got the letter you wrote to me in September. The money will be sent to the registry as soon as the war will be over. Please give my love to Johnson whom I appreciate more and more the longer I haven't seen him.

If you get this please write to me to the above address via the red cross Switzerland.

Yours

L. WITTGENSTEIN

K.7   *Briefe 62.*

Jan 4, 1915. – Date added by Keynes. Probably the date of receipt, cf. 52.

K. u. k.– *Kaiserliche and königliche,* Imperial and Royal, the style of institutions common to Austria and Hungary.

50.   **JMK – LW**

10 January 1915
Kings College
Cambridge

DEAR WITTGENSTEIN,

I am astonished to have got a letter from you. Do you think it proves that you existed within a short time of my getting it? I think so. I hope you have been safely taken prisoner by now.

Russell and I have given up philosophy for the present – I to give my services to the Govt for financial business, he to agitate for peace. But Moore and Johnson go on just as usual. Russell, by the way, brought out a new book at about the beginning of the War.

Pinsent had not joined the army by the middle of October but I have not heard since.

This is presumably the letter received by Wittgenstein on 25 January, according to his code diary: "nicht sehr lieb" ("Not specially friendly") he comments. It is of some interest that Wittgenstein scribbled logical formulae and illustrations of facts – "aRb", "cPd", and models projecting *----* on to x----x in the space left blank by Keynes, echoing the discussion of propositions and pictures in his Notebooks for this period.

give my services to the Government. – Keynes joined the Treasury on 3 August 1914 and served brilliantly until June 1919, when he left in a disagreement over the Treaty negotiations in Paris. See Roy Harrod, *The Life of J. M. Keynes* and the first volume of Robert Skidelsky's *John Maynard Keynes*.

to agitate for peace. – Russell, in Vol. II of his *Autobiography*, describes his opposition to the war as beginning precisely when Keynes left Cambridge for the Treasury but it intensified as the war proceeded. It cost him his lectureship at Trinity and earned him a spell in prison. See also Alan Ryan, *Russell, A Political Life.*

a new book. – Presumably *Our Knowledge of the External World*, on which see comments, to 35. above.

Your dear friend Békássy is in your army and your very dear friend Bliss is a private in ours.

It must be pleasanter to be at war than to think about propositions in Norway. But I hope you will stop such self-indulgence soon.

Yours

J.M. KEYNES

---

friend Békássy . . . very dear friend Bliss. – Ferenc Békássy and F. K. Bliss, the former a Hungarian nobleman, were both of them Kingsmen and members of the Society (see 39 above.) whose company Wittgenstein was known to dislike. (See *P. Levy, Moore*, pp. 268 ff.) Both fell in the war.

51. **BR – LW**

Trinity College,
Cambridge
5 Feb. 1915

MY DEAR WITTGENSTEIN

It was a *very* great happiness to hear from you – I had been thinking of you constantly and longing for news. I am amazed that you have been able to write a MS. on logic since the war began. I cannot tell you how great a joy it will be to see you again after the war, if all goes well. If only your MSS come to me, I will do my utmost to understand them and make others understand them; but without your help it will be difficult.

Your letter came about 3 weeks ago – I did not know how I should answer it, but I am enabled to by the kindness of an American who is going to Italy.

Please remember me to your mother, and tell her that you are constantly in my mind with anxious affection.

Ever yours

BERTRAND RUSSELL

This letter came to the Russell Archives from W. H. Watson, the physicist. Though sent by Russell it was returned (see 53.) and was only given to Wittgenstein after the war. In the 1930s Wittgenstein made a present of it to Watson, a Cambridge friend.

to hear from you. – Russell is referring to Wittgenstein's letter (48.) apparently of December 1914.

52.   **LW – JMK**

K.u.k. Art. Autodetachement
"Oblt. Gürth"
Feldpost No 186
[25 January 1915]

DEAR KEYNES,

Got your letter you wrote January 10th today. I'm very interested to hear that Russell has published a book lately. Could you possibly send it to me and let me pay you after the war? I'd so much like to see it. By the way, you're quite wrong if you think that being a soldier prevents me from thinking about propositions. As a matter of fact I've done a good deal of logical work lately, and hope to do a good deal more soon. – Please give my love to Johnson. The war hasn't altered my private feelings in the least (thank God!!) Or rather: I think I've grown a little milder. I wonder if Russell has been able to make anything out from the notes I gave to Moore last Easter?

Yours

L. WITTGENSTEIN

K.8   Briefe 69

For the date and for the book by Russell referred to, see comments on 50.

53.   **BR – LW**

Trinity College,
Cambridge.
10.5.15

LIEBER WITTGENSTEIN!

Dein Brief vom 13ten April ist eben jetzt angekommen – ich freue mich sehr Nachrichten von Dir zu bekommen. Als ich Deinen vorigen Brief erhielt, habe ich sofort geantwortet, zur selben Zeit als ich Deiner Mutter schrieb, aber der Brief ist nach zwei Monaten zurückgekommen – er soll zu freundlich gewesen sein! Von Deiner Mutter habe ich neulich einen sehr lieben Brief bekommen – bitte schicke ihr meinen besten Dank dafür.

Wenn Du dafür die Zeit hast, so solltest Du in Krakau einen einsamen alten Logiker besuchen, Namens M. Dziewicki, Szczepanska, 11. Er hat die "Principia Mathematica" studiert, und kennt wahrscheinlich niemand der sich mit der modernen Logik beschäftigt. Es würde ihm gewiß große Freude machen, Dich zu sehen.

Dein Brief vom 13ten April/your letter of 13 April. – This appears to be lost.

Dziewicki. – M. H. Dziewicki, who among other things taught English in Cracow, had published a paper on scholastic philosophy in the *Proceedings of the Aristotelian Society*. He was in philosophical correspondence with Russell during this period. Two postcards from Dziewicki to Wittgenstein (now in the Brenner Archiv) show that there were visits to Dziewicki's house by Wittgenstein in (apparently) June 1915 and philosophical discussion (e.g. of the problem of the contiguity of instants of time). After the war Dziewicki wrote to Russell (the letters are in the Russell Archives):

> I am glad to get news of Wittgenstein; a most genial young man, whom I was very much pleased to meet. Will you tell him how much I rejoice to know that his gloomy forebodings have not been realized.

Internal evidence suggests that "a young man of genius" is meant. Against the last quoted sentence is a note in Russell's hand: "He expected to be killed in Russia." In further letters Dziewicki requests a copy of *Tractatus Logico-Philosophicus* and later comments on the work, saying *inter alia* that its doctrine that belief is not a relation had been one of the main points of difference between him and Wittgenstein in their discussions.

Ich habe alles von Moore erhalten, was er über Tautologien etc. zu berichten hatte; es war mir aber nur in geringem Maaße verständlich. Ich hoffe aus ganzem Herzen daß Du mir nach dem Kriege alles mündlich erklären wirst. Seit der Krieg anfing, ist es mir unmöglich über Philosophie zu denken – daran wird aber wohl schließlich ein Ende sein. Ich denke fortwährend an Dich, und sende Dir die herzlichsten Wünsche.

Dein

BERTRAND RUSSELL.

English Translation

DEAR WITTGENSTEIN

Your letter of 13 April has just arrived – I am very happy to have news from you. When I received your earlier letter, I replied at once, at the same time as I wrote to your mother. But the letter came back two months later: it seems to have been too friendly! I have recently had a very kind letter from your mother – please send her my best thanks for it.

In Cracow, if you have the time for it, you should visit a lonely old logician called M. Dziewicki, Szczepanska, 11. He has studied *Principia Mathematica* and probably knows no one who has concerned himself with modern logic. It would certainly give him great pleasure to see you.

I have got from Moore everything he had to report about tautologies etc., but it was intelligible to me only in very small measure. I hope with all my heart that you will explain everything to me orally after the war. Since the war began, it has been impossible for me to think about philosophy – but no doubt that will come to an end some day. I think of you continually and send you most heartfelt wishes.

Yours

BERTRAND RUSSELL

54.   **LW – BR**

K.u.k. Werkstätte der Festung Krakau
Feldpost No 186
22.5.15.

LIEBER RUSSELL!

Erhielt heute Deinen lieben Brief vom 10.5. Dziewicki werde
ich so bald als möglich besuchen; bin schon sehr neugierig auf ihn.
Daß Du Moores Aufschreibungen nicht hast verstehen können
tut mir außerordentlich leid! Ich fühle, daß sie ohne weitere Erklärung sehr schwer verständlich sind, aber ich halte sie doch im
Wesentlichen für endgültig richtig. Was ich in der letzten Zeit
geschrieben habe wird nun, wie ich fürchte, noch unverständlicher
sein; und, wenn ich das Ende dieses Krieges nicht mehr erlebe, so
muß ich mich darauf gefaßt machen, daß meine ganze Arbeit
verloren geht. – Dann soll mein Manuskript gedruckt werden, ob
es irgend einer versteht, oder nicht! –
Die Probleme werden immer lapidarer und allgemeiner und die
Methode hat sich durchgreifend geändert. –
Hoffen wir auf ein Wiedersehen nach dem Krieg! Sei herzlichst
gegrüßt von

Deinem treuen

LUDWIG WITTGENSTEIN

R.31   *Briefe 70*

K.u.k. – See comments on 49.
Dziewicki. – See comments on 53.

English Translation

DEAR RUSSELL

Received today your kind letter of 10.5. I will visit Dziewicki as soon as possible; I'm already very curious about him.

I'm extremely sorry that you weren't able to understand Moore's notes. I feel that they're very hard to understand without further explanation, but I regard them essentially as definitive. And now I'm afraid that what I've written recently will be still more incomprehensible, and if I don't live to see the end of this war I must be prepared for all my work to go for nothing. – In that case you must get my manuscript printed whether anyone understands it or not. –

The problems are becoming more and more lapidary and general and the method has changed drastically. –

Let's hope for a reunion after the war! Warmest regards from

Your devoted friend

LUDWIG WITTGENSTEIN

55.   **LW – BR**

Frau Elsa Gröger
Gut Wangensbach
Küsnacht (Zch.)
22.10.15.

Lieber Russell!

Ich habe in der letzten Zeit sehr viel gearbeitet und, wie ich glaube, mit gutem Erfolg. Ich bin jetzt dabei das Ganze zusammenzufassen und in Form einer Abhandlung niederzuschreiben. Ich werde nun keinesfalls etwas veröffentlichen, ehe Du es gesehen hast. Das kann aber natürlich erst nach dem Kriege geschehen. Aber, wer weiß, ob ich das erleben werde. Falls ich es nicht mehr erlebe, so laß Dir von meinen Leuten meine ganzen Manuscripte schicken, darunter befindet sich auch die letzte Zusammenfassung mit Bleistift auf losen Blättern geschrieben. Es wird Dir vielleicht einige Mühe machen alles zu verstehen, aber laß Dich dadurch nicht abschrecken. Meine gegenwärtige Adresse ist:

K.u.k. Artillerie Werkstätten Zug No I
Feldpost No 12.

Hast Du Pinsent in der letzten Zeit einmal gesehen? Wenn Du Johnson siehst so grüße ihn bestens von mir. Ich denke noch immer

---

Frau Elsa Gröger. – Her address is stamped on both letter and envelope, which thus seemed to originate in neutral Switzerland and hence perhaps might arrive sooner or more securely. She was a friend (probably a cousin) of Wittgenstein's mother and lived near Zürich; later she petitioned the Vatican to secure his early release from prison-camp. See *Young Ludwig*, pp. 275 f (in the first impression of that work her surname by a misreading was given as "Gräzer").

Zusammenfassung/final summary. – This was "probably the first of about three preliminary versions of the *Tractatus* (*Young Ludwig*, p 237) Note the use, as for that work, of the description "*Abhandlung* ".

Johnson. – See 16. above and 121. below.

gerne an ihn und an unsere fruchtlosen und aufgeregten Disputa-
tionen. Möge der Himmel geben, daß wir uns noch einmal sehen!
  Sei herzlichst gegrüßt von

Deinem treuen

WITTGENSTEIN

R.32   *Briefe 74*

English Translation

DEAR RUSSELL,

  I have recently done a great deal of work and, I think, quite
successfully. I'm now in the process of summarizing it all and
writing it down in the form of a treatise. Now: whatever happens I
won't publish anything until you have seen it. But, of course, that
can't happen until after the war. But who knows whether I shall
survive until then? If I don't survive, get my people to send you all
my manuscripts: among them you'll find the final summary written
in pencil on loose sheets of paper. It will perhaps cost you some
trouble to understand it all, but don't let yourself be put off by that.
My present address is:

> K.u.k. Artillerie Werkstätten Zug No 1
> Feldpost No 12

  Have you seen anything of Pinsent recently? If you see Johnson,
please give him my best regards. I still remember him with great
pleasure, as also the fruitless and heated discussions we used to have.
Heaven grant that we may meet again sometime!
  Warmest regards from

Your devoted friend

WITTGENSTEIN

56.   **BR – LW**

34 Russell Chambers
Bury Str. W.C.
25 Nov. 1915

LIEBER WITTGENSTEIN!

Es war mir eine sehr große Freude Deinen lieben Brief zu erhalten – erst vor einigen Tagen ist er angekommen. Es freut mich ganz außerordentlich daß Du eine Abhandlung schreibst die Du veröffentlichen willst. Ich glaube kaum daß es notwendig sei bis zum Ende des Krieges zu warten. Könntest Du nicht das MS. vervielfältigen lassen und nach Amerika schicken? Professor Ralph Barton Perry, Harvard University, Cambridge, Mass., U.S.A., kennt Deine früheren logischen Theorien durch mich. Er würde mir das MS. Schicken, und ich wurde es veröffentlichen.

Seit langer Zeit habe ich weder Pinsent noch Johnson gesehen. Ich bin während diesem Winter nicht in Cambridge. Nächstes Frühjahr kehre ich zurück.

Wie schön wird es sein wenn wir uns endlich wiedersehen! Ich denke fortwährend an Dich, und wünsche Nachrichten von Dir zu bekommen. Sei glücklich, und möge der Schicksal Dich schonen!

Dein treuer

BERTRAND RUSSELL

Deinen . . . Brief/your . . . letter. – refers to 53.

Perry. – Ralph Barton Perry (1876–1957), an eminent philosopher at Harvard, where Russell in 1914 explained Wittgenstein's ideas, using a version of *Notes on Logic.*

English Translation

DEAR WITTGENSTEIN,

It was a very great pleasure for me to receive your kind letter – it arrived only a few days ago. I am absolutely delighted that you are writing a monograph and want it published. I hardly think that it is necessary to wait until the end of the war. Could you not have a copy of the manuscript made and send it to America? Professor Ralph Barton Perry, Harvard University, Cambridge, Mass., U.S.A., knows of your previous logical theories from me. He would send me the manuscript and I would publish it.

It is a long time since I have seen either Pinsent or Johnson. This winter I am not in Cambridge. I go back there next spring.

How splendid it will be when we finally meet again. I constantly think of you and want to have news of you. Be happy, and may Fate spare you!

Yours ever,

BERTRAND RUSSELL

57.   **LW – BR**

[Postcard]

Cassino
Provincia Caserta
Italia
9.2.19.

DEAR RUSSELL,

I don't know your precise address but hope these lines will reach you somehow. I am prisoner in Italy since November and hope I may communicate with you after a three years interruption. I have done lots of logical work which I am dying to let you know before publishing it.

Ever yours

LUDWIG WITTGENSTEIN

R. 33   Briefe 94

---

precise address. – The postcard was addressed by Wittgenstein to Russell c/o Dr A. N. Whitehead, University College, London.

58. **BR – LW**

Garsington Manor,
near Oxford.
2.3.19.

Most thankful to hear you are still alive. Please write on Logic,
when possible. I hope it will not be long now before a talk will be
possible. I too have very much to say about philosophy etc.

B. RUSSELL.

59.   **BR – LW**

Manor House,
Garsington, Oxford.
3.3.19.

Very glad to hear from you – had been anxious for a long time.
I shall be most interested to learn what you have done in Logic. I
hope before long it may be possible to hear all about it. Shall be glad
of further news – about your health etc.

B. RUSSELL.

A duplicate of 58., no doubt occasioned by distrust of postal connections with a
prisoner-of-war camp. In fact both postcards are postmarked 8 March on arrival in
Cassino.

60. **LW – BR**

[Postcard]

Cassino
Prov[incia] Caserta
Italia
10.3.19.

You can't imagine how glad I was to get your cards! I am afraid though there is no hope that we may meet before long. Unless you came to see me here, but this would be too much joy for me. I can't write on Logic as I'm not allowed to write more than 2 cards (15 lines each) a week. I've written a book which will be published as soon as I get home. I think I have solved our problems finally. Write to me often. It will shorten my prison. God bless you.

Ever yours

WITTGENSTEIN

R.34   *Briefe 95*

61.   **LW – BR**

[Cassino, Provincia Caserta, Italy]
13.3.19.

DEAR RUSSELL,

Thanks so much for your postcards dated 2nd and 3rd of March. I've had a *very* bad time, not knowing whether you were dead or alive! I can't write on Logic as I'm not allowed to write more than two p[ost] c[ard]s a week (15 lines each). This letter is an exception, it's posted by an Austrian medical student who goes home tomorrow. I've written a book called "Logisch-Philosophische Abhandlung" containing all my work of the last six years. I believe I've solved our problems finally. This may sound arrogant but I can't help believing it. I finished the book in August 1918 and two months after was made Prigioniere. I've got the manuscript here with me. I wish I could copy it out for you; but it's pretty long and I would have no safe way of sending it to you. In fact you would not understand it without a previous explanation as it's written in quite short remarks. (This of course means that *nobody* will understand it; although I believe, it's all as clear as crystal. But it upsets all our theory of truth, of classes, of numbers and all the rest.) I will publish it as soon as I get home. Now I'm afraid this *won't* be "before long". And consequently it will be a long time yet till we can meet. I can hardly imagine seeing you again! It will be too much! I suppose it would be impossible for you to come and see

Russell, upon receipt of this letter, copied it out by hand and had copies typed out. We know from his correspondence with Colette (Lady Constance Malleson) of 19, 23, and 24 March 1919 that he meant to send the copies to various people who might be able to help Wittgenstein, among them Keynes and G. M. Trevelyan, see 62. and 64. below and comments. Six clean copies remain in the Russell Archives because the typists at first corrected the spelling, contrary to Russell's explicit instructions. They had to do the work again and we indeed have a copy in the Wittgenstein file of the Keynes Papers, kept at King's College, Cambridge, which retains a few misspellings: "crystall", "immagine", "collossal".

me here? or perhaps you think it's colossal cheek of me even to think of such a thing. But if you were on the other end of the world and I *could* come to you I would do it.

Please write to me how you are, remember me to Dr Whitehead. Is old Johnson still alive? Think of me often!

Ever yours

LUDWIG WITTGENSTEIN

R.35   *Briefe 96*

62.   **JMK – LW**

> Delegazione italiana
> al congresso della pace
> Hotel Edouard VII
> Parigi
> 13 May 1919

MY DEAR WITTGENSTEIN,

Russell has sent me a letter of yours showing that you are a prisoner of war in Italy and have the manuscript of your book with you; – but have no safe way of dealing with it. Perhaps this is all out of date by now. But in case it is not, I am begging the Italian authorities to do all that is possible in the circumstances and to provide an absolutely safe way of conveying the MS. or other communications to Russell through me. I much hope that it may also be possible to arrange some relaxation of the usual provisions.

I should immensely like to see you again.

> Yours ever
>
> J. M. KEYNES

Keynes was in Paris for the Peace Conference, see comments on 50. above. This letter was written on a sheet of the headed writing paper of the Italian delegation. For the final attitude of the Italian authorities see comments on 64. below and *Young Ludwig*, p. 276.

63.   **LW – JMK**

Cassino
12.6.19.

My dear Keynes,

Please kindly forward the enclosed letter to Russell's address. I wish I could see him somehow or other, for I am sure he won't be able to understand my book without a very thorough explanation, which can't be written. Have you done any more work on probability? My M-S. contains a few lines about it which, I believe, – solve the essential question.

Yours ever

Ludwig Wittgenstein

!!

K.9   Briefe 98

enclosed letter. – This is 64.

work on probability. – Keynes had been working on probability for many years. For his *Treatise on Probability* see 66. below and Skidelsky's *John Maynard Keynes*, especially vol. 2, pp. 56 ff. In the *Tractatus* a logical definition of probability is given in the propositions 5.15 ff.

64. **LW – BR**

Cassino
12.6.19.

Lieber Russell!

Vor einigen Tagen schickte ich Dir mein Manuskript durch Keynes's Vermittelung. Ich schrieb damals nur ein paar Zeilen für Dich hinein. Seither ist nun Dein Buch ganz in meine Hände gelangt und nun hätte ich ein großes Bedürfnis Dir einiges zu schreiben. – Ich hätte nicht geglaubt, daß das, was ich vor 6 Jahren in Norwegen dem Moore diktierte an Dir so spurlos vorübergehen würde. Kurz ich fürchte jetzt, es möchte sehr schwer für mich sein mich mit Dir zu verständigen. Und der geringe Rest von Hoffnung mein M.S. könne Dir etwas sagen, ist ganz verschwunden. Einen Kommentar zu meinem Buch zu schreiben, bin ich, wie Du Dir denken kannst, nicht im Stande. Nur mündlich könnte ich Dir einen geben. Ist Dir irgend an dem Verständnis der Sache etwas gelegen und kannst Du ein Zusammentreffen mit mir bewerkstelligen, so bitte, tue es. – Ist dies nicht möglich, so sei so gut und schicke das M.S. so bald Du es gelesen hast auf sicherem Wege nach

ein paar Zeilen/a couple of lines. – These lines are apparently no longer extant.

Dein Buch/your book. – Russell's *Introduction to Mathematical Philosophy*, which was published in March 1919. In a letter to J. M. Keynes of 23 March 1919 Russell says that he wanted to send his "new book" to Wittgenstein but that he does not know whether this will be possible. He also says that he had written to George Trevelyan asking him whether he could do anything to obtain permission for Wittgenstein to "communicate freely about logic". Russell wonders whether Keynes could "speak to anybody about him" and concludes the letter by saying "I wish he could get permission to come to England". Trevelyan did obtain, through Dr Filippo de Filippi, permission for Wittgenstein to receive books. Filippi recommended sending them by letter post and it seems that this book was sent in parts (*ist . . . ganz in meine Hände gelangt* ["has reached me *in toto*"]). There was some residual difficulty about letters, which perhaps accounts for the fact that Wittgenstein sent his typescript to Russell through Keynes (cf. 63.).

Wien zurück. Es ist das einzige korrigierte Exemplar, welches ich besitze und die Arbeit meines Lebens! Mehr als je brenne ich *jetzt* darauf es gedruckt zu sehen. Es ist bitter, das vollendete Werk in der Gefangenschaft herumschleppen zu müssen und zu sehen, wie der Unsinn draußen sein Spiel treibt! Und ebenso bitter ist es zu denken daß niemand es verstehen wird, auch wenn es gedruckt sein wird! – Hast Du mir jemals seit Deinen zwei ersten Karten geschrieben? Ich habe nichts erhalten.

Sei herzlichst gegrüßt und *glaube nicht, daß alles Dummheit ist was Du nicht verstehen wirst.*

Dein treuer

LUDWIG WITTGENSTEIN

R.36   *Briefe 99*

English Translation

DEAR RUSSELL,

Some days ago I sent you my manuscript through Keynes's intermediacy. At that time I enclosed only a couple of lines for you. Since then your book has reached me *in toto* and I'd very much like to write some things to you. – I should never have believed that the stuff I dictated to Moore in Norway six years ago would have passed over you so completely without trace. In short, I'm now afraid that it might be very difficult for me to reach any understanding with you. And the small remaining hope that my manuscript might mean something to you has completely vanished. As you can imagine, I'm in no position to write a commentary on my book. I could only give you one orally. If you attach any importance whatsoever to understanding the thing and if you can manage to arrange a meeting with me, then please do so. – If that isn't possible, then be so good as to send the manuscript back to Vienna by a safe route as soon as you've read it. It is the only corrected copy I possess and is my life's work! *Now* more than ever I'm burning to see it in print. It's galling to have to lug the completed work round in captivity and to see how nonsense has a clear field outside! And it's equally galling to think that no one will understand it even if it does get printed! – Have you written to me at all since your first two postcards? I've received nothing.

Warmest regards and *don't think that everything that you won't understand is a piece of stupidity.*

Your devoted friend

LUDWIG WITTGENSTEIN

65.   **BR – LW**

> 70, Overstrand Mansions,
> Prince of Wales Road,
> Battersea, S. W.
> 21 June 1919

DEAR WITTGENSTEIN

Your letter reached me today, but your MS. has not come yet. It is true that what you dictated to Moore was not intelligible to me, and he would give me no help. I think probably it is true that I shan't understand your MS till I see you, but it will be easier to get understanding from your talk if I have read the MS carefully first. At the moment, I could not get a passport to go abroad, but that won't last. I think probably it will be possible for us to meet at Christmas time, but it is not likely to be possible sooner.

I wrote only two post-cards, as I thought letters would not be allowed. But I wrote innumerable letters about you, trying to get greater freedom for you. They bore some slight fruit, but not as much as I hoped. I also wrote to your mother, but the letter was returned to me! – Please don't be discouraged about my understanding your work. Throughout the war I did not think about philosophy, until, last summer, I found myself in prison, and beguiled my leisure by writing a popular text-book, which was all I could do under the circumstances. Now I am back at philosophy, and more in the mood to understand.

I shall read your MS the moment I get it, and return it. What will be the address to which it is to be returned? All friendship and

---

Your letter. – That of 12 June (63.) is evidently meant. Possibly an answer by Russell to Wittgenstein's letter of 13 March, which has been lost.

innumerable letters. – See comments on 61. and 63.

popular text book – *Introduction to Mathematical Philosophy*, the only book which Russell wrote during his time in prison, must be the text-book in question.

affection from me to you. Don't be discouraged – you will be understood in the end.

Yours ever

B. RUSSELL.

66.   **JMK – LW**

King's College
Cambridge
28 June 1919

MY DEAR WITTGENSTEIN,

Your book has safely reached me and I am forwarding it immediately to Russell. As soon as peace is safely signed, is there any good likelihood of our seeing you in England?

I had nearly finished my book on Probability in the summer of 1914 and most of it, indeed, was actually in print. But the war stopped all such thoughts. I hope now soon to take it up again and at last publish early next year.

Yours ever

J. M. KEYNES

Probability. – The book was published by Macmillan in 1921.

67.   **BR – LW**

70, Overstrand Mansions
Prince of Wales Road,
Battersea, S.W.
13 August 1919

DEAR WITTGENSTEIN,

I have now read your book twice carefully. – There are still points I don't understand – some of them important ones – I send you some queries on separate sheets. I am convinced you are right in your main contention, that logical props are tautologies, which are not true in the sense that substantial props are true. I do not understand why you are content with a purely ordinal theory of number, nor why you use for the purpose an ancestral relation, when you object to ancestral relations. This part of your work I want further explained. Also you do not state your reasons against classes. *I am sure you are right in thinking the book of first-class importance.* But in places it is obscure through brevity. I have a most intense desire to see you, to talk it over, as well as simply because I want to see you. But I can't get abroad as yet. Probably you will be free to come to England before I am free to go abroad. – I will send back your MS when I know where to send it, but I am hoping you will soon be at liberty.

All best wishes. Do write again soon.

Yours ever,

B. RUSSELL

[The separate sheet with queries:]
Wittgenstein
2. What is the difference between Tatsache and Sachverhalt?
3. "Das logische Bild der Tatsachen ist der Gedanke." Yes, I agree. But a Gedanke is a Tatsache: what are its constituents and components, and what is their relation to those of the pictured Tatsache?

Letters

3.331. The theory of types, in my view, is a theory of correct symbolism:
(a) a simple symbol must not be used to express anything complex; (b)
more generally, a symbol must have the same structure as its meaning.

4 & 4.001. "Der Gedanke ist der sinnvolle Satz." "Die Gesamtheit der
Sätze ist die Sprache." Does a Gedanke consist of words? Compare 3
(above).

4.112. I agree strongly with this number.

4.1272. I suppose this hangs together with the rejection of identity. It is
awkward to be unable to speak of Nc'V. One could still say

$$(\exists \phi) \ . \ Nc'\hat{x}(\phi x) > V$$
$$(\phi) \quad . \ Nc'\hat{x}(\phi x) \leq V$$

and I should have thought that from such props one could obtain a meaning
for "there are at least 2 Gegenstände" – for you, "$(\exists x, y, \phi) . \phi x . \phi y$ "
would suffice – and similar statements. There are things that puzzle me
in this number and the next.

4.211. I gather no elementary prop is negative.

4.51. It is necessary also to be given the prop that *all* elementary props are
given.

5.15. This theory of probability seems to me right.

5.3 All props results of truth-operations on elementary props? How about
generality?

5.453. No numbers in logic? Why?

5.53 seq. On identity. I agree with this. But the connection with the
axiom of infinity seems dubious. See remark on 4.1272 above.

6. "General truth-function: $[\bar{p}, \bar{\xi}, N(\bar{\xi})]$"
Yes, this is *one* way. But could one not do equally well by making $N(\bar{\xi})$ mean "at least one value of ξ is false", just as one can do
equally well with ~p∨~q and with ~p.~q as fundamental? I feel as if the
duality of generality and existence persisted covertly in your system.

6.03. "General form of integer: $[0, \xi, \xi, +1]$". You only get finite ordinals.
You deny classes, so cardinals collapse. What happens to $\aleph_0$? If you said
classes were superfluous in *logic* I would imagine that I understood you,
by supposing a distinction between logic and mathematics; but
when you say they are unnecessary in *mathematics* I am puzzled. E.g.
something true is expressed by $Nc'Cl'\alpha = 2^{Nc'\alpha}$. How do you re-state this
prop?

I agree with what you say about induction, causality, etc.; at least, I can find no ground for disagreeing.

English Translation of German passages in the queries

The Ramsey–Ogden version, not always felicitously, but under the influence of Russell and Wittgenstein himself, adopts the following translations:

2. *Tatsache*, fact. *Sachverhalt*, atomic fact.
3. "The logical picture of the facts is the thought."
4. "The thought is the significant proposition."
4.001. "The totality of propositions is the language."
4.1272. *Gegenstände*, objects.

68.   **LW – BR**

Cassino
19.8.19.

DEAR RUSSELL,

Thanks so much for your letter dated 13 August. As to your queries, I can't answer them *now*. For firstly I don't know always what the numbers refer to, having no copy of the M.S. here. Secondly some of your questions want a very lengthy answer and you know how difficult it is for me to write on logic. That's also the reason why my book is so short, and consequently so obscure. But that I can't help. – Now I'm afraid you haven't really got hold of my main contention, to which the whole business of logical prop[osition]s is only a corollary. The main point is the theory of what can be expressed (gesagt) by prop[osition]s – i.e. by language – (and, which comes to the same, what can be *thought*) and what can not be expressed by prop[osition]s, but only shown (gezeigt); which, I believe, is the cardinal problem of philosophy.

I also sent my M.S. to Frege. He wrote to me a week ago and I gather that he doesn't understand a word of it all. So my only hope is to see *you* soon and explain all to you, for it is VERY hard not to be understood by a single soul!

Now the day after tomorrow we shall probably leave the Campo Concentramento and go home. Thank God! – But how can we meet as soon as possible? I should like to come to England, but you can imagine that it's rather awkward for a German to travel to England now. (By far more so, than for an Englishman to travel to Germany.) But in fact I didn't think of asking you to come to Vienna now, but it would seem to me the best thing to meet in Holland or Switzerland. Of course, if you can't come abroad I will do my best to get to England. Please write to me as soon as possible about this point, letting me know when you are likely to get the permission of coming abroad. Please write to Vienna IV. Alleegasse

16. As to my M.S., please send it to the same address; but only if there is an absolutely safe way of sending it. Otherwise please keep it. I should be very glad though, to get it soon, as it's the only corrected copy I've got. – My mother wrote to me, she was very sorry not to have got your letter, but glad that you tried to write to her at all.

Now write soon. Best wishes.

Ever yours

LUDWIG WITTGENSTEIN

P.S. After having finished my letter I feel tempted after all to answer some of your simpler points:

(1) "What is the difference between Tatsache and Sachverhalt?" Sachverhalt is, what corresponds to an Elementarsatz if it is true. Tatsache is , what corresponds to the logical product of elementary prop[osition]s when this product is true. The reason why I introduce *Tatsache* before introducing *Sachverhalt* would want a long explanation.

(2) " . . . But a Gedanke is a Tatsache: what are its constituents and components, and what is their relation to those of the pictured Tatsache?" I don't know *what* the constituents of a thought are but I know *that* it must have such constituents which correspond to the words of Language. Again the kind of relation of the constituents of thought and of the pictured fact is irrelevant. It would be a matter of psychology to find it out.

(3) "The theory of types, in my view, is a theory of correct symbolism: (a) a simple symbol must not be used to express anything complex; (b) more generally, a symbol must have the same structure as its meaning." That's exactly what one can't say. You cannot prescribe to a symbol what it *may* be used to express. All that a symbol CAN express, it MAY express. This is a short answer but it is true!

(4) Does a Gedanke consist of words? No! But of psychical constituents that have the same sort of relation to reality as words. What those constituents are I don't know.

(5) "It is awkward to be unable to speak of Nc'V̄." This touches the cardinal question of what can be expressed by a prop[osition], and what can't be expressed, but only shown. I can't explain it at length here. Just think that, what you want to *say* by the apparent prop[osition] "there are 2 things" is *shown* by there being two names which have different meanings (or by there being one name which may have two meanings). A prop[osition] e.g. φ(a, b) or (∃φ, x, y).φ(x, y) doesn't say that there are two things, it says something quite different; *but whether it's true or false, it* SHOWS what you want to *express* by saying: "there are 2 things".

(6) Of course no elementary prop[osition]s are negative.

(7) "It is necessary also to be given the prop[osition] that all elementary prop[osition]s are given." This is not necessary, because it is even *impossible.* There is no such prop[osition]! That all elementary prop[osition]s are given is SHOWN by there being none having an elementary sense which is not given. This is again the same story as in No 5.

(8) I suppose you didn't understand the way, how I separate in the old notation of generality what is in it truth-function and what is purely generality. A general prop[osition] is A truth-function of *all* PROP[OSITION]S of a certain form.

(9) You are quite right in saying that "N(ξ̄)" may also be made to mean ~p ∨~q ∨~r∨~ . . . . But this doesn't matter! I suppose you don't understand the notation of "ξ̄ ". It does not mean "for all values of ξ . . . ". But all is said in my book about it and I feel unable to write it again. Try to understand it till we meet, I never thought I could write such long explanations as I've done now.

Ever yours,

L.W.

R.37   *Briefe 100*

69.   **LW – BR**

Wien XVII.
Neuwaldeggerstr[aße] 38
30.8.19.

LIEBER RUSSELL!

Verzeih', daß ich Dich mit einer dummen Bitte belästige: Ich bin
jetzt mit einer Kopie meines M.S.s zu einem Verleger gegangen, um
den Druck endlich in die Wege zu leiten. Der Verleger, der natürlich
weder meinen Namen kennt, noch etwas von Philosophie versteht,
verlangt das Urteil irgend eines Fachmanns, um sicher zu sein, daß das
Buch wirklich wert ist, gedruckt zu werden. Er wollte sich deshalb an
einen seiner Vertrauensmänner hier wenden (wahrscheinlich an einen
Philosophie-Professor). Ich sagte ihm, nun, daß hier niemand das
Buch beurteilen könne, daß *Du* aber vielleicht so gut sein würdest,
ihm ein kurzes Urteil über den Wert der Arbeit zu schreiben;
was, wenn es günstig ausfällt, ihm genügen wird um den Verlag
zu übernehmen. Die Adresse des Verlegers ist: Wilhelm Braumüller
XI. Servitengasse 5 Wien. Ich bitte Dich nun, dorthin ein paar
Worte, so viel Du vor Deinem Gewissen verantworten kannst, zu
schreiben:

Auch an mich schreib, bitte, recht bald! Wie es Dir geht, wann
Du auf den Continent kommen kannst, etc., etc. Wie Du siehst
bin ich aus der Gefangenschaft zurück, ich bin aber doch noch
nicht ganz normal. Aber das wird schon kommen. Sei herzlichst
gegrüßt!

Dein treuer

LUDWIG WITTGENSTEIN

R.38   *Briefe102*

XI. Servitengasse.– In fact IX. Servitengasse.

English Translation

DEAR RUSSELL,

Forgive me if I burden you with a tiresome request. I've now been to a publisher with a copy of my manuscript in order to get its printing finally under way. The publisher, who naturally neither knows my name nor understands anything about philosophy, requires the judgment of some expert in order to be sure that the book is really worth printing. For this purpose he wanted to apply to one of the people he relies on here (probably a professor of philosophy). So I told him that no one here would be able to form a judgment on the book, but that *you* would perhaps be kind enough to write him a brief assessment of the value of the work, and if this happened to be favourable that would be enough to induce him to publish it. The publisher's address is: Wilhelm Braumüller, XI Servitengasse 5, Vienna. Now please write him a few words – as much as your conscience will allow you to.

Please write to me too, very soon – how you are, when you can come to the continent, etc., etc. As you can see, I'm back from prison-camp. I'm not quite normal yet, though. But that will come soon enough. Warmest regards.

Your devoted friend

LUDWIG WITTGENSTEIN

70.   **BR – LW**

70, Overstrand Mansions,
Prince of Wales Road,
Battersea, S. W.
8.9.19.

DEAR WITTGENSTEIN

Thank you for your letter and explanations, which have helped me a great deal. I am re-reading your book, and will return it as soon as I can do so safely, with remarks. I am very very much impressed by it, though whether it is definitive I don't yet feel sure.

This letter is only about meeting. The only plan that I can see is to try to meet at The Hague at Christmas time – it is doubtful whether I can get leave, for, as you may know, I have fallen out with the Government – but I will do all I possibly can to get permission. I can't come sooner as I have lectures to give, and getting permission will take a long time. Please let me know whether you would probably be able to come to Holland at Christmas or soon after – I could manage a week, if the government will let me go.

I will write later about your book. I hope you are at liberty now and back in Austria – Has the war injured you in any way?

Yours ever

BERTRAND RUSSELL

your letter. – That of 19 August (68.). Wittgenstein's letter of 30 August from Vienna and freedom (69.) had clearly not yet arrived.

71. **BR – LW**

70, Overstrand Mansions,
Prince of Wales Road,
Battersea, S.W
12.9.19.

DEAR WITTGENSTEIN

I have written to your publisher, praising your book in the highest terms. I hope the letter will reach him. – I wrote to you a few days ago, to your old address, saying that if I can obtain permission I will come to Holland at Christmas for a week to see you – I can't manage sooner or longer, worse luck. I am very thankful you are free – let me have personal news of your health, experiences etc. as soon as it is possible. Warmest good wishes.

Yours ever

B. RUSSELL.

---

your publisher. – Braumüller. See letter 69.

72. **LW – BR**

6.10.19.

LIEBER RUSSELL!

Herzlichen Dank für Deinen Brief vom 12.9. Auch mein Verleger hat schon längst Dein Empfehlungsschreiben bekommen, hat mir aber noch immer nicht geschrieben, ob, und unter welchen Bedingungen, er mein Buch nimmt (der Hund!). Ich glaube *bestimmt* zu Weihnachten in den Haag kommen zu können. Nur ein unvorsehbares Ereignis könnte mich daran hindern. Ich habe mich entschlossen Lehrer zu werden und muß dazu noch einmal eine sogenannte Lehrerbildungsanstalt besuchen. Dort sitzen lauter Buben von 17–18 Jahren und ich bin schon 30. Das giebt sehr komische Situationen und oft auch *sehr* unangenehme. Ich fühle mich oft unglücklich! – Mit Frege stehe ich in Briefwechsel. Er versteht kein Wort von meiner Arbeit und ich bin schon ganz erschöpft vor lauter Erklärungen.

Wie geht es Dr Whitehead und Johnson? Schreibe bald.

Dein treuer

LUDWIG WITTGENSTEIN

P.S. Wann kannst Du mir voraussichtlich mein M.S. zurückschicken? Meine Adresse ist jetzt:

Wien III., Untere Viaduktgasse 9 bei Frau Wanicek

Aber auch Briefe an meine alte Adresse erreichen mich. Ich wohne nämlich nicht mehr bei meiner Mutter. Ich habe mein ganzes Geld weggeschenkt und werde bald versuchen, mir selbst etwas zu verdienen. *Oft* denke ich an Dich!

L.W.

R. 39   Briefe 105

English Translation

Dear Russell,

Warmest thanks for your letter of 12.9. My publisher too received your testimonial long ago but has still not written to me to say whether and under what conditions he will take my book (the swine!). I think I'll *certainly* be able to come to The Hague at Christmastime. Only some unpredictable occurrence could prevent me. I have made up my mind to become a teacher and so must go back to school at a so-called Teachers' Training College. The benches are full of boys of 17 or 18 and I've reached 30. That leads to some very funny situations – and many *very* unpleasant ones too. I often feel miserable! – I'm in correspondence with Frege. He doesn't understand a single word of my work and I'm thoroughly exhausted from giving what are purely and simply explanations.

How are Dr Whitehead and Johnson? Write soon.

Your devoted friend,

Ludwig Wittgenstein

P.S. When do you think you can send me back by MS? My address now is:

Vienna III., Untere Viaduktgasse 9 bei Frau Wanicek

but letters to my old address will also reach me. The fact is, I'm not living at my mother's any more. I've given all my money away and am shortly going to try to earn something for myself. I think of you *often*!

L.W.

73.   **BR – LW**

> 70, Overstrand Mansions,
> Prince of Wales Road,
> Battersea, S.W.
> 14.10.19

DEAR WITTGENSTEIN

Thanks for your letter, which arrived today. I will send back your book in a few days: I was waiting to know which address to send it to. I have not written things in the blank pages, except once or twice, because talk will be much better. I studied the book rather carefully, and I think now I do fairly understand it. But we shall see. I shall send it to your new address.

It is terrible to think of your having to earn your living, but I am not surprised by your action. I am much poorer too. They say Holland is very expensive but I suppose we can endure a week of it without going bankrupt. I find the time that would suit me best would be before Christmas, about Dec. 13–20 – I ought to be back in England for Christmas. I will see about getting permission, and shall assume that date. It may turn out that Switzerland would be better. – Tell your publisher from me that he is a low scoundrel! My dear Wittgenstein it will be a joy to see you again after all these years – In all friendship,

> Yours ever,
>
> BERTRAND RUSSELL

I have not written . . . except once or twice. – This is true of the Engelmann typescript (TS 202), now in the Bodleian Library, Oxford.

your action. – Wittgenstein had given away all his money.

74.   LW – BR

1.11.19.

Lieber Russell!

Ich besorge mir jetzt den Paß für Holland und werde Dich am 10 ᵗᵉⁿ Dezember im Haag treffen. Mit dem Geld hat es allerdings eine gewisse Schwierigkeit; eine Woche wird mich aber auf keinen Fall umbringen. – Nun habe ich aber eine Idee, weiß allerdings nicht, ob sie durchführbar ist: Ich habe nämlich seinerzeit, als ich von Cambridge nach Norwegen gezogen bin, alle meine Sachen in Cambridge bei einem Möbelhändler deponiert (seinen Namen habe ich vergessen, es war nicht der Lilies sondern einer in der Nähe von Magdalene College). Es waren viele Bücher, darunter auch ein paar wertvolle, ein Teppich, etc. *Sind nun alle diese Sachen schon verfallen?* Wenn nicht, so hätte ich eine große Bitte an Dich: nämlich, sie zu verkaufen und mir das Geld nach Holland mitzubringen. Bitte sei so gut und schreibe mir, ob das überhaupt möglich ist.

Ich freue mich unbeschreiblich auf unser Wiedersehen.

Sei herzlichst gegrüßt von Deinem treuen

Ludwig Wittgenstein

Meine Adresse ist jetzt   ;   Wien, XIII, St. Veitgasse 17
                                            bei Frau Sjögren.

Hast Du schon das M.S. abgeschickt?

L.W.

Möbelhändler / furniture dealer. – The dealer was B. Jolley & Sons. Russell bought the books and the furniture ("the best bargain I ever made" he says in his *Autobiography*, vol. II, p. 100). Some at least of the books remained in Russell's library and have now joined the Russell Archives at McMaster University.

P.P.S. Etwas ÄUSSERST WICHTIGES fällt mir ein: Unter meinen Sachen befinden sich auch eine Menge Tagebücher und Manuscripte diese sind ALLE zu verbrennen!!!

R.40   *Briefe 108*

English Translation

DEAR RUSSELL,

   I am now getting my passport for Holland and will meet you in The Hague on 10 December. To be sure there are certain difficulties over money but whatever happens a week won't kill me. – A thought occurs to me, however, though I don't know whether it's practicable. The thing is that at the time I moved from Cambridge to Norway, I stored all my things in Cambridge at a furniture dealer's. (I've forgotten his name. It wasn't Lilies but one near Magdalene College.) There were a good few books, including a couple of valuable ones, a carpet, etc. *Now: have I lost all claim to these things?* If not, then I'd like to ask a great favour of you – i.e. to sell them and to bring the money to Holland for me. Please be so good as to write to me if this is at all possible.
   I look forward more than I can say to our meeting.
   Warmest regards from your devoted friend

LUDWIG WITTGENSTEIN

My address now is :   Vienna XIII, St Veitgasse 17
                              bei Frau Sjögren.
   Have you sent the MS yet?
P.P.S. Something EXTREMELY IMPORTANT has just occurred to me. Among my things there are a lot of journal-notebooks and manuscripts. These are ALL to be burnt!!!

75. **BR – LW**

> 70, Overstrand Mansions,
> Prince of Wales Road,
> Battersea, S. W.
> 13.11.19

DEAR WITTGENSTEIN

Your MS. has been posted to the address you gave in your last letter – it was posted only two days ago, as there were a number of difficulties at the Post Office. I am looking forward to seeing you more than I can say. It is of course *possible* that I may be refused a passport – if so I will let you know at once.

The furniture dealers you mention must be B. Jolley & Son, Bridge Str., Camb. I have written to them saying I have your authority to have your things sold, but I think you should write to them also, otherwise they may refuse to accept my authority. If the sale is not yet completed when I come to Holland, I can give you in advance whatever the furniture, books etc. are judged to be worth. They ought easily to pay your expenses.

In all friendship and affection,

> Your
>
> B. RUSSELL.

write to them also – No letter from Wittgenstein to the dealers is known. See also Wittgenstein to Russell, 27 November 1919 (78.)

judged to be worth. – The dealers valued the furniture at £80. See 77.

76. **LW – BR**

LIEBER RUSSELL!

Heute erhielt ich das M.S. Vielen Dank. Ich habe es bisher nur flüchtig durchgesehen und nur zwei Bemerkungen von Deiner Hand gefunden. Über alles werden wir sprechen, wenn wir uns im Haag treffen, Meinen Pass habe ich bereits und die Einreisebewilligung von Holland werde ich hoffentlich auch bekommen. Ich kann es schon gar nicht mehr erwarten, Dich zu sehen, Hast Du meinen letzten Brief erhalten? Ich bat Dich in ihm meine Sachen in Cambridge, falls sie noch existieren, zu verkaufen und mir den Erlös mit nach Holland zu bringen, da ich mit dem Geld einige Schwierigkeiten habe.

Bitte schreibe bald, Meine Adresse ist: Wien XIII, St. Veitgasse 17 bei Frau Sjögren.

Sei herzlichst gegrüßt

von Deinem treuen

LUDWIG WITTGENSTEIN

R.41 *Briefe 110*

English Translation

DEAR RUSSELL,

I received the MS today. Many thanks. So far I've only leafed through it and found only two remarks in your handwriting. We shall talk about everything when we meet in The Hague. I have my passport already and hope to get the Dutch entry-permit also. Already I can hardly wait to see you. Did you get my last letter? In it I asked you to sell my things in Cambridge, if they still exist, and to bring the proceeds to Holland for me, because I have some difficulties with money.

Please write soon. My address is: Vienna XIII, St Veitgasse 17 c/o Frau Sjögren.

Warmest regards from your devoted friend

LUDWIG WITTGENSTEIN

77.   **BR – LW**

> 70 Overstrand Mansions
> Battersea S.W.
> 24 Nov. '19

DEAR WITTGENSTEIN

I have got my passport but find great difficulties over the Dutch visa, as I dare say you do too. It seems not impossible that we may not be both able to get visas. If I fail, I will wire to you the one word "impossible". In that case, we shall have to wait till Easter, and then meet in Switzerland. I shall be *very* sorry if that happens. But I find (what I didn't know) that Switzerland is much easier to get to than Holland. – Jolley, at Cambridge, offers £80 for your furniture, not including the books. If I go back to Cambridge, which I may do, I should probably be glad to take your furniture, or part of it. Would it suit you if I paid you £100 for the furniture and books (not including any special books that you might want returned[ )] and then I could arrange with Jolley what I wanted to keep. I don't know whether it is legally possible to pay you yet, but I will find out. You would have to write to

B. Jolley & Son, Bridge Sir. Camb.

to say you had sold the furniture and books to me and they were to deal with me.

Please let me know as soon as you possibly can whether you can get your visa. It will be a very great disappointment if we have to put off meeting till the spring.

> Yours ever
>
> BERTRAND RUSSELL.

78.   **LW – BR**

Wien XIII
St. Veitgasse 17 bei Frau Sjögren
27.11.19.

LIEBER RUSSELL!

Dank' Dir bestens für Deinen Brief. Wenn Du nur in den Haag kommen kannst! Bitte TELEGRAPHIERE mir sofort wenn Du es weißt, da ich bereits den Pass habe und angab, daß ich vom 13ten–20ten im Haag zu sein beabsichtige. Eine neuerliche Änderung des Termins würde große Schwierigkeiten machen. Also bitte, laß mich nicht auf Deine Nachricht warten! – Mit dem Möbelhändler

About his encounter with Wittgenstein, Russell wrote to Lady Ottoline from The Hague on 20 December:
I have much to tell you that is of interest. I leave here today, after a fortnight's stay, during a week of which Wittgenstein was here, and we discussed his book every day. I came to think even better of it than I had done; I feel sure it is a really great book, though I do not feel sure it is right. I told him I could not refute it, and that I was sure it was either all right or all wrong, which I considered the mark of a good book; but it would take me years to decide this. This of course didn't satisfy him, but I couldn't say more.
    I had felt in his book a flavour of mysticism, but was astonished when I found that he has become a complete mystic. He reads people like Kierkegaard and Angelus Silesius, and he seriously contemplates becoming a monk. It all started from William James's *Varieties of Religious Experience*, and grew (not unnaturally) during the winter he spent alone in Norway before the war, when he was nearly mad. Then during the war a curious thing happened. He went on duty to the town of Tarnov in Galicia, and happened to come upon a bookshop which however seemed to contain nothing but picture poscards. However, he went inside and found that it contained just one book: Tolstoy on The Gospels. He bought it merely because there was no other. He read it and re-read it, and thenceforth had it always with him, under fire and at all times. But on the whole he likes Tolstoy less than Dostoewski (especially Karamazov). He has penetrated deep into mystical ways of thought and feeling, but I think (though he wouldn't agree) that what he likes best in mysticism is its power to make him stop thinking. I don't much think he will really become a monk – it is an idea, not an intention. His intention is to be a teacher. He gave all his money to his brothers and sisters, because he found earthly possessions a burden. I wish you had seen him.

hast Du ganz recht, es ist Jolley. Ich glaube aber, er wird schon Deine Bevollmächtigung anerkennen. –

Ich habe jetzt erneute Schwierigkeiten wegen meines Buches. Niemand will es verlegen. Erinnerst Du Dich noch, wie Du mich immer drängtest etwas zu veröffentlichen: und jetzt, wo ich es möchte, geht es nicht. Das soll der Teufel holen!

Wann immer Du in den Haag kommst, laß, bitte, Deine Adresse auf der Österreichischen Gesandtschaft. Dort werde ich sie erfahren.

Sei herzlichst gegrüßt von Deinem immer

treuen

LUDWIG WITTGENSTEIN

R.42   Briefe 112

English Translation

DEAR RUSSELL,

Thank you very much for your letter. If only you are able to come to The Hague! Please WIRE me immediately you know because I've got my passport already and have stated my intention of being in The Hague from the 13th to the 20th. A new change of date would give rise to great difficulties. So please don't keep me waiting for your news! – You're quite right about the furniture dealer. It is Jolley. But I think he'll be satisfied with the authority you've got. –

The difficulties with my book have started up again. Nobody wants to publish it. Do you remember how you were always pressing me to publish something? And now when I should like to, it can't be managed. The devil take it!

Whenever you do arrive in The Hague, please leave your address at the Austrian Legation. I'll find it there.

Warmest regards from your devoted friend

as ever

LUDWIG WITTGENSTEIN

79.   **BR – LW**

70, Overstrand Mansions,
Prince of Wales Road,
Battersea, S. W.
27.11.19

DEAR WITTGENSTEIN

I have my passport and visa; I informed the authorities that my business was to see you. I suggest your arriving *Dec. 11*, as I am not quite sure what day I shall get away. I will buy your furniture from you, which will pay your expenses. I don't know where I shall stay, but will have a letter at *Poste Restante* addressed to you, to say where I am staying, if you arrive after me. If you arrive first, you can do the same. I can't tell you how much I look forward to seeing you – you have been in my thoughts so much all through this long time.

Yours ever

BERTRAND RUSSELL.

letter at Poste Restante. – See the two notes from Russell, below.

80.   **BR – LW.**

Hotel Twee Steeden
(Hotel des deux Villes)
Buitenhof

DEAR WITTGENSTEIN

  This is my address. I have got here without misadventure and I
hope you will. Come on here straight the moment you arrive. It
will be joy to see you again.

Yours ever

B.R.

81.   **BR – LW**

> Hotel Twee Steden
> (= des deux Villes)
> Buitenhof, Den Haag

Dear Wittgenstein

This is my address – Come here as quick as you can after your arrival in The Hague – I am impatient to see you – We will find some way to get your book published in England if necessary.

Yours ever

B.R.

---

my address. – Russell presumably left one of the two messages at the Poste Restante and the other, as requested in Wittgenstein's letter of 27 November 1919 (78.), at the Austrian Embassy.

82.   **LW – BR**

LIEBER RUSSELL!

Herzlichen Dank für Deine Bücher; sie werden mich beide interessieren. Wenige Tage nach meiner Ankunft in Wien wurde ich krank, aber jetzt geht es schon wieder. Von meinen vorhabenden Verlegern habe ich noch keine Antwort auf die Mitteilung, daß Du meinem Buch mit einer Einleitung nachhelfen willst. Sobald ich etwas erfahre, schreibe ich Dir.

Wie geht es Dir? Bist Du in Cambridge?

Ich habe unser Beisammensein *sehr* genossen und ich habe das Gefühl daß wir in dieser Woche sehr viel wirklich gearbeitet haben. (Du nicht auch?)

Sei vielmals gegrüßt

von Deinem treuen

LUDWIG WITTGENSTEIN

R. 43   Briefe 119

Deine Bücher / your books. – the letter makes reference to two books. It is a reasonable conjecture that they were *Our Knowledge of the External World* and the collection of essays, *Mysticism and Logic.*

in Cambridge. – Russell was living in London at this time.

English Translation

DEAR RUSSELL,

Many thanks for your books. Both of them will be interesting for me. A few days after arriving in Vienna I fell ill but now I'm more or less all right again. I've still no answer from my various prospective publishers to the information that you're willing to come to the aid of my book with an introduction. As soon as I hear anything, I'll write to you.

How are you? Are you in Cambridge?

I enjoyed our time together *very* much and I have the feeling (haven't you too?) that we did a great deal of real work during that week.

Best regards from your devoted friend

LUDWIG WITTGENSTEIN

83.   **LW – BR**

Wien XIII
St. Veitgasse 17 bei Frau Sjögren
19.1.20.

LIEBER RUSSELL!

Heute erhielt ich die Nachricht, daß der Verlag von Reclam in Leipzig aller Wahrscheinlichkeit nach mein Buch nehmen will. Ich werde also mein M.S. aus Innsbruck kommen lassen und es an Reclam schicken. Wann aber kommt Deine Einleitung?! Denn ohne sie kann ja der Druck nicht beginnen. *Wenn* Du also gewillt bist, sie zu schreiben, so bitte tue es so bald als möglich und lasse mich wissen ob, und wann ich Dein M.S. erwarten darf. Ich vegetiere hier ohne viel Freude am Leben. Schreib mir bald.

Dein treuer

LUDWIG WITTGENSTEIN

R. 44   Briefe 122

English Translation

DEAR RUSSELL,

I have had word today that the Leipzig publisher Reclam is prepared, in all probability, to take my book. So I will get my MS sent from Innsbruck and will forward it to Reclam. But when is your introduction going to arrive?! Because the printing can't begin without it. So: *if* you're prepared to write it, please do so as soon as possible and let me know whether and when I can expect your MS. I am vegetating here and not enjoying life very much. Write to me soon.

Your devoted friend

LUDWIG WITTGENSTEIN

84.   **BR – LW**

> 70, Overstrand Mansions,
> Prince of Wales Road,
> Battersea, S.W.
> February 2nd, 1920.

Herr Ludwig Wittgenstein
Wien, XIII St. Veitgasse 17.

DEAR WITTGENSTEIN,

I have broken my collarbone and am therefore obliged to dictate this letter.

I am very glad to hear that Reclam will probably take your book. I waited to begin writing the introduction until I knew you had a publisher, since the introduction would have had to be quite different if it had been written for publication in England. I will get it done as soon as I possibly can, but I do not think it can be finished for another six weeks. You may, however, absolutely count upon it, and tell your publishers so.

I am very sorry to hear you have been ill.

I do not go back to Cambridge until October.

Keynes, as you may have heard, has written a book of the very greatest importance on the economic consequences of the peace. It is having a great effect upon opinion here, and is likely to do much good.

An answer to Wittgenstein's letters of 8 and 19 January (82. and 83.).

another six weeks. – The Introduction was sent in the middle of March. See letter 86.

I loved our time together at the Hague, and was very happy, both in seeing you and in our discussions.

Yours ever,

BERTRAND RUSSELL

85. **LW – BR**

19.3.20

LIEBER RUSSELL!

Es ist lange her seit Du von mir gehört hast. Wie steht's mit der Einleitung? Ist sie schon fertig? Und wie geht es mit Deinem Schlüsselbein, wie hast Du es Dir denn gebrochen? Wie gern möchte ich Dich wieder sehen. Ich bin nicht mehr im Stande mir neue Freunde zu erwerben und die alten verliere ich. Das ist schrecklich traurig. Fast täglich denke ich an den armen David Pinsent. Denn, so sonderbar das klingt, ich bin fast allen Menschen zu dumm!

Schreib mir bald einmal und schicke auch Deine Einleitung.

Dein trauriger

LUDWIG WITTGENSTEIN

R.45   *Briefe 126*

English Translation

DEAR RUSSELL,

It is a very long time since you heard from me. How are things with the introduction? Is it finished yet? And how is your collarbone? How did you manage to break it? How much I'd like to see you again! I'm no longer in any condition to acquire new friends and I'm losing my old ones. It's terribly sad. Nearly every day I remember poor David Pinsent. Because, however odd it sounds, I'm too stupid for nearly everybody.

Do write to me soon and also send your introduction.

Yours sadly,

LUDWIG WITTGENSTEIN

86.   **BR – LW**

> 70 Overstrand Mansions
> Prince of Wales Road
> Battersea
> London, S.W.
> March 19th, 1920.

DEAR WITTGENSTEIN,

I am sending you at last the introduction which I promised you three months ago. I am sorry to have been so long about it, but breaking my collarbone made me stupid. I am assuming that you will translate it into German. When I have put in brackets "quote number so-and-so", I have meant that it seemed an appropriate place to insert your actual words in the passages referred to. I did not think it worth while to translate your words into English and have you translate them back into German. If there is anything unsatisfactory to you in my remarks, let me know, and I will try to amend it.

How are you? I should like news of you.

Yours affectionately,

BERTRAND RUSSELL.

87.   **LW – BR**

9.4.20.

LIEBER RUSSELL!

Besten Dank für Dein Manuscript. Ich bin mit so manchem darin nicht ganz einverstanden; sowohl dort, wo Du mich kritisierst, als auch dort, wo Du bloß meine Ansicht klarlegen willst. Das macht aber nichts. Die Zukunft wird über uns urteilen. Oder auch nicht – und wenn sie schweigen wird, so wird das auch ein Urteil sein. – Die Einleitung wird jetzt übersetzt und geht dann mit der Abhandlung zum Verleger. Hoffentlich nimmt er sie! – Hier gibt es wenig Neues. Ich bin so dumm wie gewöhnlich. Meine Adresse ist jetzt: Wien III. Rasumofskygasse 24 (bei Herrn Zimmermann). Sei herzlichst gegrüßt!

Dein treuer

LUDWIG WITTGENSTEIN

R. 46   Briefe 127

English Translation

DEAR RUSSELL,

Thank you very much for your manuscript. There's so much of it that I'm not quite in agreement with – both where you're critical of me and also where you're simply trying to elucidate my point of view. But that doesn't matter. The future will pass judgment on us – or perhaps it won't, and if it is silent that will be a judgment too. – The introduction is in the course of being translated and will then go with the treatise to the publisher. I hope he will accept them! – There's nothing much new here. I am as stupid as usual. My address is now: Vienna III., Rasumofskygasse 24 (c/o Herr Zimmermann). Warmest regards from your devoted friend

LUDWIG WITTGENSTEIN

88.   **LW – BR**

6.5.20.

LIEBER RUSSELL!

Sei für Deinen lieben Brief herzlich bedankt. Nun wirst Du aber auf mich böse sein, wenn ich Dir etwas erzähle; Deine Einleitung wird nicht gedruckt und infolgedessen wahrscheinlich auch mein Buch nicht. – Als ich nämlich die deutsche Übersetzung der Einleitung vor mir hatte, da konnte ich mich doch nicht entschließen sie mit meiner Arbeit drucken zu lassen. Die Feinheit Deines englischen Stils war nämlich in der Übersetzung – selbstverständlich – verloren gegangen und was übrig blieb war Oberflächlichkeit und Mißverständnis. Ich schickte nun die Abhandlung und Deine Einleitung an Reclam und schrieb ihm, ich wünschte nicht daß die Einleitung gedruckt würde, sondern sie solle ihm nur zur Orientierung über meine Arbeit dienen. Es ist nun höchst wahrscheinlich, daß Reclam meine Arbeit daraufhin nicht nimmt (obwohl ich noch keine Antwort von ihm habe). Aber darüber habe ich mich bereits beruhigt; und zwar mit folgendem Argument, das mir unantastbar erscheint: Meine Arbeit ist nämlich entweder ein Werk ersten Ranges, oder sie ist kein Werk ersten Ranges. Im zweiten – wahrscheinlicheren – Falle bin ich selbst dafür, daß sie nicht gedruckt werde. Und im ersten ist es ganz gleichgültig ob sie 20 oder 100 Jahre früher oder später gedruckt wird. Denn wer fragt danach ob z.B. die Kritik der reinen Vernunft im Jahre 17x oder y geschrieben worden ist! Ja, eigentlich brauchte sie in diesem Falle auch nicht gedruckt zu werden. – Und nun sei nicht bös! Es war vielleicht undankbar von mir, aber ich konnte nicht anders.

deutsche Übersetzung / German translation. – This, as far as we have been able to ascertain, was *not* the translation which was eventually printed with Wittgenstein's book by Ostwald in 1921. Ostwald seems to have had another translation made from Russell's English original. Cf *Prototractatus*, Historical Introduction, pp. 28–9. and G. H. v. W., *Wittgenstein*, p. 100

Sei herzlichst gegrüßt

von Deinem treuen

LUDWIG WITTGENSTEIN

Es wäre herrlich wenn Du im Sommer nach Wien kämst!

R. 47   Briefe 129

English Translation

DEAR RUSSELL,

Many thanks indeed for your kind letter. But now you'll be angry with me when I tell you something: Your Introduction is not going to be printed and as a consequence my book probably won't be either. – You see, when I actually saw the German translation of the Introduction, I couldn't bring myself to let it be printed with my work. All the refinement of your English style was, obviously, lost in the translation and what remained was superficiality and misunderstanding. Well, I sent the treatise with your Introduction to Reclam and wrote saying that I didn't want the Introduction printed, it was meant to serve only for his own orientation in relation to my work. It is now highly probable that as a result Reclam won't accept my work (though I've had no answer from him yet). But I've already comforted myself on that score, by means of the following argument, which seems to me unanswerable. Either my piece is a work of the highest rank, or it is not a work of the highest rank. In the latter (and more probable) case I myself am in favour of its not being printed. And in the former case it's a matter of indifference whether it's printed twenty or a hundred years sooner or later. After all, who asks whether the Critique of Pure Reason, for example, was written in 17x or y. So really in the former case too my treatise wouldn't need to be printed. – And now, don't be angry! Perhaps it was ungrateful of me but I couldn't do anything else.

Warmest regards from your devoted friend

LUDWIG WITTGENSTEIN

It would be marvellous if you could come to Vienna in the summer.

89.   **BR – LW**

> 70, Overstrand Mansions,
> Prince of Wales Road,
> Battersea, S. W.
> 1.7.20.

DEAR WITTGENSTEIN

I returned yesterday from Russia (where there are no posts) and found your letter waiting for me. I don't care twopence about the introduction but I shall be really sorry if your book isn't printed. May I try, in that case, to have it printed in England or America?

I have 2 months' letters to answer so I mustn't write more. Best love, now and always.

> Yrs aff.

> B.R.

your letter. – That of 6 May (88.).

Russia. – Russell visited Russia in May and June 1920 as an unofficial member of a Labour Party Delegation.

90.   **LW–BR**

Wien III
Rasumofskygasse 24/II
bei Herrn Zimmermann
7.7.20

LIEBER RUSSELL!

Dank Dir vielmals für Dienen lieben Brief! Reclam hat mein Buch natürlich nicht genommen und ich werde vorläufig keine weitere Schritte tun, um es zu publizieren. Hast Du aber Lust es drucken zu lassen, so steht es Dir ganz zur Verfügung und *Du kannst damit machen, was Du willst.* (Nur wenn Du am Text etwas änderst, so *gib an, daß die Änderung von Dir ist.*) Heute habe ich mein Zeugnis bekommen und kann jetzt Lehrer werden. Wie es mir gehen wird – wie ich das Leben ertragen werde – weiß Gott allein. Am besten wäre es vielleicht, ich könnte mich eines Abends hinlegen und nicht mehr aufwachen. (Vielleicht aber gibt es auch noch etwas besseres für mich.) Wir werden ja sehen. –
Sei herzlichst gegrüßt

von Deinem treuen

LUDWIG WITTGENSTEIN

R.48   Briefe 133.

English Translation

DEAR RUSSELL,

Very many thanks for your kind letter, Reclam has, naturally, not accepted my book and for the moment I won't take any further

---

*mein Zeugnis/ my certi*ficate. – Wittgenstein's certificate from the teacher's training college in Vienna which he attended in the academic year 1919–20.

steps to have it published. But if you feel like getting it printed, it is entirely at your disposal and *you can do what you like with it.* (Only, if you change anything in the text, *indicate that the change was made by you.*)

Today I got my certificate, and I can now become a teacher. How things will go for me – how I'll endure life – God only knows. The best for me, perhaps, would be if I could lie down one evening and not wake up again. (But perhaps there is something better left for me.) We shall see.

Warmest regards from your devoted friend

LUDWIG WITTGENSTEIN

91.   **LW – BR**

LIEBER RUSSELL!

Eine Freundin meiner Schwester, Frau Margarethe Faber, hält sich gegenwärtig für kurze Zeit in London W, 6, Berkeley street auf. Könntest Du ihr den Inhalt jener Kassette schicken, die ich Dir, als ich nach Norwegen ging, übergab? Wenn es Dir keine Mühe macht, so, bitte, tue es. Ist aber die Kassette jetzt nicht in Deiner Hand, so macht es nichts; es wird sich schon einmal Gelegenheit bieten, die Sachen zu schicken. Wenn Du sie jetzt an Frau Faber schickst, so bitte schreibe Deinen Namen auf das Packet, damit man es Dir zurückschicken kann, im Falle Frau Faber bereits abgereist wäre.

Wenn Du wieder einmal Zeit hast, so schreib' auch Deinem

treuen

LUDWIG WITTGENSTEIN

R.49   Briefe 134

English Translation

DEAR RUSSELL

A lady who is a friend of my sister's, Frau Margarethe Faber, is at the moment in London (6 Berkeley St, W) for a short stay. Could

Frau Margarethe Faber. – A friend of Wittgenstein's sister, Helene, member of a distinguished Anglo-Austrian family.

Kassette/casket. – Nothing is known of this but it probably contained keepsakes.

you send her the contents of the casket I entrusted to you when I left for Norway? Please do this, if it's no trouble. But if the casket is not to hand at the moment, it doesn't matter. There's bound to be an opportunity to send the things sometime. If you do send them to Frau Faber now, please write your name on the parcel so that it can be sent back to you if she should already have left.

When you have time again, please also write to

Your devoted friend

LUDWIG WITTGENSTEIN

92. **LW – BR**

LIEBER RUSSELL!

Vor ein paar Tagen erhielt ich eine Einladung vom Trinity College zu einem Diner, das am 30. September stattfinden soll. Es wurde gewiß nicht für möglich gehalten, daß ich wirklich kommen könnte; trotzdem hat mich die Einladung sehr gefreut. Möchtest Du so gut sein, und in meinem Namen beim junior Bursar absagen, da ich die Form einer solchen Absage nicht weiß.

Ich verbringe jetzt meine Ferien als Gärtnergehilfe in der Gärtnerei des Stiftes Klosterneuburg bei Wien. Ich muß den ganzen Tag über fest arbeiten; und das ist gut. – Im Inneren geht es mir nicht besonders. – Wann werden wir uns wiedersehen? Vielleicht nie. Täglich denke ich an Pinsent. Er hat mein halbes Leben mit sich genommen. Die andere Hälfte wird der Teufel holen. Bis dahin bin ich immer

Dein treuer

LUDWIG WITTGENSTEIN

R.50   *Briefe 136*

English Translation

DEAR RUSSELL,

A few days ago I received an invitation from Trinity College to a dinner to be held on 30 September. It was surely not thought possible that I could actually come, but none the less the invitation gave me a great deal of pleasure. Could you be so good as to write to the Junior Bursar on my behalf declining the invitation, because I don't know the right form for such a thing?

At the moment I'm spending my holidays as a gardener's assistant in the nurseries of the monastery of Klosterneuburg near Vienna. I have to work solidly the whole day through, which is good. – My inner life is nothing to write home about. – When shall we see one another again? Perhaps never. Every day I think of Pinsent. He took half my life away with him. The devil will take the other half. In the meantime I am, as always,

Your devoted friend

LUDWIG WITTGENSTEIN

93.   **LW – BR**

LIEBER RUSSELL!

Dank' Dir für Deinen lieben Brief! Ich habe jetzt eine Anstellung bekommen; und zwar als Volksschullehrer in einem der kleinsten Dörfer; es heißt Trattenbach und liegt 4 Stunden südlich von Wien im Gebirge. Es dürfte wohl das erste mal sein, daß der Volksschullehrer von Trattenbach mit einem Universitätsprofessor in Peking korrespondiert. Wie geht es Dir und was trägst Du vor? Philosophie? Dann wollte ich, ich könnte zuhören und dann mit Dir streiten. Ich war bis vor kurzem *schrecklich bedrückt* und lebensmüde, jetzt aber bin ich etwas hoffnungsvoller und jetzt hoffe ich auch, daß wir uns wiedersehen werden.

Gott mit Dir! Und sei herzlichst gegrüßt von Deinem

treuen

LUDWIG WITTGENSTEIN

Meine Adresse ist:
L. W. Lehrer,
Trattenbach bei Kirchberg am Wechsel
Nieder-Österreich

R. 51   *Briefe 138*

Peking. – Russell had gone to China early in the autumn of 1920; he returned to England at the end of August 1921.

English Translation

DEAR RUSSELL,

Thank you for your kind letter. I have now obtained a position: I am to be an elementary-school teacher in a tiny village called Trattenbach. It's in the mountains, about four hours' journey south of Vienna. It must be the first time that the schoolmaster at Trattenbach has ever corresponded with a professor in Peking. How are you? And what are you lecturing on? Philosophy? If so, I wish I could attend and could argue with you afterwards. A short while ago I was *terribly depressed* and tired of living, but now I am slightly more hopeful, and one of the things I hope is that we'll meet again.

God be with you! Warmest regards from

Your devoted friend

LUDWIG WITTGENSTEIN

My address is:
L.W. Schoolmaster
Trattenbach bei Kirchberg am Wechsel
Nieder-Österreich

94.   **BR – LW**

> Government University,
> Peking
> 11.2.1921

MY DEAR WITTGENSTEIN,

I have been meaning to write you, ever since I got your letter of Sep. 20, which it gave me real happiness to get. I wonder how you like being an elementary school-teacher and how you get on with the boys. It is honest work, perhaps as honest as there is, and everybody now-a-days is engaged in some form of humbug, which you escape from.

I like China and the Chinese – they are lazy, good-natured, fond of laughter, very like nice children – they are very kind and nice to me. All the nations set upon them and say they mustn't be allowed to enjoy life in their own way – They will be forced to develop an army and navy, to dig up their coal and smelt their iron, whereas what they want to do is to make verses and paint pictures (very beautiful) and make strange music, exquisite but almost inaudible, on many-stringed instruments with green tassels. Miss Black and I live in a Chinese house, built around a courtyard: I send you a picture of me at the door of my study. My students are all Bolsheviks, because that is the fashion; they are annoyed with me for not being more of a Bolshevik myself. They are not advanced enough for mathematical logic. I lecture to them on Psychology, Philosophy, Politics and Einstein. Once in a way I have them to an evening party and they let off fire-works in the courtyard – they like this better than lectures. – I leave China in July, spend a month in Japan, and then come back to London – 70 Overstrand Mansions, S.W. 11, will always find me.

your letter of Sep. 20.–93.

Miss Black sends all sorts of messages. Best love, my dear Ludwig – I shall hope to see you again, perhaps next year. I suppose by then it will be possible to travel to Trattenbach. Be as happy as you can!

Ever yours affectionately

BERTRAND RUSSELL

Miss Black. – Dora Black, who had been at The Hague with Russell and whom Russell married after their return from the journey to China. See also 96. and 97.

95. **BR – LW**

Government University
Peking.
3 June 1921

DEAR WITTGENSTEIN

Your letter of the 2nd April reached me yesterday.

Your manuscript is quite safe. I left it in England in the hopes of getting it printed, I do not know with what success. It is in the hands of Miss Wrinch of Girton, who is a good mathematician and a student of mathematical logic.

I am sorry you find the people in your neighbourhood so disagreeable. I don't think average human nature is up to much anywhere, and I dare say wherever you were you would find your neighbours equally obnoxious.

I have been in bed for the last ten weeks with a severe illness, but am now nearly well, and am returning to England this summer, so address there if you write again.

I am determined to get your manuscript published, and if it has not been achieved during my absence, I will take the matter in hand as soon as I return.

I wish you could come to England some time and pay me a visit, but I suppose that would be very difficult for you. I shall have to come to Trattenbach which, from the picture, looks quite a pretty place.

Best love, my dear Wittgenstein

Yours ever,

BERTRAND RUSSELL.

letter of the 2nd April. – This letter is lost. It evidently enclosed a picture postcard of Trattenbach.

Miss Wrinch. – On her share in the publication history of the Tractatus see letter 97.

96.   **LW – BR**

23.10.21.

LIEBER RUSSELL!

Verzeih, daß ich Dir erst jetzt auf Deinen Brief aus China antworte. Ich habe ihn sehr verspätet erhalten. Er traf mich nicht in Trattenbach und wurde mir an verschiedene Orte nachgeschickt, ohne mich zu erreichen. – Es tut mir sehr leid, daß Du krank warst; und gar schwer! *Wie geht es denn jetzt?!* Bei mir hat sich nichts verändert. Ich bin noch immer in Trattenbach und bin nach wie vor von Gehässigkeit und Gemeinheit umgeben. Es ist wahr, daß die Menschen im Durchschnitt nirgends sehr viel wert sind; aber hier sind sie viel mehr als anderswo nichtsnutzig und unverantwortlich. Ich werde vielleicht noch dieses Jahr in Trattenbach bleiben, aber länger wohl nicht, da ich mich hier auch mit den übrigen Lehrern nicht gut vertrage. (Vielleicht wird das wo anders auch nicht besser sein.) Ja, *das wäre schön*, wenn Du mich einmal besuchen wolltest. Ich bin froh zu hören, daß mein Manuskript in Sicherheit ist. Wenn es gedruckt wird, wird's mir auch recht sein. – Schreib mir bald ein paar Zeilen, wie es Dir geht, etc., etc.

Sei herzlich gegrüßt
von Deinem treuen

LUDWIG WITTGENSTEIN

Empfiehl mich der Miss Black.

R. 52   *Briefe 147*

English Translation

DEAR RUSSELL,

Forgive me for only now answering your letter from China. I got it after a very long delay. I wasn't in Trattenbach when it arrived and it was forwarded to several places before it reached me. – I am very sorry that you have been ill – and seriously ill! *How are you now, then?* As regards me, nothing has changed. I am still at Trattenbach, surrounded, as ever, by odiousness and baseness. I know that human beings on the average are not worth much anywhere, but here they are much more good-for-nothing and irresponsible than elsewhere. I will perhaps stay on in Trattenbach for the present year but probably not any longer, because I don't get on well here even with the other teachers (perhaps that won't be better in another place). Yes, *it would be splendid* if you would visit me sometime. I am glad to hear that my manuscript is in safety. And if it's printed, that will suit me too. –

Write me a few lines soon, to say how you are, etc., etc.

Warmest regards from
your devoted friend

LUDWIG WITTGENSTEIN

Remember me to Miss Black.

97. **BR – LW**

(Permanent Address)
31 Sydney Street
London S.W. 3
5.11.21

MY DEAR WITTGENSTEIN

I was very glad to hear from you. First, I have to tell you about your MS. As you know, I left it to Miss Wrinch to deal with while I was in China. After various failures, she got it accepted by Ostwald for his Annalen der Naturphilosophie; the proofs have just come, and I suppose it will be published in about 2 months. I had thought she was only going to try English publishers, so I left her my introduction, which Ostwald is also printing. I am sorry, as I am afraid you won't like that, but as you will see from his letter, it can't be helped. It is also going to appear in English in a new philosophical library published by Kegan Paul, but probably that won't be for nearly a year. In English it will appear as a separate book. This is due to Ogden (of the Cambridge Mag[azine].) who has taken a lot of trouble about it.

As for me, I am now married to Miss Black, and expecting a child in a few days. We have bought this house, and got your furniture from Cambridge, which we like *very* much. The child will probably be born in your bed. There were a great many books of yours, as well as various boxes and parcels from engineering firms which you had never opened. If ever you come to see us, I will give you back

---

For the early publication history of the *Tractatus* see *Young Ludwig* pp. 296–9.

Ostwald.–Wilhelm Ostwald (1853–1932), physical chemist, publisher of a series of scientific classics and something of a crank. (See letter 98.)

Ogden.–C. K. Ogden (1889–1957) editor and student of language in general, founded the *Cambridge Magazine* in 1912. For his part in the publication of the *Tractatus* see L. Wittgenstein, *Letters to C. K. Ogden*.

any of your books that you may want. Your things are worth much more than I paid for them, and I will pay you more whenever you like. I didn't know when I bought them how much I was getting. In particular, if you could ever manage to come to England, you must let me pay the expenses of your journey as further payment for your furniture. I do wish you would come – the prospective child will make it a little more difficult for me to travel. I am quite well again now. I forget whether I told you that in Peking I was in the German hospital, and looked after by German Doctors. They were wonderfully skilled and kind and careful, and one of them, Dr. Esser, became a great friend of us both. I also made friends with an Austrian named Brandauer, who knew you by name. He had been a prisoner in Siberia.

I am very sorry you find the people of Trattenbach so trying. But I refuse to believe they are worse than the rest of the human race; my logical instinct revolts against the notion.

Do consider seriously coming to see us whenever you have long enough holidays. Best love, as always.

Yours ever

BERTRAND RUSSELL

98. **LW – BR**

28.11.21.

LIEBER RUSSELL!

Dank Dir vielmals für Deinen lieben Brief. Ehrlich gestanden: es freut mich, daß mein Zeug gedruckt wird. Wenn auch der Ostwald ein Erzscharlatan ist! Wenn er es nur nicht verstümmelt! Liest Du die Korrekturen? Dann bitte sei so lieb und gib acht, daß er es genau so druckt, wie es bei mir steht. Ich traue dem Ostwald zu, daß er die Arbeit nach seinem Geschmack, etwa nach seiner blödsinnigen Orthographie, verändert. Am liebsten ist es mir, daß die Sache in England erscheint. Möge sie der vielen Mühe die Du und andere mit ihr hatten würdig sein! –

Du hast recht: nicht die Trattenbacher allein sind schlechter, als alle übrigen Menschen; wohl aber ist Trattenbach ein besonders minderwertiger Ort in Österreich und die *Österreicher* sind – seit dem Krieg – bodenlos tief gesunken, daß es zu traurig ist, davon zu reden! So ist es. – Wenn Du diese Zeilen kriegst, ist vielleicht schon Dein Kind auf dieser merkwürdigen Welt. Also: ich gratuliere Dir und Deiner Frau herzlichst. Verzeih' daß ich so lange nicht geschrieben habe; auch ich bin etwas kränklich und riesig beschäftigt. Bitte schreibe wieder einmal wenn Du Zeit hast. Von Ostwald habe ich keinen Brief erhalten. Wenn alles gut geht werde ich Dich mit tausend Freuden besuchen!

Herzlichste Grüße,

Dein

LUDWIG WITTGENSTEIN

R. 53   *Briefe* 148.

English Translation

DEAR RUSSELL,

Many thanks for your kind letter! I must admit I am pleased that my stuff is going to be printed. Even though Ostwald is an utter charlatan. As long as he doesn't tamper with it! Are you going to read the proofs? If so, please take care that he prints it exactly as I have it. He is quite capable of altering the work to suit his own tastes – putting it into his idiotic spelling, for example. What pleases me most is that the whole thing is going to appear in England. I hope it may be worth all the trouble that you and others have taken with it. You are right: the Trattenbachers are not uniquely worse than the rest of the human race. But Trattenbach is a particularly insignificant place in Austria and the *Austrians* have sunk so miserably low since the war that it's too dismal to talk about. That's what it is. – By the time you get this letter your child will perhaps already have come into this remarkable world. So: warmest congratulations to you and your wife! Forgive me for not having written to you for so long. I too haven't been very well and I've been tremendously busy. Please write again when you have time. I have not had a letter from Ostwald. If all goes well, I will come and visit you with the greatest of pleasure.

Warmest regards,

Yours

LUDWIG WITTGENSTEIN

99. **BR – LW**

31 Sydney Str.
London S.W. 3
24.12.21

DEAR WITTGENSTEIN

Thanks for your letter. Ostwald had already printed before I saw the proofs – I think it must be out by now. Ogden has done all the business, and is going ahead with getting your work published in English. The publication is all arranged for. The publisher will be Kegan Paul. The translation is being done by two young men at Cambridge who know mathematical logic, and I am telling them all that you and I agreed on as regards translations of terms. What I saw of Ostwald's stuff was all right, and not in his "insane" orthography. In the English publication, we are trying to get the German text also printed, but I am not sure whether the publisher will agree.

Our boy was born on Nov. 16, and flourishes. He is called John Conrad (the latter after the novelist of that name, who is a friend of mine). My wife is now quite recovered and we are both very happy.

I am very sorry to hear you are not well. Remember that we shall both be overjoyed if you can ever come to see us, and that it will be easy to pay all your expenses by selling a few of your things

---

two young men. – One was F. P. Ramsey. Who the other was we have not been able to find out. Perhaps Russell wrongly supposed that R. B. Braithwaite (1900–90, scholar, later Fellow of King's College, Cambridge and still later holder of the Knightbridge Chair of Moral Philosophy), who in fact knew little German at that time, was going to assist with the translation.

While C. K. Ogden, who always speaks of "translators" in the plural, clearly took many of the final decisions and discussed them with Wittgenstein, it is probably inaccurate to refer to him as the translator of the work. It has, of course, long been clear, and these letters of Russell's make it additionally so, that Ogden deserves great credit for ensuring the work's publication.

which are of no use to me. Your property was worth much more than Jolley pretended. Your books alone were worth £100, and I don't see why I should swindle you because Jolley understated the value of your things. £300 would have been a fair price. I will send you the extra £200 if you will accept it, or give you back anything of yours that you want when you come, whichever you prefer.

Best wishes for the New Year, and much love.

Yrs ever

BERTRAND RUSSELL

Jolley understated the value. – Wittgenstein's reaction to the offers made by Russell is unknown. But see 100. about Wittgenstein's willingness to let Russell pay for his expenses in connection with a planned meeting.

100. **BR – LW**

31 Sydney Street S.W. 3
7.2.22

DEAR WITTGENSTEIN

I was very glad to get your letter the other day, with your nice message to the little boy, which, as you suggested, I conveyed by appropriate symbols other than words. He flourishes, and gives us both great happiness.

I wonder you haven't heard from Ostwald. Have you written to him to tell him your address? If not, I don't suppose he knows it. I have heard nothing further about publication of your book, either here or in Germany, but I will find out next time I see Ogden.

We intend to go to Germany and Switzerland next August. If you have holidays then, I hope we could see you then – it would be easier for you, I suppose, than coming to England. In Switzerland we intend to stay with my brother's wife, who used to be Gräfin Arnim. I am sure she would be delighted to have you too, if you could come. I am *very* glad you will let me pay your expenses. If you *can* come to England sooner, do.

I liked China much better than Europe – the people are more civilized – I keep wishing I were back there. I lectured to them on all sorts of topics, but what they liked best was mathematical logic.

I wish you didn't have to work so hard at elementary teaching – it must be very dreary. Would you like me to bring your journals and note-books when we next meet? Take care of yourself – With love,

Yours ever

BERTRAND RUSSELL

your letter. – This letter is apparently lost.

your journals and note-books. – See Wittgenstein's letter to Russell, 1 November 1919 (74.). For Wittgenstein's reaction to Russell's question, see the next letter.

101. **LW – BR**

[1922]

LIEBER RUSSELL,

Dank' Dir für Dienen lieben Brief! Nein, von Ostwald habe ich noch nichts gehört. Ich dachte übrigens er wußte meine Adresse durch den der ihm mein Manuskript geschickt hat. Nun, das ist übrigens ganz gleichgültig wenn er die Geschichte nur überhaupt druckt und nicht zu viele Druckfehler hinein macht. Ich bin in der letzten Zeit auch sehr niedergeschlagen. Nicht, daß mir das Lehren an der Volksschule zuwider ist. Im Gegenteil! Aber SCHWER ist es, daß ich in diesem Lande Lehrer sein muß, wo die Menschen so ganz und gar hoffnungslos sind. Ich habe in diesem Ort nicht eine Seele mit der ich ein wirklich vernünftiges Wort sprechen könnte. Wie ich das auf die Dauer aushalten werde weiß Gott! Ich glaub' Dir's gern daß auch Du es in China schöner gefunden hast als in England obwohl es in England zweifellos noch tausendmal besser ist als bei uns. – Du weißt wie ich mich freuen würde Dich zu sehen. Wenn mich die Frau Deines Bruders aufnimmt komme ich mit Freuden zu Euch. Meine Tagebücher und Notizen verwende, bitte, zum einheizen. Wenn Du täglich 2–3 Blätter zum Feueranzünden benützt werden sie bald aufgebraucht sein und ich hoffe sie werden gut brennen. Also – weg damit! – Bitte empfiehl mich Deiner Frau und grüß den kleinen Buben. Und schreibe wieder einmal.

Deinem

L. WITTGENSTEIN

This is Wittgenstein's reply to 100. It is undated.
Tagebucher und Notizen/journals and notebooks. – We must assume that Russell complied with Wittgenstein's wish and destroyed this material.

P.S. Hast Du zufällig unter Deinen Büchern die "religiösen Streit-schriften" von Lessing? Wenn ja so lies sie bitte! Ich glaube sie werden Dich interessieren und Dir gefallen. Ich liebe sie sehr! Dein L.W.

English Translation

DEAR RUSSELL,

Thank you for your kind letter. No, I have not yet heard anything from Ostwald, though I did think he knew my address from the person who sent him my manuscript. But, anyway, that is completely unimportant, just as long as he really prints the thing and does not introduce too many misprints.

I have been very depressed in recent times too. Not that I find teaching in the elementary school distasteful: quite the contrary. But what's HARD is that I have to be a teacher in this country where people are so completely and utterly hopeless. In this place I have not a single soul with whom I could talk in a really sensible way. How I shall support that in the long run, God knows! I readily believe that you too found things better in China than in England, though England still is without a doubt a thousand times better than here where I am. –

You know how happy I should be to see you. If your brother's wife will have me I will gladly come to see you all. Please use my journals and notebooks for kindling. If you take 2 or 3 pages a day to light the fire, they will soon be used up, and I hope they burn well. Away with them, I say! Please remember me to your wife and give my greetings to the little boy. And write another letter to

Your

L. WITTGENSTEIN

P.S. Do you happen to have among your books the "Religious Controversies" of Lessing? If so, please read them. I think they will interest you and give you pleasure. I like them very much. Yours L.W.

102. **BR – LW**

Till July 25 [1922]:
Sunny Bank, Treen, Penzance
31 Sydney Street
London S.W.3

DEAR WITTGENSTEIN

I have heard from my brother's wife, and she will be delighted if you will come to her Chalet in Switzerland when we are there – about 8th to 20th of August, but I will let you know the exact date later – certainly 15th ±ε. The address of her chalet is
Chalet Soleil, Randogne sur Sierre.
I have never been there, but I think it is above the Simplon railway, by a funicular. It will be a great happiness to see you again. My sister-in-law writes novels – they used to be all about Germany – "Elizabeth and her German garden" was the first. She used to live in Pommern. She has quarrelled with my brother, who is difficult as a husband.

Ogden is getting on with your book, which I gather he will print both in English and German. I suppose it will be out in October. I have never read Lessing's "religiöse Streitschriften" – I think they are among your books which I have in town – I will look when I get home. I am sorry you have such a depressing life. All Europe is horrible since the war, but I suppose it is worse in Austria than here. One gathers that England, Germany and Russia jointly are going to fight France – so it goes on.

---

my brother's wife. – A letter of May 1922 to Russell from his sister-in-law is preserved which begins "I shall love to have Wittgenstein at the chalet". As far as is known Wittgenstein's visit to Switzerland did not come off. In August 1922, however, Russell and Wittgenstein met in Innsbruck.

The little boy is lovely – At first he looked exactly like Kant, but now he looks more like a baby – Best wishes from my wife. With love,

Yours ever

BERTRAND RUSSELL.

103.   **LW – BR**

[November or December 1922]

LIEBER RUSSELL!

Schon lange habe ich von Dir nichts mehr gehört und Dir nicht mehr geschrieben, und heute schreibe ich Dir hauptsächlich, weil ich ein Anliegen an Dich habe: Ich will Dich, wie man bei uns sagt "anpumpen". Wie Du weißt ist mein Buch vor ein paar Wochen erschienen. Ich habe vom Verlag 3 Exemplare gekriegt, möchte aber noch 3 haben, da ich es noch einigen Leuten schenken soll. Würdest Du nun die Güte haben und mir 3 Exemplare kaufen und schicken? Das Geld dafür werde ich Dir dann schicken, aber vielleicht nicht auf einmal, sondern ratenweise, wenn ich nur erst weiß, wie ich es machen kann. Zu Weihnachten werde ich mich in Wien darüber erkundigen. Natürlich gilt meine Bitte nur für den Fall, daß Dir die Auslage GAR KEINE Schwierigkeiten macht; denn die Angelegenheit ist ja nicht *sehr* wichtig. Im Falle, daß Du die Bücher besorgen kannst wäre es mir am liebsten Du tätest es recht bald! – Ich bin jetzt in einem anderen Nest, wo es freilich auch nicht besser ist als in dem Vorigen. Es ist schwer mit den Menschen zu leben! Aber es sind ja eigentlich gar keine Menschen sondern 1/4 Tiere und 3/4 Menschen.

Schreib mir bald; auch wie es Dir geht.

Grüße Deine liebe Frau herzlich von mir.

Dein treuer

LUDWIG WITTGENSTEIN

vor ein paar Wochen erschienen/ appeared a few weeks ago. – The book was published by Kegan Paul in November. The letter, which is undated, must be from November or December 1922.

Meine Addresse ist:
    L.W. bei Frau Ehrbar
    Puchberg am Schneeberg
    Nieder-Österreich

English Translation

DEAR RUSSELL,

It is a long time since I have heard from you or written to you
and today I am writing chiefly because I have a favour to ask of you:
I want (as we say here) "to put the bite on you". As you know my
book appeared a few weeks ago. I have had 3 copies from the
publisher, but should like another 3 copies because there are more
people whom I need to present copies to. Would you very kindly
buy three copies and send them to me? The money for them I will
send you later, probably not all at once, but in instalments, as soon
as I know how I can manage it. I will find out about that in Vienna
at Christmas. Obviously the request only holds good as long as
the outlay does not cause you any difficulties AT ALL, because the
matter is not *very* important. If you really can get me the books,
the best thing for me would be if you could do it straightaway! – I
am now in another hole, though, I have to say, it is no better than
the old one. Living with human beings is hard! Only they are not
really human, but rather 1/4 animal and 3/4 human.

Do write soon, also to tell me how things are with you.

Give my very best wishes to your wife.

Yours ever

LUDWIG WITTGENSTEIN

My address is:
    L.W. c/o Frau Ehrbar
    Puchberg am Schneeberg
    Lower Austria

104.   **LW – BR**

7.4.23
Puchberg am Schneeberg, N.Ö.

LIEBER RUSSELL!

Ich habe lange nichts mehr von Dir gehört und auch nicht geschrieben weil es wenig neues gibt und auch weil ich etwas krank war. Meine Nerven sind durch die Arbeit und viele Aufregung recht herunter gekommen und oft fürchte ich, daß sie es nicht bis zu den Ferien aushalten werden. – Vor kurzer Zeit erhielt' ich "The Meaning of Meaning". Gewiß ist es auch Dir geschickt worden. Ist das nicht ein miserables Buch?! Nein, so leicht ist die Philosophie doch nicht! Dafür sieht man aber, wie leicht es ist, ein dickes Buch zu schreiben. Das ärgste ist die Einleitung des Professor Postgate Litt.D. F.B.A. etc. etc., Etwas so albernes habe ich selten gelesen. – Ein wenig neugierig bin ich auf Ritchies Buch, das er mir schicken will (wie mir Ogden schreibt). Ritchie war ein netter Mensch und ich würde mich freuen von ihm zu hören.

Schreib auch Du wieder einmal, wie es Euch allen geht und was Dein kleiner Bub macht; ob er schon fleißig Logik studiert. Sei herzlich gegrüßt und grüße auch Deine liebe Frau

von Deinem

LUDWIG WITTGENSTEIN

"*The Meaning of Meaning*". – by C. K. Ogden and I. A. Richards published by Kegan Paul in 1923.

Postgate. – J. P. Postgate (1853–1926), classical scholar, who also permitted himself some remarks on the relations between language and reality. His preface was dropped from subsequent editions of *The Meaning of Meaning* At the time of this letter he was in retirement in Cambridge from the Professorship of Latin at the University of Liverpool.

Ritchie. – A. D. Ritchie (1892–1967), physiologist and philosopher, then Fellow of Trinity College, Cambridge, later Professor of Logic and Metaphysics at Edinburgh. The book referred to is evidently *Scientific Method*, published by Kegan Paul in the same series as the *Tractatus* and *The Meaning of Meaning*.

Letters

English Translation:

DEAR RUSSELL,

I have not heard anything more from you for a long time and I have also not written, because there was little that was new and also because I have been rather unwell. The work and all the excitement have got my nerves completely down and I am often afraid that I shall not be able to hold out until the holidays. –

A short time ago I received *The Meaning of Meaning*. Doubtless it has been sent to you too. Is it not a miserable book?! No, no, philosophy, after all, is not as easy as that! But it does show how easy it is to write a thick book. The worst thing is the Introduction by Professor Postgate, Litt.D., F.B.A., etc. etc. I have rarely read anything so stupid –

I am a bit curious about Ritchie's book, which he means to send me (so Ogden writes). Ritchie was a nice person and I should be happy to hear from him.

Now it is for you to write me another letter telling me how things are going for you and yours and what your little boy is doing. Is he already a keen student of logic? Warmest greetings to you with messages also to your wife,

Yours

LUDWIG WITTGENSTEIN

105.   **LW – JMK**

[1923]

DEAR KEYNES!

Thanks so much for sending me the "Reconstruction in Europe". I should have preferred though to have got a line from you personally, saying how you are getting on, etc. Or, are you too busy to write letters? I don't suppose you are. Do you ever see Johnson? If so, please give him my love. I should so much like to hear from him too (*not* about my book but about himself).

So do write to me sometime, if you will condescend to do such a thing.

Yours sincerely

LUDWIG WITTGENSTEIN

K 10   *Briefe 154*

Reconstruction in Europe. – Published in the *Manchester Guardian Commercial* for 18 May 1922, but Keynes's reply (letter 112) seems to show that this letter was sent in 1923.

106.   **LW – FPR**

[1923]

DEAR MR RAMSEY,

I've got a letter from Mr Ogden the other day saying that you may possibly come to Vienna in one of these next months. Now as you have so excellently translated the Tractatus into English I have

This is the English section of a letter drafted by Wittgenstein, no doubt in answer to a proposed visit by Ramsey, who was to go to Austria in the Long Vacation (summer) of 1923. Ramsey in fact came to see Wittgenstein at Puchberg in September 1923 and stayed for a couple of weeks. During that time they spent several hours each day reading the *Tractatus*, with Wittgenstein explaining his thoughts to Ramsey. In the course of these discussions Wittgenstein also made numerous changes and corrections in the English translation and some in the German text. They were all written down in Ramsey's copy of the book, where they can still be studied.

Ramsey has given a vivid account of his encounter with Wittgenstein in two letters which are preserved. The one was to John Maynard Keynes, the other to Ramsey's mother. The relevant passages from the letter to his mother, dated Puchberg am Schneeberg, 20th September 1923 read as follows:

Wittgenstein is a teacher in the Village school. He is very poor, at least he lives economically. He has one tiny room whitewashed, containing a bed, wash-stand, small table and one hard chair and that is all there is room for. His evening meal which I shared last night is rather unpleasant coarse bread butter and cocoa. His school hours are 8 to 12 or 1 and he seems to be free all the afternoon.

He looks younger than he can possibly be; but he says he has bad eyes and a cold. But his general appearance is athletic. In explaining his philosophy he is excited and makes vigorous gestures but relieves the tension by a charming laugh. He has blue eyes.

He is prepared to give 4 or 5 hours a day to explaining his book. I have had two days and got through 7 (+ incidental forward references) out of 80 pages. And when the book is done I shall try to pump him for ideas for its further development which I shall attempt. He says he himself will do nothing more, not because he is bored, but because his mind is no longer flexible. He says no one can do more than 5 or 10 years work at philosophy. (His book took 7). And he is sure Russell will do nothing more important. His idea of his book is not that anyone by reading it will understand his ideas, but that some day someone will think them out again for himself, and will derive real pleasure from finding in this book their exact expressions. I think he exaggerates his own verbal inspiration, it is much more careful than I supposed but I think it

no doubt you will be able to translate a letter too and therefore I am going to write the rest of this one in German.

reflects the way the ideas came to him which might not be the same with another man.

He has already answered my chief difficulty which I have puzzled over for a year and given up in despair myself and decided he had not seen. (It is not in the 1st 7 pages but arose by the way.) He is great. I used to think Moore a great man but beside W!

He says I shall forget everything he explains in a few days; Moore in Norway said he understood W completely and when he got back to England was no wiser than when he started.

It's terrible when he says "Is that clear" and I say "no" and he says "Damn it's *horrid* to go through that again". Sometimes he says, I can't see that now we must leave it. He often forgot the meaning of what he wrote within 5 minutes, and then remembered it later. Some of his sentences are intentionally ambiguous having an ordinary meaning and a more difficult meaning which he also believes.

He is, I can see, a little annoyed that Russell is doing a new edition of Principia because he thought he had shown R that is was so wrong that a new edition would be futile. It must be done altogether afresh. He had a week with Russell 4 y[ea]rs ago.

Ramsey also sent a postcard to Ogden:

L. W. explains his book to me from 2–7 every day. It is most illuminating; he seems to enjoy this and as we get on about a page an hour I shall probably stay here a fortnight or more. He is very interested in it, though he says that his mind is no longer flexible and he can never write another book. He teaches in the village school from 8 to 12 or 1. He is very poor and seems to lead a very dreary life having only one friend here [Rudolf Koder, then schoolteacher at Puchberg, life-long friend of Wittgenstein's, *Ed*.], and being regarded by most of his colleagues as a little mad.

F.P.R.

The "week with Russell" referred to seems to have been the meeting at the Hague in December 1919 (see 78. and comments), which suggests that the meeting in Innsbruck in August 1922 (see 102.) did not occasion serious discussion.

107.   **FPR – LW**

Trinity
15 October 1923

DEAR WITTGENSTEIN,

I had a letter the other day from the waiter in the hotel at
Puchberg, containing a bill I had not paid. (It was hardly my fault
as the proprietor's son assured me I had paid everything). I sent him
a cheque, but I'm afraid he may have some difficulty in cashing it.
Would you be so good as to see if it is all right, and if not, let me
know and explain the difficulty so that I can solve it if possible by
some other method of payment? I'm sorry to trouble you but I
don't think it will be much trouble as my cheque ought to do, if he
waits till the bank has sent it over here.

I haven't seen Keynes yet to ask him about your degree.

I went to Salome at the Opera in Vienna; it was most beautifully
staged and I entirely agree about the Opera House. I stayed in
Vienna 3 days and enjoyed myself looking at pictures and buildings.

In this letter and the following one (108.) Wittgensstein seems to have underlined
one or two words or phrases as a kind of *aide–mémoire*. These passages have not
been italicized. But see note on 109.

degree. – Clearly Wittgenstein wished to complete and have conferred the degree
he was working for in 1913–14. See 45. above and 108. below.

Opera House in Vienna. – A work of architecture of which Wittgenstein had a high
opinion, see the reference to its architect in *Culture and Value*, p. 74.

my other copy of the Tractatus. – For the work of Wittgenstein and Ramsey on the
text and translation of this work, see 116. below and C. Lewy in *Mind* 76, (1967):
417–23. The copy now sent is presumably 'other' than the one marked up with
their corrections.

I haven't started work on numbers yet as I have been busy preparing stuff to teach my women pupils. They pretend to understand more than I expected; but whether they do really, I don't know.

I am sending you my other copy of Tractatus at the same time as this letter.

Russell and his wife have just produced a book on "The Prospects of Industrial Civilisation" and he alone one called "The A.B.C. of the Atom"!

I have been talking to a man who knows Baron von Schrenck Notzing; he had seen the materialization happening and taken photographs of it which he showed to me; they were astonishing. He is very smart and has detected a lot of very clever frauds but he is sure these things are genuine.

I am afraid the fare from Vienna to London is rather more than I thought. My ticket was K1,940,000.

I haven't yet found myself out in having forgotten anything you explained to me.

Yours ever

FRANK RAMSEY

of the Atom.–Actually "of Atoms".

Schrenk-Notzing. – Albert von S.-N. (1862–1929) was one of the first to apply the methods of natural science to the study of materialization and other parapsychological phenomena. These were much discussed in Vienna in the twenties – particularly by members of the Vienna Circle (see Karl Menger, *Reminiscences of the Vienna Circle*, p. 59) and figure from time to time in Wittgenstein's correspondence.

He is very smart. – Presumably the man Ramsey talked to is meant.

108.   **FPR – LW**

Trinity
11 November 1923

DEAR WITTGENSTEIN,

Thanks for your letter.

I have good news for you. If you will pay a visit to England, there is £50 (=K16,000,000) available to pay your expenses. So do, please, come. I imagine you would prefer to come in your summer holiday, which I think you said was July and August. The disadvantage of that time is that it is vacation in Cambridge, and the time when people in England take their holidays, so that the people you would like to see might be scattered all over the place. It occurred to me that if, as you said was possible, you were leaving your present school at the end of the academic year, you might perhaps leave two months earlier, and come to England for May and June, or longer, or part of those months. The Cambridge summer term is April 22nd to June 13th.

I asked Keynes about your degree, and the position seems to be this. The regulations have changed so that it is no longer possible to obtain a B.A. by keeping six terms and submitting a thesis. Instead you can obtain a Ph.D. by 3 years and a thesis. If you could come here for another year, you could probably get permission to count your two previous years and so obtain a Ph.D. But that is the only possibility.

I have not been doing much towards reconstructing mathematics; partly because I have been reading miscellaneous things, a little Relativity and a little Kant, and Frege. I do agree that Frege is wonderful; I enjoyed his critique of the theory of irrationals in the Grundgesetze enormously. I should like to read Ueber die Zahlen

---

advertisement. – This reproduces some of the sarcasms of the Preface, as printed in G. Frege, *Collected Papers.* (Oxford, 1984), pp. 249–51. A translation is given below.

des Herrn H. Schubert but haven't yet found a copy only this wonderful advertisement which I'm sure you would like to read again.

"Der Verfasser knüpft seine Betrachtungen an die Darstellung, die Herr Schubert in der Encyklopädie der mathematischen Wissenschaften von den Grundlagen der Arithmetik gegeben hat. Er entdeckt darin eine Methode und ein Prinzip, die vielleicht schon früher von anderen Forschern benutzt, aber, wie es scheint, noch nie als solche besonders in Auge gefasst und ausgesprochen worden sind; die Methode, störende Eigenschaften durch Absehen von ihnen zum Verschwinden zu bringen, und das Prinzip der Nichtunterscheidung des Verschiedenen, wie der Verfasser es nennt, das mit sehr interessanten histrionalen Eigenschaften der Zahlen enge zusammenzuhängen scheint. Indem der Verfasser das Wesen dieser Methode und dieses Prinzips genau in Worte auszusprechen und ihre Tragweite in helles Licht zu setzen sucht, glaubt er den Weg für weiter unabsehbare Fortschritte gebahnt zu haben."

But I am awfully idle; and most of my energy has been absorbed since January by an unhappy passion for a married woman, which produced such psychological disorder, that I nearly resorted to psychoanalysis, and should probably have gone at Christmas to live in Vienna for 9 months and be analysed, had not I suddenly got better a fortnight ago, since when I have been happy and done a fair amount of work.

I think I have solved all problems about finite integers, except such as are connected with the axiom of infinity, but I may well be wrong. But it seems to me too difficult to discuss by post, except that perhaps when I get an account of it written out I will send it to you. I wish you were here; do come in the Summer. Have you noticed the difficulty in expressing without $=$ what Russell expresses by $(\exists x) : fx.x \neq a$?

I am reading The Brothers Karamazov, I think the scene described by Ivan between Christ and the Inquisitor is magnificent.

Yours ever

F. P. RAMSEY

Has Ogden sent you my review *of Tractatus* in *Mind* ? if not, and you would like it I will send it to you, but it is not at all good and you must remember I wrote it before coming to see you.

English translation of the quotation from Frege

The author's reflections take as their starting-point the account of the foundations of arithmetic which Mr Schubert has given in the Encyclopaedia of the Mathematical Sciences. The author discovers there a method and a principle which perhaps have been used earlier by other investigators but, it seems, have never before been expressly studied and fully spelt out. This is the method of making distressing properties disappear by ignoring them and the principle of not distinguishing the different, as the author calls it, which appears to be intimately connected with interesting histrionic properties of numbers. By trying to give the essence of this method and this principle a precise formulation in words and to shed clear light on their scope, he thinks he has paved the way for as yet incalculable advances.

my review. – *Mind* 32, (1923): 465–78 (reprinted in Ramsey's posthumous *The Foundations of Mathematics*, 1931 (but not in subsequent collections) and in I. M. Copi and R. M. Beard edd, *Essays on Wittgenstein's Tractatus*, New York, 1966).

109. **FPR – LW**

27 December 1923

DEAR WITTGENSTEIN,

Thanks for your letter; I'm sorry you have been ill and depressed. First, *the £50 belong to Keynes.* He asked me not to say so straight away because he was afraid you might be less likely to take it from him than from an unknown source, as he has never written to you. I can't understand why he hasn't written, nor can he explain, he says he must have some "complex" about it. He *speaks of you with warm affection and very much wants to see you again.* And also, apart from that, if you would like to come to England he would not like you to be unable to for want of money, of which he has plenty.

I quite understand your fear of not being fit for society, but you mustn't give it much weight. I could get lodgings in Cambridge and you need not see more of people than you like or feel able to. I can see that staying with people might be difficult as you would inevitably be with them such a lot, *but if you lived by yourself you could come into society gradually.*

I don't want you to take this as endorsing your fear of boring or annoying people, for I know *I myself want to see you awfully,* but I just want to say that if you have such a fear surely it would be all right if you were not staying with anyone but lived alone at first.

In this and the following letter from Ramsey the underlining (represented in print by italics) gives every sign of being not the sender's expression of emphasis but rather the recipient's expression of interest or appreciation. However it has been reproduced precisely for its interest as such.
See also note on 107

"complex". – Invoked to explain Keynes's reluctance to answer 105. above, see also 110. and 112.

I don't know how long you could live here on the £50, but I am sure it would be long enough to make it worth while for you to come.

I think Frege is more read now, two great mathematicians *Hilbert and Weyl* have been writing on the *foundations of mathematics* and *pay compliments to Frege,* appear in fact to have appreciated him to some extent. His unpopularity would naturally go as the generation he criticized dies.

I was silly to think I had solved those problems. I'm always doing that and finding it a mare's nest. (Moore does the same.) I will write to you about it soon at length, but I am afraid you will think my difficulties silly. I didn't think there was a real difficulty about $\exists x : fx.x \neq a$ i.e. that it was *an objection to your theory of identity,* but I didn't see how to express it, because I was under the silly delusion that if an x and an a occurred in the same proposition the x could not take the value a. I had also a reason for wanting it not to be possible to express it. But I will try to explain it all in about a fortnight from now, because it ought to help me to get clearer about things, and you may be able to put me right and may be interested. If I had anything of importance to say you would, I know, be interested, but I don't think I have.

I have been trying a lot to prove a proposition in the Mengenlehre either $2^{\aleph_0} = \aleph_1$, or $2^{\aleph_0} \neq \aleph_1$, which it is no one knows but I have had no success.

---

proposition in the Mengenlehre. – This proposition (and hence also its negation) were first proved to be independent of the axioms of Set Theory (*Mengenlehre*) by P. J. Cohen in 1963.

I made the acquaintance of your nephew Stonborough, whom I like.

I hear Russell is going to America to lecture.

I do hope you are better and no longer depressed and exhausted and will come to England.

Yours ever

FRANK RAMSEY

Thanks for giving me the expression fa. $\supset$. $(\exists x, y)$. fx . fy : ~fa $\supset$ $(\exists x)$fx.

your nephew Stonborough. – Thomas S., later Dr. phil., elder son of Wittgenstein's sister Margaret, was at the time an undergraduate at Trinity College.

Russell going to America to lecture. – This was planned for January and February 1924 but delayed by illness and Russell in fact arrived there on 1 April 1924 and gave popular lectures for nine weeks, the first of a series of such visits, which, he took some pleasure in avowing, were for the purpose of making money to support his family life and (later) his school: see Ronald Clark, *Life of Bertrand Russell*, p. 415, and Russell's *Autobiography*, vol. II, pp. 152ff.

the expression fa etc. – In an unpublished paper on "Identity" Ramsey uses this expression, altering only the order of the main conjuncts, to say in Wittgenstein's notation (i.e. one without identity but with conventions to prevent distinct free variables taking the same value) what is said in the notation of *Principia Mathematica* by "$(\exists x): x \neq a.fx$" (roughly: something other than a has f). Providing this translation is the problem mentioned by Ramsey in 108.

110.   **FPR – LW**

Trinity
20 February 1924

MY DEAR WITTGENSTEIN,

Thanks for your letter; except that I think you might enjoy it, *I no longer want you to come here this summer, because I am coming to Vienna*, for some and perhaps the whole of it! I can't say exactly when or for how long, but very likely, next month, so I shall hope to see you quite soon now.

This is for various reasons: I hope to settle permanently in Cambridge, but as I have always lived here, I want to go away for a time first, and have the chance now for six months. And if I live in Vienna I can learn German, and come and see you often, (unless you object) and *discuss my work with you*, which would be most helpful. Also I *have been very depressed* and done little work, and have *symptoms so closely resembling some of those described by Freud* that I shall probably *try to be psychoanalysed, for which Vienna would be very convenient*, and which would make me stay there the whole six months. *But I'm afraid you won't agree with this.*

As announced here, Ramsey did in fact go to Vienna in March 1924 after the end of the Lent Term. He returned to Cambridge in time to take up his position as a lecturer and a fellow of King's at the beginning of Michaelmas Term. Most of the time he spent in Vienna, where he was being psycho-analysed. He dined regularly at the house of Wittgenstein's sister, Margaret Stonborough. We have evidence of four visits (in one case probably abortive, see 114.) to Wittgenstein himself: in March, May, and July at Puchberg and in late September, just before going back to England, at Otterthal, the third and last of the villages in Lower Austria in which Wittgenstein worked as a schoolmaster. The first visit, which was within a week of his arrival, he describes to his mother as follows (letter of 30 March 1924):

> I stayed a night at Puchberg last weekend. Wittgenstein seems to me tired, though not ill; but it isn't really any good talking to him about work, he won't listen. If you suggest a question he won't listen to your answer but starts thinking of one for himself. And it is such hard work for him like pushing something too heavy uphill.

For the underlining (italics) in this letter, see note on 109.

Keynes still means to write to you; it really is a disease — his procrastination; but he doesn't (unlike me) take such disabilities so seriously as to go to Freud! He very much hopes you will come and see him.

I haven't seen *Johnson* for a long time but I am going to tea with his sister soon, and unless he is ill I will give him your love (last time I went there he was ill). *The third part of his Logic is to be published soon.* It deals with Causation.

I am so sorry you *are using up all your strength* struggling with your surroundings; *it must be terribly difficult with the other teachers.* Are you staying on in Puchberg? When I saw you, you *had some idea of leaving if it got too impossible, and becoming a gardener.*

I can't write about work, it is such an effort when my ideas are so vague, and I'm going to see you soon. Anyhow I have done little except, I think, made out the proper solution rather in detail of *some of the contradictions which made Russell's Theory of Types unnecessarily complicated, and made him put in the Axiom of Reducibility. I went to see Russell a few weeks ago,* and am reading the manuscript of the new stuff he is putting into the Principia. You *are quite right that it is of no importance;* all it really *amounts to is a clever proof of mathematical induction without using the axiom of reducibility.* There are no fundamental changes, identity just as it used to be. *I felt he was too old: he seemed to understand and say "yes" to each separate thing,* but it made no impression so that 3 minutes afterwards he *talked on his old lines. Of all your work be seems now to accept only this: that it is nonsense to put an adjective where a substantive ought to be which helps in his theory of types.*

He indignantly denied ever having said that vagueness is a characteristic of the physical world.

He has 2 children now and is very devoted to them. *I liked him very much.* He does not really think *The Meaning of Meaning* important, but he wants to help Ogden by encouraging the sale of it. He wrote a review of it, from which the quotation you saw was taken, in a political weekly.

I had a *long discussion with Moore* the other day, who has *grasped more of your work than I should have expected.*

I'm sorry I'm not getting on better with the foundations of mathematics; I have got several ideas but they are still dim.

I hope you are well, and as happy as you can be under the circumstances. It gives me great pleasure that probably I shall see you soon.

Yours ever

FRANK RAMSEY

111.   **FPR – JMK**

Wien I
Mahlerstrasse 7
Tür 27
Austria
24/3/24

DEAR MAYNARD,

The Puchberg address is right for Wittgenstein. I went to see him yesterday; he was very pleased to have your books, and sends you his love.

He also asked me to write to you about the possibility of his coming to England, because he is afraid he could not express himself adequately in English and you would not understand if he wrote in German. I think he could express himself all right but it would be a great effort and so I said I would try for him. He talked about it to Richard but does not trust Richard to report him faithfully.

He has definitely decided that he wouldn't like to come and stay in Cambridge. July and August are almost the only holiday he gets in the year, and he generally spends them living almost alone in Vienna contemplating. He prefers Vienna to Cambridge unless he has some special reason for going to Cambridge, which could only be to see people. The people in England he wants to see are few; Russell he can no longer talk to, Moore he had some misunderstanding with, and there really only remain you and Hardy, and perhaps Johnson whom he would just like to see, but obviously they wouldn't get on. I shan't be coming back to England till October.

To come to Cambridge and just go out to tea and see people, is, he thinks, not merely not worth while, but positively bad because such intercourse would merely distract him from his contemplation without offering any alternative good; because he feels that he

Richard. —R.B. Braithwaite, see 99.

couldn't get into touch with people, even you whom he likes very much, without some effort on both sides and unless he were to see them a good deal.

It comes to this: that, while he would like to stay with you in the country and try to get intimate with you again, he won't come to England just to have a pleasant time, because he would feel it so futile and not enjoy it.

I think he is right about this, but I feel it a pity too, because if he were got away from his surroundings and were not so tired, and had me to stimulate him, he might do some more very good work; and he might conceivably have come to England with that in view. But while he is teaching here I don't think he will do anything, his thinking is so obviously frightfully uphill work as if he were worn out. If I am here during his summer holiday I might try to stimulate him then.

So I'm afraid he won't come to England this year, nor can I advise him to, unless you would like to ask him to stay with you in the country, in which case he would come. (It occurred to him that that was what he would like to do; I didn't suggest it.)

I hope I have made his point of view clear; it is just the opposite of what I imagined. When he wrote that he was afraid of staying with anyone as he might find it difficult and be a bore, I at once thought he might nevertheless like to live alone and see people occasionally. But that he won't do as he thinks he would not understand the people he saw nor they him at once or at all, unless he saw them constantly, as he would staying with them. On the other hand I think he has decided that it would be worth while trying, in spite of the chance of complete failure, if you were to ask him to stay with you.

I'm afraid I think you would find it difficult and exhausting. Though I like him very much I doubt if I could enjoy him for more than a day or two, unless I had my great interest in his work, which provides the mainstay of our conversation.

But I should be pleased if you did get him to come and see you, as it might possibly get him out of this groove.

Yours ever

FRANK RAMSEY

112.   **JMK – LW**

46, Gordon Square
Bloomsbury
29 March 1924

MY DEAR WITTGENSTEIN,

A whole year has passed by and I have not replied to your letter.
I am ashamed that this should have been so. But it was not for want
of thinking about you and of feeling very much that I wanted to
renew signs of friendship. The reason was that I wanted to try to
understand your book thoroughly before writing to you; yet my
mind is now so far from fundamental questions that it is impossible
for me to get clear about such matters. I still do not know what to
say about your book, except that I feel certain that it is a work of
extraordinary importance and genius. Right or wrong, it dominates
all fundamental discussions at Cambridge since it was written.

I have sent you in a separate package copies of the various books
which I have written since the war. *Probability* is the completion of
what I was doing before the war, – I fear you will not like it. Two
books on the Peace Treaty, half economic and half political, a book
on Monetary Reform (which is what I most think about just now).

---

various books. – For *Probability* see comments on 63. and 66. above. The other books
were: *The Economic Consequences of the Peace*, 1919 (see 115.), *A Revision of the
Treaty*, 1922, and *A Tract on Monetary Reform*, 1923.

I should like immensely to see and talk with you again. Is there a chance that you will pay a visit to England?

Yours truly and affectionately

J. M. KEYNES

You may like to see the enclosed paper about a memorial to Pinsent.

I would do anything in my power which could make it easier for you to do further work.

---

memorial to Pinsent. – It is not known what was intended. There is a stone to Pinsent and his brother in the church at Dry Sandford, near Oxford, where his mother lived, but Cambridge friends are unlikely to have been involved in that.

113.   **FPR – LW**

[Spring 1924]

DEAR WITTGENSTEIN

I am sure you really need a rest, and as it is a fine day am going up Schneeberg.

I hope you will come to lunch to-morrow, or, if not, after; but you need not answer this as I shall be in anyhow.

Yours

F. P. RAMSEY

Briefe 164

A stay of several days in Puchberg is clearly involved, so this letter may really be from 1923 (see notes on 106.). If from 1924 then perhaps it dates from May ("fine day"), when indeed a week-end visit did take place, for Ramsey wrote to his mother in that month:

I spent last weekend at Puchberg. Wittgenstein seemed more cheerful: he has spent weeks preparing the skeleton of a cat for his children, which he seemed to enjoy. But he is no good for my work.

114. **FPR – LW**

[Spring 1924]

DEAR WITTGENSTEIN,

As I was passing through here with some friends on a walk, I thought I would leave this money I owe you. I hope you are well.

Yours ever

F. P. RAMSEY

Briefe 165

Probably a later occasion than 113. Indeed Ramsey this time does not seem to have stayed in Puchberg at all ("passing through"). Very likely the date is late June or early July, because Wittgenstein used the reverse of the sheet to write a draft of 115. below.

115.   **LW – JMK**

Puchberg am Schneeberg
4.7.24.

MY DEAR KEYNES

Thanks awfully for sending me your books and for your letter dated 29./3. I have postponed writing to you so long because I could not make up my mind as to whether to write to you in English or in German. Writing in German makes things easy for me and difficult for you. On the other hand if I write in English I am afraid the whole business may become hopeless at MY End already. Whereas you might find somebody to translate a German letter to you. If I have said all I've got to say I'll end up in English.

Also: Zuerst möchte ich Ihnen noch einmal für die Bücher und Ihren lieben Brief danken. Da ich sehr beschäftigt bin und mein Gehirn für alles Wissenschaftliche ganz unaufnahmsfähig ist, so habe ich nur in *einem* der Bücher gelesen ("The economic consequences [of the peace]"). Es hat mich sehr interessiert, obwohl ich von dem Gegenstand natürlich so gut wie nichts verstehe. Sie schreiben, ob Sie etwas tun könnten, um mir wieder wissenschaftliches Arbeiten zu ermöglichen: Nein, in dieser Sache läßt sich nichts machen; denn ich habe selbst keinen starken inneren Trieb mehr zu solcher Beschäftigung. Alles was ich wirklich sagen mußte, habe ich gesagt und damit ist die Quelle vertrocknet. Das klingt sonderbar, aber es ist so. – Gerne, *sehr* gerne möchte ich Sie wiedersehen; und ich weiß, daß Sie so gut waren, mir Geld für einen Aufenthalt

---

The draft on the reverse of 114. agrees with the letter sent until Wittgenstein says. "you might not find anybody to translate my letter. But now I thought I would have to try after all and write in English. Well: It was very kind indeed of you to invite me to stay in England during the summer. Now the absolute truth about the matter is this: 1) I should like very much to see you again. On the other hand 2) I'm afraid I shall probably disappoint you because I have changed so much since we met last. Especially I am no longer capable to do any good . . ." [Here, at the end of the sheet, the draft as we have it breaks off.]

in England zuzusichern. Wenn ich aber denke, daß ich von Ihrer Güte nun wirklich Gebrauch machen soll, so kommen mir allerlei Bedenken: Was soll ich in England tun? Soll ich nur kommen um Sie zu sehen und mich auf alle mögliche Weise zu zerstreuen? I mean to say shall I just come to be nice? Now I don't think at all that it isn't worth while being nice – if only I could be REALLY nice – or having a nice time – if it were a VERY nice time indeed.

But staying in rooms and having tea with you every other day or so would not be *nice enough*. But then I should pay for this little niceness with the great disadvantage of seeing my short holidays vanish like a phantom without having the least profit – I don't mean money – or getting any satisfaction from them. Of course staying in Cambridge with you is much nicer than staying in Vienna alone. But in Vienna I can collect my thoughts a little and although they are not worth collecting they are better than mere distraction.

Now it wouldn't seem impossible that I could get more out of you than a cup of tea every other day that's to say that I could really profit from hearing you and talking to you and in this case it would be worth while coming over. But here again there are great difficulties: We haven't met since 11 years. I don't know if you have changed during that time, but *I* certainly have tremendously. I am sorry to say I am no better than I was, but I am *different*. And therefore if we shall meet you may find that the man who has come to see you isn't really the one you meant to invite. There is no doubt that, even if we *can* make ourselves understood to one another, a chat or two will *not* be sufficient for the purpose, and that the result of our meeting will be disappointment and disgust on your side and disgust and despair on mine. – Had I any definite work to do in England and were it to sweep the streets or to clean anybody's boots I would come over with great pleasure and then nicety could come by itself in course.

There would be a lot more to say about the subject but it's too difficult to express it either in English or in German. So I'd better make an end. I thought when I began to write that I should write this letter altogether in German but, extraordinarily enough, it has proved more natural for me to write to you in broken English than in correct German.

Herzliche Grüße! Yours ever

LUDWIG WITTGENSTEIN

P.S. Please give my love to Johnson if you see him.

K. 11   *Briefe 166*

English Translation of German section

So: first I should like to thank you once again for the books and for your kind letter. Since I'm very busy and my brain is quite incapable of absorbing anything of a scientific character, I've only read parts of *one* of the books ("The economic consequences of the peace"). It interested me very much, though of course I understand practically nothing about the subject. You ask in your letter whether you could do anything to make it possible for me to return to scientific work. The answer is, No: there's nothing that can be done in that way, because I myself no longer have any strong inner drive towards that sort of activity. Everything that I really *had* to say, I have said, and so the spring has run dry. That sounds queer, but it's how things are. – I'd like – *very much* – to see you again and I know that you've been so kind as to guarantee me money for a stay in England. But when I think that I ought really to avail myself of your kindness, all sorts of misgivings occur to me; what am I to do in England? Shall I come just in order to see you and to amuse myself in every way possible?

116. **FPR – LW**

Mahlerstrasse 7/27
Wien I
15 September 1924

DEAR WITTGENSTEIN,

I wonder if it would be convenient to you if I came to Puchberg to see you next week end ie the 20th. Please say frankly whether you would be bored or pleased to see me. I don't much want to talk about mathematics as I haven't been doing much lately.

I had a letter from Ogden with a large enclosure for you from an American business man, who patronisingly thinks your book not so bad and sends you some stuff of his own, which I will bring or send. There's nothing in it.

Ogden also asked me to get from you, if possible, while I was here any corrections in case there should be a second edition of your book. (This is not really likely.) I have got marked in my copy a lot of corrections we made to the translation, and 4 extra propositions you wrote in English. Obviously I think the corrections to the translation should be made in a new edition, and the only doubt is about the extra propositions; and also you might have something else you would like altered. But it isn't worth while taking much trouble about it yet as a second edition is unlikely. It is merely, I think, that Ogden thought that it might save possible future correspondence for us to talk about it now.

I am here till October 3rd. I don't know if I knew when I last

---

Puchberg. – With the new school year Wittgenstein had in fact moved to Otterthal, which necessitated a change in arrangements, for which see 117.

corrections . . . extra propositions. – The former were inserted in the second impression (1933), the latter not: for both see the article by C. Lewy cited in comments on 107. above.

saw you or told you that I have been made a fellow and lecturer in mathematics at King's starting with this coming term.

Yours ever

FRANK RAMSEY

117. **FPR – LW**

22 October [but in fact September] 1924

DEAR WITTGENSTEIN

Thanks very much for your letter: I will come on Thursday (25th).
I shall get to Gloggnitz 11.18, so I suppose to Ottertal about 1.

Yours ever,

F. P. RAMSEY

Briefe 168

Though dated 22.10.24, clearly enough despite Ramsey's rather approximate hand,
this letter must be from September, when indeed the 25th was a Thursday. Ramsey
was to leave for Cambridge on 3 October, see 116. and notes.

Gloggnitz. – A railway station on the line from Wiener Neustadt to Bruck an der
Mur. From it one crosses over a quite impressive range of hills into the valley of
the Feistritz where Trattenbach, the village of Wittgenstein's first school, and
Otterthal, that of his third and last, lie.

118.   **JMK – LW**

27.12.24.
46, Gordon Square
Bloomsbury

MY DEAR WITTGENSTEIN

I was happy to get your letter of last July, and, though I was sorry you wouldn't come here, I agreed with your reasons, – I think that what you said is true. It is true that it would be no good on either side to meet in Cambridge *casually*. The only satisfactory way would be, if the conditions were such that conversation was unnecessary unless desired; – as for example, if you were to stay with me in the country when I was working (I generally take a house in August and September). Then perhaps you could work too, – and at any rate be just as morose as you might feel inclined, without upsetting anybody. Perhaps sometime under such conditions you will come?

Yours ever (with much feeling)

J. M. KEYNES

Briefe 169

119.   **LW – JMK**

8.7.25.

DEAR KEYNES,

Some weeks ago I got a letter from a friend of mine in Manchester inviting me to stay with him some time during my holidays. Now I'm not yet quite decided about whether I shall come or not but I should rather like to, if I could also see *you* during my stay (about the middle of August). Now please let me know FRANKLY if you have the slightest wish to see me. If you give me a negative answer I shan't mind in the least. Please write to me as *soon* as possible, as my holidays are rather short and I shall hardly have time enough to arrange for my journey.

Yours ever

LUDWIG WITTGENSTEIN

My address is:
    L. W. bei Dr. Hänsel
    Wien V., Kriehubergasse 25.

K. 12   Briefe 176

---

a friend of mine in Manchester. – W. Eccles (see 35. above): Wittgenstein had written to him suggesting a visit on 7 May 1925, see *Briefe* no. 175.

120.   **LW – JMK**

[July or August 1925]

DEAR KEYNES,

Thanks so much for your letter. I will come to London on the 16th at 10^h 40 in the evening (via Boulogne–Folkestone). Please let me meet you in London as I don't like the idea of travelling about in England alone now. If you will send me some money for the journey I shall be very glad. I'm awfully curious how we are going to get on with one another. It will be exactly like a dream.

Yours ever

LUDWIG WITTGENSTEIN

K. 13   Briefe 177

121. **LW – JMK**

7.8.25.

DEAR KEYNES,

Thanks very much for your letter and the £10. I will travel by Dieppe–Newhaven as you suggest and shall arrive at Newhaven on Tuesday 18th in the morning by the boat which leaves Dieppe at midnight.

Auf Wiedersehen!

Yours ever

L. WITTGENSTEIN

K. 14   *Briefe 178*

Arrival at Newhaven (in Sussex) enabled Wittgenstein to go directly (or more probably to be easily met and brought) to the house that Keynes with his newly-married wife, Lydia Lopokova, had taken nearby. There, later the same day, Ramsey also came. Wittgenstein made further visits, to W. Eccles in Manchester and to Cambridge, to see W. E. Johnson, for whom he had a great fondness. Johnson wrote to Keynes on 24 August saying:

> Tell Wittgenstein that I shall be very pleased to see him once more; but I must bargain that we don't talk on the foundations of Logic, as I am no longer equal to having my roots dug up.

122. **LW – JMK**

MY DEAR KEYNES,

Thanks so much for your letter! I am still teacher and don't want any money at present. I have decided to remain teacher, as long as I feel that the troubles into which I get that way, may do me any good. If one has toothache it is good to put a hot-water bottle on your face, but it will only be effective, as long as the heat of the bottle gives you some pain. I will chuck the bottle when I find that it no longer gives me the particular kind of pain which will do my character any good. That is, if people here don't turn me out before that time. If I leave off teaching I will probably come to England and look for a job there, because I am convinced that I cannot find anything at all possible in *this* country. In this case I will want your help.

Please remember me to your wife.

Yours ever

LUDWIG

Give my love to Johnson, if you see him.

K. 15   Briefe 184

The letter reflects the difficulties of Wittgenstein's life as a schoolteacher. After a severe crisis with the people in his environment and the school authorities he resigned his post at the end of April 1926, and did not return to school-teaching.

Wien 2.7.1927

DEAR MR. RAMSEY,

Prof. Schlick lent me your book, The foundations of Math. & asked me to give him my opinion about it. As I don't agree with one of your main points I told Prof. Schlick my objections & I think I ought to let you know them too; for I'm sure you would oblige Prof. Schlick greatly by writing to him your answer to my criticism. I will now try to explain my point.

You define x = y by

$$(\varphi_\varepsilon) : \varphi_\varepsilon x = \varphi_\varepsilon y \text{ - - - - - - - - - - - - } Q(x,y)$$

& you justify this Definition by saying that Q(x, y) is a tautology

---

The first and last paragraphs of this letter are handwritten by Wittgenstein, the remainder is typed, with some manuscript alterations by Wittgenstein. The late Herbert Feigl recalled an occasion in his lodgings when Carnap typed a letter for Wittgenstein, presumably the present one. Among Friedrich Waismann's papers there was a carbon copy of this typed portion, naturally without the corrections. It is printed in F. Waismann, *Wittgenstein and the Vienna Circle* pp. 189ff. The coldness of this letter ("Mr." Ramsey, and the suggestion that a reply will be a favour to Schlick, not to Wittgenstein himself) is best explained by the reply that Ramsey did in fact send to Schlick (22 July 1927, see also comments on 124.). The following is the relevant passage:

> I had a letter the other day from Mr. Wittgenstein criticizing my paper "The Foundations of Mathematics" and suggesting that I should answer not to him but to you. I should perhaps explain what you may not have gathered from him, that last time we met we didn't part on very friendly terms, at least I thought he was very annoyed with me (for reasons not connected with logic) so that I did not even venture to send him a copy of my paper. I now hope very much that I have exaggerated this, and that he may perhaps be willing to discuss various questions about which I should like to consult him. But from the tone of his letter and the fact that he gave no address I am inclined to doubt it.

your book. – Actually an article with this title in *Proceedings of the London Mathematical Society*, ser. 2, vol. 125, part 5, reprinted in Ramsey's posthumous *The Foundations of Mathematics*, 1931, *Foundations*, 1978, and now *Philosophical Papers*, 1990, where the passage objected to occurs on p. 53, p. 204, and p. 216 respectively.

whenever "x" and "y" have the same meaning, and a contradiction, when they have different meanings.

I will try to show that this definition won't do nor any other that tries to make x = y a tautology or a contradiction.

It is clear that Q(x, y) is a logical product. Let "a" and "b" be two names having different meanings. Then amongst the members of our product there will be some such that f(a) means p and f(b) means ~p. Let me call such a function a critical function f_k. Now although we know that "a" and "b" have different meanings, still to say that a = b cannot be nonsensical if a ≠ b is to have any sense. For if a = b were nonsensical the negative proposition, i.e. that they have the same meaning, would be nonsensical too, *for the negation of nonsense is nonsense.* Now let us suppose, wrongly, that a = b, then, by substituting a for b★ in our logical product the critical function $f_k(a)$ becomes nonsensical (being ambiguous) and, consequently, the whole product too. On the other hand, let "c" and "d" be two names having the same meaning, then it is true that Q(c, d) becomes a tautology. But suppose now (wrongly) c ≠ d, Q(c, d) remains a tautology still, for there is no critical function in our product. And even if it could be supposed (which it cannot) that c = d; surely a critical function f_k (such that f_k means p[,]$f_k(d)$ means ~p) cannot be supposed to exist, for the sign f_k in this case becomes meaningless. Therefore, if x = y were a tautology or a contradiction and correctly defined by Q(x, y), Q(a, b) would not be contradictory, but nonsensical (as this supposition, if it were the supposition that "a" and "b" had the same meaning, would make the critical function nonsensical). And therefore ~Q(a, b) would be nonsensical too, for the negation of nonsense is nonsense.

In the case of c and d, Q(c, d) remains tautologous, even if c and d could be supposed to be different (for in this case a critical function cannot even be supposed to exist).

I conclude: Q(x, y) is a very interesting function, but cannot be substituted for x = y.

The mistake becomes still clearer in its consequences, when you try to say "there is an individual". You are aware of the fact that the supposition of there being no individual makes

$$(\exists x).x = x \qquad\qquad\qquad E$$

"absolute nonsense". But if E is to say "there is an individual" ~E says: "there is no individual". Therefore from ~E follows that E is nonsense. Therefore ~E must be nonsense itself, and therefore again so must be E.

The case lies as before. E, according to your definition of the sign " =" may be a tautology right enough, but does not say "there is an individual". Perhaps you will answer: of course it does not say "there is an individual" but it *shows* what we really mean when we say "there is an individual". But this is not shown by E, but simply by the legitimate use of the symbol $(\exists x)$ . . ., and therefore just as well (and as badly) by the expression ~$(\exists x).x = x$. The same, of course, applies to your expressions "there are at least two individuals" and so on.

That's all I've got to say. My objections are so very simple that I can hardly make myself believe that you haven't noticed & refuted those difficulties yourself. Still I can't help thinking that they are real difficulties.

Yours sincerely

L. WITTGENSTEIN

* which must be legitimate if we have given a = b the right meaning

Briefe 189

124. FPR – LW

King's College
Cambridge
[July-August 1927.]

DEAR WITTGENSTEIN,

Thank you very much for sending me your criticism of my paper. I hope you don't mind my answering to you as well as to Prof. Schlick, because he won't know whether my answer is any good, I'm afraid (judging by his book *Allgemeine Erkenntnislehre* which contains some sad rubbish), (but he may have got clearer since then). I am very sorry not to have sent you my paper myself before, but I didn't like to because you were so annoyed with me when we were at Keynes', and I didn't think the paper would interest you much.

Calling, as you do, $\varphi_\varepsilon, : \varphi_\varepsilon\, x \equiv \varphi_\varepsilon\, y,$ Q(x, y)

I say (1) Q(x, y) is a tautology whenever "*x*", "*y*" have the same meaning, and contradiction when they have different meanings.

rpspectively.

This is what seems to be the later of two drafts of a reply to 123. The draft closes with the cancelled sentence: "But the other convention seems to me as good as yours." It seems that Ramsey did not actually send it (see comments on 123.) but wrote instead to Schlick, who in turn communicated the answer to Wittgenstein in a letter dated 15 August 1927. The philosophical part of the Ramsey letter (faithfully transmitted by Schlick) is printed in *Wittgenstein and the Vienna Circle*, pp. 189–91 along with a later comment (9 December 1931) by Wittgenstein on this argument with Ramsey. Ramsey's letter to Schlick is in the Vienna Circle Archive in Haarlem. Both of Ramsey's drafts for a letter to Wittgenstein are printed in F.P. Ramsey, *Notes on Philosophy, Probability and Mathematics*, edited by Maria Carla Galavotti, Naples: Bibliopolis, 1991), p. 341ff.

Allgemeine Erkenntnislehre. – Springer, Berlin, 1/1918, 2/1925. E. T. *The General Theory of Knowledge* Lasalle, IL: Open Court, 1974).

(2) that therefore we may define $x = y .=. Q(x, y)$ Df.

Now I gather you are not disputing (1); (or are you?) but saying that granting (1) the definition is wrong. If by that you mean that $Q(x, y)$ does not *say* that x and y are identical, I entirely agree. All I contend is that substituting $Q(x, y)$ for $x = y$ in general propositions in which $x = y$ is part of the function generalized (in Russell's notation) will give the whole proposition the right sense.

Thus in the example on p. 351–2 of my paper.

$$(\exists\ m, n) : \hat{x}\ (\varphi\ x) \in m\ .\ \hat{x}\ (\psi\ x) \in n\ .\ m^2 = n^3 + 2$$

if we put for $m^2 = n^3 + 2$

$$Q(m^2, n^3 + 2)$$

we shall get the right meaning for the whole proposition or (a more simple case)

$$(\exists\ x) : fx\ .\ x \neq a$$

means the same as $(\exists\ x) : fx\ .\ \sim Q(x, a)$.

So also $Q(x, a) .\vee. Q(x, b)$ defines a class whose only members are a and b [,] just as $x = a .\vee. x = b$ was used by Russell to.

If you admit $Q(x, y)$ as a legitimate symbol at all it seems to me this must be all right.

I also agree with what you say about $(\exists\ x) . x=x$, but don't feel so clear about $(\exists\ x, y) : x \neq y$ etc. because if we adopt the convention that "x", "y" may take the same value the legitimate use of "$\exists\ x, y$" is possible even if there is only 1 individual, and the difference between there being only 1 individual and there being

---

pp. 351–2, p. 19, p. 170, p. 180 in book form (see comments on 123.).

used by Russell to.– to do, i.e. to define the class in question.

more does not seem to be shown by whether $(\exists\, x, y) : {\sim}Q(x, y)$ is a contradiction or a tautology.

I expect you will say that that is obviously foolish because we ought to adopt your convention and write not

$$(\exists\, x, y) : \sim Q(x, y)$$

but $(\exists\, x, y) : \sim Q(x, y) : \vee: \sim (\exists\, x) . \sim Q(x, x)$

and there being more than 1 indiv[idual] would then be shown by the legitimate use of $(\exists\, x, y)$ in your sense.[1]

---

[1] [Struck out:] But the other convention seems to me as good as yours. [After this the draft breaks off.]

Briefe 190

125.   **LW – JMK**

[Summer 1927]
Wien III.
Parkgasse 18

My Dear Keynes,

It's ages since you have heard from me. I haven't even thanked you
for your little book about Russia which you sent me about a year
and a half ago. I won't try to explain my long silence: there were
lots of reasons for it. I had a great many troubles one overlapping
the other and postponed writing until they would be all over. But
now I have interrupted my troubles by a short holiday and this is
the occasion to write to you. I have given up teaching long ago
(about 14 months)* and have taken to architecture. I'm building a
house in Vienna. This gives me heaps of troubles and I'm not even
sure that I'm not going to make a mess of it. However I believe it
will be finished about November and then I might take a trip to
England if anybody there should care to see me. I should VERY
much like to see you again and meanwhile to get a line from you.
About your book I forgot to say that I liked it. It shows that you
know that there are more things between heaven and earth etc.

little book about Russia. – *A Short View of Russia*, published by the Hogarth Press in
December 1925. One of its ideas, that Soviet Communism, for all its detestable
faults, "might represent the first stirrings of a great religion", is probably what
earned Wittgenstein's favourable comment.

house in Vienna. – This is the house (Parkgasse 18 or Kundmanngasse 19) which
Wittgenstein built for his sister Margaret Stonborough. It is described and illus-
trated in many books and brochures, most recently and most fully in Paul
Wijdeveld, *Ludwig Wittgenstein, Architect*, (London: Thames and Hudson, 1994).

Please remember me to your wife.

Yours ever

LUDWIG

* I couldn't stand the hot bottle any longer.

K.17   *Briefe 191*

the hot bottle. – See 122.

126.   **LW – JMK**

Wien III
Kundmanngasse 19
[1928]

MY DEAR KEYNES,

I've just finished my house that has kept me entirely busy these
last two years. Now however I will have some holidays and
naturally want to see you again as soon as possible. The question is,
would you mind seeing me. If not, write a line. I could come to
England in the first days of December but not before, as I must first
set to rights part of my anatomy. Enclosed you will find a few
photos of my house and hope you won't be too much disgusted by
its simplicity.

Yours ever

LUDWIG

Write soon!

K.18   Briefe 192

parts of my anatomy. – It is not known to us to what sort of bodily ailment this
phrase makes reference.

127.   **LW – JMK**

[Telegram]

3 December 1928

AM STILL UNABLE TO TRAVEL LETTER FOLLOWS
LUDWIG

Briefe 193

128.   **LW – JMK**

Wien III
Kundmanngasse 19
[December 1928]

MY DEAR KEYNES,

I had to postpone my trip, as my health was not quite strong
enough in the first days of this month. But I am nearly well now
and want to come to England in the beginning of January. Please
write a line letting me know if I can see you then.

Yours ever

LUDWIG

K.20   Briefe 194

129.   **LW – FPR**

[Early 1929]

DEAR RAMSEY,

I saw Braithwaite yesterday to ask him what exactly Dr. Broad had told him & this morning I went to see Mr. Priestley. He said that he couldn't remember having talked to you about my dissertation & if he had, that he could never have said with any certainty the book would count as he is only the secretary of the Board of research studies & it is not for him to decide the matter. He thinks however that there will be no difficulty about it in the meeting of the Board of research studies if the report from the moral science board should be favorable. In any case he will be so kind to talk to the authorities Sorley & Broad about it & let me know if there is

---

This letter is printed from a draft found among Wittgenstein's papers. The manuscript contains, perhaps unsurprisingly, an unusually large number (even for Wittgenstein) of second thoughts and spelling mistakes ("whent", "cann't", "Soreley", "Braithwait") which we have not reproduced.

Braithwaite. – See 99. At this point Braithwaite was Secretary of the Faculty Board of Moral Science.

Broad. – C. D. Broad (1887–1971) at the time University Lecturer, later Knightbridge Professor of Moral Philosophy at Cambridge.

Priestley. – Raymond Edward Priestley (1886–1974), Sir Raymond, as he later became, was at this time Secretary to the General Board. He was to be a close friend of Wittgestein's. He left Cambridge in 1935 and was in succession Vice-Chancellor of the Universities of Melbourne and of Birmingham.

the book. – The issue was whether Wittgenstein's *Tractatus Logico-Philosophicus* would be accepted as a dissertation for the degree of Ph.D. of the University of Cambridge. In the event it was so accepted and Wittgenstein received the title of Doctor.

Sorley. – W. R. Sorley (1855–1935) was Knightbridge Professor of Moral Philosophy at the time.

anything for me to do. So I believe the matter is in good hands now & I dont worry about it any longer.

A thing which is of much greater importance to me & was so on Saturday evening, is, that I still can't understand the way you behaved in this matter, that's to say I can't understand how, being my supervisor & even – as I thought – to some extent my friend having been very good to me you couldn't care two pins whether I got my degree or not. So much so, that you didn't even think of telling Braithwaite that you had told me my book would count as a dissertation. (I afterwards remembered one day talking to you about it in hall & you saying "it would be absurd to write another thesis now straightaway".) – Now you'll want to know why I write to you all this. It is not to reproach you nor to make fuss about nothing but to explain why I was upset on Saturday & couldn't have supper with you. It is always very hard for a fellow in my situation to see that he can't rely on the people he would like to rely on. No doubt this is due to a great extent to the difference of nationalities: What a statement seems to imply to me it doesn't to you. If you should ever live amongst foreign people for any length of time & be dependent on them you will understand my difficulty.

Yours

Ludwig

P.S. I find on looking at my College bills that I have informed you wrongly about the fees; they are altogether only 59 £ not 70 or 80 as I thought.

Briefe 197

130.   **FPR – LW**

[Spring 1929]

DEAR LUDWIG

I really think it will be all right about your degree and that you need not worry.

As for my own part in the matter I am extremely distressed to hear you find me unreliable, for I really don't think I have let you down in anything I have done or not done, and it seems to me there must be some misunderstanding between us.

Until my recent talk with Braithwaite I had no doubt that your book would count as a dissertation and that you would get your degree for it. I have talked about it to Moore and to Braithwaite previously, assuming that this was so, as I think they assumed too and only questioning the detail of whether the preface would do for a summary. This confidence was founded originally on my conversation with Priestley which seemed to me conclusive, for though he has no authority to bind the board I did not think his view of the matter was in the least likely to be questioned.

As I say, I had no doubts on the matter till I was told by Braithwaite that Broad was doubtful and was going to think it over. I did not take this very seriously, thinking that Broad was likely to change his mind being possibly actuated by a slight degree of malice which often prompts people to say something unpleasant which they never carry into act. Nor did I see anything I could usefully do; I do not know Broad well enough to be confident of improving matters by talking to him, supposing there to be any possibility of malice on his part; and when the matter came up at the Moral Sciences Board, I knew Moore, at any rate, would do everything possible in your interest.

The text of this letter is based on a fair copy in Ramsey's hand which the late R. B. Braithwaite found among his Ramsey papers. We suppose that Ramsey either sent another copy of the letter to Wittgenstein or made the same points verbally.

What exactly I said to Braithwaite I don't remember, but my conversation with Priestley I'm sorry to say didn't enter my head. Though it was my original reason for thinking the book would certainly do I had forgotten it for the moment. As to my "not telling Braithwaite that I had told you the book would count as a dissertation", I am very sorry if he didn't get that impression and indeed rather surprised. I did not say so in so many words but I thought he knew it. For instance I remember telling him once of a conversation I had with Moore as to whether you ought to write a summary, from which it must have been clear (since all that was in question was a summary of the book) that both Moore and I took for granted that the book would do for a dissertation and were only doubtful about whether the preface would do for a summary.

Where I think you may be right to reproach me, is not for anything I have done or not done but for my attitude of mind, which was, I am very sorry to say, rather casual. I did not at first realise how much you wanted a degree or the sacrifices you were making for it, and when I did fully realise what a monstrous cheat it would be if you didn't get one after all, I was afraid I had unnecessarily alarmed you since I thought the risk of anything going wrong was infinitesimal, and therefore tried to make as little of it as possible in what must have seemed the most unsympathetic way. I also felt that if anything did go wrong it might be through some fearful muddle and not through villainy as you naturally supposed. Though I thought Broad might be actuated by malice I did not know that he was, and I did not feel that I had behaved badly, and so I got too much drawn into making excuses.

But, Ludwig, it really isn't true that I didn't care twopence whether you got your degree. I may not have realised how much it mattered, but I did mind about it, and I don't know how you can suppose I didn't. I must express myself very obscurely and I get drawn into making excuses of a foolish kind. But it hurts me that you should suppose I don't feel the warmest friendship for you, or that you cannot rely on me

If, after all, your book is not accepted as a dissertation, I shall have made the most serious mistake in thinking my conversation with

Priestley proved that it would; but if, as I still think very unlikely, it should come to that I do hope you will believe that it was only a mistake and forgive me for it and for whatever else I have done or failed to do.

Yours ever

Frank Ramsey

Briefe 198

131.   **LW – JMK**

[May 1929]

DEAR KEYNES,

It is very difficult for me to write this letter to you. Please try to understand it before you criticize it. (To write it in a foreign language makes it still more difficult.) But I feel I could not come to you as you wanted me to without beginning to give and perhaps to ask for long explanations which I am sure you wouldn't like. When I saw you *last* I was confirmed in a view which had arisen in me last term already: you then made it very clear to me that you were tired of my conversation etc. *Now please don't think that I mind that!* Why shouldn't you be tired of me, I don't believe for a moment that I can be entertaining or interesting to you. What I *did* mind was to hear through your words an undertone of grudge or annoyance. Perhaps these are not exactly the right words but it was that sort of thing. I couldn't make out for some time what could be the cause of it all, until a thought came into my head which was by an accident proved to be correct. It was this: I thought probably you think that I cultivate your friendship amongst other reasons to be able to get some financial assistance from you if I should be in need (as you imagined I might be some day). This thought was *very* disagreable to me. I was however proved right in this way: In the beginning of this term I came to see you and wanted to return you some money you had lent me. And in my clumsy way of speaking I prefaced the act of returning it by saying "Oh, first I want money" meaning "first I want to settle the money business" or some such phrase. But you naturally misunderstood me and consequently made a face in which I could read a whole story. And what followed this, I mean our conversation about the society, showed

---

the society. – Clearly a reference to the discussion club known as "The Society" or "The Apostles". Cf. comment to 39.

me what amount of negative feelings you had accumulated in you against me. Now this could never prevent me from having tea with you; I would be very glad if I could suppose that your grudge for which I could not see any good reason had passed away. But the second remark in your letter seems to show me that you don't want to see me as my friend but as my benefactor. But I don't accept benefactions except from my friends. (That's why I accepted your help three years ago in Sussex.)

If some day you should want me to have tea with you without talking over my finances I will gladly come. – Please don't answer this letter unless you can write a *short* and *kind* answer. I did not write it to get explanations from you but to inform you about how I think. So if you can't give me a kind answer in three lines, no answer will please me best.

Yours ever

LUDWIG

K.21   *Briefe 199*

---

three years ago. – Since this presumably refers to Wittgenstein's visit to England in 1925, he ought to have written "four" and not "three".

132. **JMK – LW**

King's College,
Cambridge.
May 26 1929

DEAR LUDWIG,

What a maniac you are! Of course there is not a particle of truth
in anything you say about money. It never crossed my mind at the
beginning of this term that you wanted anything from me except to
cash a cheque or something of that kind. I have never supposed it
possible that you could want any money from me except in
circumstances in which I should feel it appropriate to give it. When I
mentioned your finances in my note the other day, it was because
I had heard that you were bothered with heavy unexpected fees
and I wanted, if this was so, to examine a possibility which I think
I suggested to you when you first came up, namely that some help
might conceivably be got out of Trinity. I had considered whether
it could be a good thing for me to do anything myself, and had
decided on the whole better not.

No – it was not "an undertone of grudge" that made me speak
rather crossly when last we met; it was just fatigue or impatience
with the difficulty, almost impossibility, when one has a conversation about something affecting you personally, of being successful
in conveying true impressions into your mind and keeping false
ones out. And then you go away and invent an explanation so
remote from anything then in my consciousness that it never
occurred to me to guard against it!

The truth is that I alternate between loving and enjoying you and
your conversation and having my nerves worn to death by it. It's
no new thing! I always have – any time these twenty years. But
"grudge" "unkindness" – if only you could look into my heart,
you'd see something quite different.

Well, if you can forgive me sufficiently, will you come and dine

with me in hall to-night (I shall be away nearly all next week)? –
When you can talk or not talk about cash, just as you feel inclined.

Yours ever

JMK

K.21   *Briefe 200*

133.   **LW – GEM**

[Cambridge]
Saturday
[15 June 1929]

DEAR MOORE,

Mr Butler wrote to me on Thursday to see him about the research-grant and to explain what exactly it was I wanted, and what were my plans for the future. – I did my best to explain it but don't feel sure that I have succeeded in making myself clear. I therefore, in this letter, want to state again as clearly as I can my position, to guard against all possibilities of misinterpretation.

I am in the middle of a bit of research work which I don't want to break off as it seems to me hopeful. I possess all in all about 100 £ which will carry me through the vacations and perhaps another month or two; but I mustn't use up all I've got, to leave some reserve for the time of looking round for a job. – I therefore ask the College to grant me say 50 £ which would enable me to go on with my philosophical work till, at least, Xmas. If it should turn out, that in this time I have been able to produce good work – as judged by anybody the College would consider an expert in the matter – and *if*, further, I should feel capable of continuing my work with success, *then* I propose to ask the College again for some sort of subvention.

The date of the letter is by Moore.

Mr Butler. – J. R. M. Butler, later Sir James (1889–1975), then Tutor in Trinity College, later Regius Professor of Modern History at Cambridge.

On 19 June 1929 the Council of Trinity College authorised a grant of £100 to be made to Wittgenstein to enable him to carry on his research at Cambridge. £50 was to be paid at Midsummer and £50 at Michaelmas.

Anybody who knew Wittgenstein will find this letter and the next extremely characteristic of their author.

Now Mr Butler asked me, how long, I thought, this might go on. – I can't answer this question, because I don't know, how long I will be able to produce good work. (For all I know – though I don't think it's likely – I may cease tomorrow.) But, I think, this question rests on a misunderstanding of what I really want. Let me explain this: Supposing I was run over by a bus today and then were to see my tutor and say: "I'm now a cripple for lifetime, couldn't the College give me some money to support me." Then it would be right to ask the question: "And how long do you propose this to go on, and when will you be self- supporting?" But this is *not* my case. I propose to do work, and I have a vague idea, that the College in some cases encourages such work by means of research grants, fellowships, etc. That's to say, I turn out some sort of goods and *if* the College has any use for these goods, I would like the College to enable me to produce them, as long as it *has* use for them, and as long as I *can* produce them. – If, on the other hand, the College has no use for them, that puts an end to the question.

Yours ever

LUDWIG WITTGENSTEIN

M.11　　*Briefe 201*

134.   **LW – GEM**

Tuesday
[18 June 1929]

DEAR MOORE,

This is a P.S. to my last letter. I met Mr Butler in the street today and he asked me 1.) whether you knew all about my financial position (I said, you did) 2.) Whether I had no other sources of getting money (I said, no) 3.) Whether I had not got relations who *could* help me (I said, I had and had told you so). Now as it somehow appears as if I tried to conceal something, will you please accept my written declaration that: not only I have a number of wealthy relations, but also that they would give me money if I asked them to. BUT THAT I WILL NOT ASK THEM FOR A PENNY. (Unless – of course – they owed me money.) Also I will add, that this is not a mere caprice of mine.

Yours ever

LUDWIG WITTGENSTEIN

M.12   *Briefe 202*

135. **LW – BR**

Wednesday
[July 1929]

DEAR RUSSELL,

On Saturday the 13th I will read a paper to the Aristotelian Society in Nottingham and I would like to ask you if you could possibly manage to come there, as your presence would improve the discussion *immensely* and perhaps would be the only thing making it worth while at all. My paper (the one *written* for the meeting) is "Some remarks on logical form", but I intend to read something else to them about generality and infinity in mathematics which, I believe, will be greater fun*. – I fear that whatever one says to them will either fall flat or arouse *irrelevant* troubles in their minds and questions and therefore I would be much obliged to you if you came, in order – as I said – to make the discussion worth while.

Yours ever

L. WITTGENSTEIN

*though it may be all Chinese to them.

R. 54   Briefe 203

The Joint Session of the Aristotelian Society and the Mind Association was held in University College, Nottingham 12–15 July 1929. Wittgenstein's written contribution "Some Remarks on Logical Form" was published under that title in the Supplementary Volume IX to the *Proceedings of the Aristotelian Society* for 1929, pp. 162–71
Russell's Appointments Diary does not show that he went to Nottingham.

136.   **LW – GEM**

[Probably 4 February 1930]

DEAR MOORE,

I wanted to come and see you today, partly to ask your advice in a few things concerning College etc. But I have got a bad cold and think I ought to stay at home. Could you come and have tea with me tomorrow (Wednesday) or, if that isn't possible the day after? I hope you aren't ill too. If you can come either day don't bother to reply.

Yours

LUDWIG WITTGENSTEIN

6 Granchester Rd

Briefe 196

Moore dates this to January or February, without a year, but in those months of 1929 Wittgenstein certainly had not moved to this address (actually Grantchester Rd.). From October 1929 Wittgenstein regularly went to tea with Moore on Tuesdays and his pocket diary shows a cancellation of Moore for 4 February and the entry "Moore tea" for the following day. The College business may have had to do with the renewal of the Research Grant mentioned in 134. On 7 March Moore was authorized by the Council of Trinity College to obtain reports on Wittgenstein's work, see also 138. (Another possible date would be 5 November 1929, where again the pocket diary has "Moore" on Tuesday (not cancelled, however) and "Moore bei mir" ["Moore at my place"] for Wednesday 6 November.).

137.   **LW – GEM**

[March or April 1930]

DEAR MOORE,

I am in Vienna now, doing the most loathsome work of dictating a synopsis from my manuscripts. It is a terrible bit of work and I feel wretched doing it. I saw Russell the other day at Petersfield and, against my original intention, started to explain to him Philosophy. Of course we couldn't get very far in two days but he seemed to understand a *little* bit of it. My plan is to go and see him in Cornwall on the 22nd or 23rd of April and to give him the synopsis and a few explanations. Now my lectures begin on Monday the 28th and I want to know if it is all right if I come to Cambridge not before the 26th. Please write to me about this as soon as possible as I have to

synopsis.–Refers to the typescript of *Philosophishe Bemerkungen* mentioned in 138. It was prepared on the basis of Wittgenstein's large manuscript volumes I, II, III, and part of IV (nos. 105–8 in G.H.v.W.'s catalogue).

Philosophy.– The capital letter may indicate a work or planned work of Wittgenstein's though the manuscript volumes use rather the title *Philosophische Bemerkungen* or *Betrachtungen*. Moore of course cannot yet have seen a typescript.

Petersfield.– The Beacon Hill School which Russell and Dora Black had founded in 1927 was near the town of Petersfield in Hampshire. Wittgenstein had gone to see Russell there, probably between 14 and 16 March, just before leaving for Austria. On his return, after Easter Sunday (20 April), he again went to see Russell, who was then on holiday in Cornwall. See 138, and comments.   Russell wrote to Moore both before the former meeting and after the latter. In the earlier letter (11 March) he said:

> I do not see how I can refuse to read Witttgenstein's work and make a report on it. At the same time, since it involves arguing with him, you are right that it will require a good deal of work. I do not know anything more fatiguing than disagreeing with him in an argument.

make my plans accordingly. I am kindhearted therefore I wish you a good vacation although I haven't a good one myself.

Yours ever

LUDWIG WITTGENSTEIN

Address:
  L.W. bei Dr Wollheim
  IV. Prinz Eugen Str. 18
  Austria Wien

M.13   Briefe 204

The first of the subsequent letters (5 May) expresses essentially the same judgement as that contained in Russell's formal report (for which see comments on 138). In a later letter (8 May), telling Moore that he had sent this report in to the College Council, he comments:

  I find I can only understand Wittgenstein when I am in good health, which
  I am not at the present moment.

(Letters in the G. E. Moore collection of Cambridge University Library.)See also comments on 138. below.
Wollheim.– Oskar Wollheim was a family friend of Wittgenstein's later brought safely to New York by Wittgenstein's sister. Possibly the rest of the family were already in Neuwaldegg and Wittgenstein stayed in town in order to dictate. Only one meeting with Schlick and Waismann (22 March) is recorded in this vacation.

138.   **LW – BR**

[Cambridge]
[April 1930]

DEAR RUSSELL,

Still in the motorcar to Penzance I thought of a notation I have used in my M.S. which you can't possibly understand as – I believe – it's explained nowhere: I use the sign $\underline{II}'$. Now first of all I must say that where you find two capital I like this II this means π for I had no π on my typewriter. Now π' is a prescription derived from the prescription π (i.e. the prescription according to which we develop the decimal extension of π) by some such rule as the following: "Whenever you meet a 7 in the decimal extension of π replace it by a 3" or "Whenever you get to three 5's in that extension replace them by 2"etc. In my original M.S. I denoted this sort of thing by $^5\bar{\pi}^{\ 3}$ and I'm not sure whether I haven't used this sign in a place of my typewritten M.S. too. – Of course there are probably lots and lots of such details which make the paper unintelligible, quite apart from the fact that it is unintelligible in any case. Another instance occurs to me just now: When I write " π_4" I mean π developed to 4 places in some given system, say, the decimal system. Thus $\pi_1 = 3$, $\pi_2 = 3.1$ in the decimal system. I can't think of anything else to write in the moment. I feel depressed and terribly muddled in my head which is partly due to

---

The references are to one copy of the typescript, which was posthumously published under Wittgenstein's eventual title *Philosophische Bemerkungen* (Oxford: Basil Blackwell, 1964). After dictating it in Vienna during the Easter Vacation (see 137.), Wittgenstein took a copy of it to Russell in Cornwall. At Moore's request Russell and J. E. Littlewood reported on the work for the College Council. Russell's report is highly interesting. It is printed in full in his *Autobiography*, vol. II, p. 199 f.

the Cambridge climate which it always takes me several days to get accustomed to. I feel there must be almost as many faults as words in this letter, but I can't help it.

Yours ever

L. WITTGENSTEIN

R. 55   *Briefe 205*

139.   **LW – GEM**

Dear Moore,

Thanks so much for the good news. I'm very grateful to the Council for its munificence.

I'm glad to hear you are enjoying your holidays. I don't yet enjoy mine, for I haven't yet been able to do any proper work, partly, I believe, due to the oppressive heat we've had here during the last week or so, and partly because my brain simply won't work. I hope to God this state won't last long. It is very depressing when all the lights are put out as if there had *never* been any burning. However, I dare say it'll pass over. – Would you be so very kind and take the Midsummer £50 for me and send them on to my Address? If it's not too much trouble for you I should be very much obliged if you would.

I hope your vacation will continue satisfactorily and that mine will soon be all right too. I'd be very glad if you would let me hear from you again some time how you're getting on, etc.

Yours ever

Ludwig Wittgenstein

M.14   *Briefe 206*

grateful to the Council. – On the basis of reports from Russell and J. E. Littlewood the Council of Trinity College had granted Wittgenstein another £100 to enable him to continue his research at Cambridge. See comments to 138.

Address. – Refers evidently to Wittgenstein's address during the Long Vacation, which he spent in Austria.

140.   **LW – GEM**

26.7.
[1930?]

DEAR MOORE,

This is to tell you that I have only just now begun to do any
proper work at all. Until about a week ago I hardly did any and
what work I did wasn't any good. I can't imagine what could have
been the matter with me, but I felt both extremely excitable and
incapable of sticking to any thought. It may have been some sort of
tiredness or the climate, for we had a terrible hot South wind
blowing almost all the time which has a bad effect on many people.
However I hope it's over now, I'm in the country again since about
10 days, in the same place where I was last year and I'm quite alone
at present. – I have received the £50 from Trinity. My life now is
very economical, in fact as long as I'm here there is no possibility of
spending any money. I hope you're getting on all right.

Yours ever

LUDWIG WITTGENSTEIN

M.15   *Briefe 207*

The annotation about the year with the question mark is by Moore. There is every
reason to believe that it is correct.

same place. – On the Hochreit. Cf. also 141. Wittgenstein's pocket diary shows that
he went there on 17 July.

141.   **LW – GEM**

[1930]

DEAR MOORE,

Thanks for your letter. I'm sorry you have such trouble at home. These illnesses are a bl[oody] nuisance. – My work is getting on moderately well but not more than that, I hardly ever feel quite alive. The weather is tolerable though rather changeable. Desmond Lee, whom you know, came to Austria and stayed with my people near where I live for a few days. We talked about you and wondered whether you'd like the place. And I almost think you would. I'm going to stay here as long as possible to get something done.

Yours ever

L. WITTGENSTEIN

M.16   *Briefe 208*

Lee. – H. D. P. (later Sir Desmond) Lee (1908–1993), then an undergraduate and student of classics at Corpus Christi College, Cambridge. Lee stayed with Wittgenstein's family on the Hochreit in 1930. Wittgenstein himself was living in a gamekeeper's cottage on the estate.

142.   **LW – GEM**

[Postcard with view of Hochreith (despite Vienna postmark)]

8.9.30 [postmark]

DEAR MOORE,

We have glorious weather since about a fortnight and my work is getting on rather well. This is another view of the place where I live. I hope you're having a good time too.

Yours ever,

LUDWIG WITTGENSTEIN

Wittgenstein's pocket diary indicates that he stayed on the Hochreith until 20 September.

143.   **LW – JMK**

[December 1930]

MY DEAR KEYNES,

Thanks so much for your congratulations. Yes, this fellowship business is very gratifying. Let's hope that my brains will be fertile for some time yet. God knows if they will – I hope to see you again some day before the end of this academic year anyhow.

Yours ever

LUDWIG

K.22   *Briefe 209*

fellowship. – Refers to Wittgenstein's appointment to a Fellowship at Trinity College in December 1930.

144.   LW – GEM

23.8.31.

DEAR MOORE,

Thanks for your letter. I can quite imagine that you don't admire Weininger very much, what with that beastly translation and the fact that W. must feel very foreign to you. It is true that he is fantastic but he is *great* and fantastic. It isn't necessary or rather not possible to agree with him but the greatness lies in that with which we disagree. It is his enormous mistake which is great. I.e. roughly speaking if you just add a "~" to the whole book it says an important truth. However we better talk about it when I come back. – I've had a very busy time since I left Cambridge and have done a fair amount of work. Now I want you to do me a favour: I don't intend to give any formal lectures this term as I think I must reserve all my strength for my own work. I will however have *private* (unpaid) discussions with students if there are any who want them. That's to say I don't want to be mentioned in the lecture list this term but at the same time Braithwaite could tell his students (and you can tell yours) that if any of them wish to have conversations with me I will arrange times with them. Please write a line to Braithwaite to explain this before the beginning of September. During the first month of the vac we had terribly hot weather and now it's abominably cold and rainy. I'm sorry to hear that the

---

Weininger. – Otto Weininger (1880–1903) was an author whom Wittgenstein greatly admired. The book here referred to is probably the English translation of Weininger's most famous work, *Geschlecht und Charakter* (*Sex and Character*).

private discussions. – Throughout the academic year 1931–2 Wittgenstein held (unpaid) conversation classes but did not give formal lectures.

weather in England depresses you, I'm not as fit as I ought to be
either.

Yours ever

Ludwig Wittgenstein

M.17   *Briefe 213*

145.   **LW – JMK**

[October 1931]

Dear Keynes,

I'm so sorry I can't see you at tea time on Friday as I've got a class every Friday at 5 o/c. Could you have tea with me on Sunday 25ᵗʰ, or Saturday next 31ˢᵗ, or Sunday 1ˢᵗ November? I hope to see you soon.

Yours ever

Ludwig

Briefe 210

This letter is undated but the dates and days of the week mentioned correspond only in 1931.

146.   **LW – GEM**

[22 Feb. 1932]
Monday

DEAR MOORE,

I can't come to tea with you tomorrow as I go to London to see the French Exhibition. Some people are taking me there in their car. I look forward hearing you on Friday. I'm sorry I wasn't well enough to hold my class last Friday.

Yours ever

LUDWIG WITTGENSTEIN

Briefe 215

Dated by a reference in Wittgenstein's pocket diary.

147.   **LW – GEM**

Saturday

[1933]

D EAR M OORE ,

Enclosed please find the proof of my letter to Mind. I have made
no corrections. Please read it through and see whether there is
anything to be altered. I wonder whether the comma after "*Now*"
in line 8 is necessary and that after "*print*". If not I'd rather leave
them out. Also the comma after "*think*" three lines below seems to
me not necessary.

Yours ever

L UDWIG W ITTGENSTEIN

M.19   *Briefe 216*

letter to Mind. – The letter is dated Cambridge, 27 May 1933 and was published in
the July issue of *Mind* for that year. Moore was then Editor of *Mind*. In the letter
Wittgenstein disclaimed responsability for views and thoughts attributed to him in
a recent publication. The first two but not the third of the suggested alterations
were made in the printed text, which may also be found in L. Wittgenstein,
Philosophical Occasions, ed. James C. Klagge and Alfred Nordmann, p. 156.

148.   **LW – GEM**

Monday
[October 1933]

DEAR MOORE,

I think I ought to let you know that I am not going to come to
tea with you on Tuesdays. I ought to have written this to you 2 or
3 weeks ago and in fact I wrote a letter to you about a fortnight ago
but destroyed it again. Then I left Cambridge for a week and
postponed writing to you and forgot about it. Please forgive me my
negligence.

I also want you to know that my reason for not coming is a lack
of friendliness which you showed on two occasions, the second
when we last met. (You weren't *un*friendly.) Your behaviour then
made me think that the way we used to meet wasn't quite the right
expression of our actual relation. I know this is expressed very badly
but you'll understand me.

If you will allow me occasionally to turn up at your at home after
tea I'll do so.

Yours

LUDWIG WITTGENSTEIN

M.20   Briefe 217

So dated by Moore although the weeks that have elapsed suggest a date further into
the academic year.

at home. – Moore's "at homes" were occasions on which philosophical topics were
taken up for discussion.

149.   **LW – GEM**

Saturday

[December 1933?]

DEAR MOORE,

This is the estimate. None of my lectures is over 1200 words and if we have them printed on foolscap they will each cost 4/6 that's to say 20 copies will cost that. Now I don't know exactly how many lectures there will be as possibly I might decide to dictate three times a week next term instead of only twice as I did this term. I dictated only 10 times this term so on the whole there will be about 52 lectures this academic year at the most, and these will cost between 11 and 12 pounds. If we only print 15 copies of each lecture, and there is no earthly reason why we should have more, they'll cost 10% less, i.e. *about* £ 10.

Yours

LUDWIG WITTGENSTEIN

I wish you and Mrs Moore a happy Christmas and New Year.

M.21   Briefe 218

The lectures are those which Wittgenstein dictated to his class in the academic year 1933–4 and of which a small number of copies were mimeographed and circulated. They have become known under the name The Blue Book (See comments on 159. and 160.). The estimate of the cost of duplication was probably given to Moore in connexion with an application to the Faculty Board for assistance.

150.   **LW – GEM**

Monday
[September 1934]

DEAR MOORE,

Thanks for your letter. I wish to God you would attend my
classes! It would give me ever so much more of a chance to make
things clear, to you *and* to others. Would you come if I promised
to provide a very comfortable chair and tobacco and pipecleaners?
I came up a week ago and am leaving for Ireland on Friday and shall
be back again on October 1st. I shall try to see you on Tuesday Oct.
2nd, i.e. I'll call and see if you are in. – I'm extremely sorry about
Priestley!

Yours

LUDWIG WITTGENSTEIN

M. 22   Briefe 219

Dated by Moore

classes. – Moore seems not to have attended Wittgenstein's classes in 1934–5.

Priestley. – See note on 129. Priestley was to leave for Melbourne at the end of
1934.

151.   **LW – GEM**

[13 May 1935]
Monday

DEAR MOORE,

I'm not going to send Miss Ambrose to you this afternoon. On
second thought I don't think it would be the right thing. If you will
allow me I shall see you tomorrow.

Yours ever

LUDWIG WITTGENSTEIN

Briefe 220

Miss Ambrose. – Later Alice Ambrose Lazerowitz, an American pupil of Wittgenstein's, was one of those to whom he dictated his notes, in particular "The Brown
Book". For the point or points at issue see notes on 153.

152.   **LW – GEM**

Trinity College
Cambridge
16th May 1935

DEAR MOORE,

This is only to confirm the statement I made in our conversation
last Tuesday that I am resigning as Miss Ambrose's examiner for her
Ph.D. degree.

Yours

LUDWIG WITTGENSTEIN

Briefe 221

examiner for her Ph.D. degree. – The Faculty Board had already, on 7 May, provided
for Wittgenstein's replacement (should he in the event decline to serve) by
Braithwaite.

153. **LW – GEM**

18 May [1935]

DEAR MOORE,

I am returning Miss Ambrose's M.S. – After her conversation with you on Thursday she wrote me a letter in which she gave me cheek. – I didn't answer it, only sent it back to her with the remark: 'Don't destroy this letter, it may interest you some day to reread it'. – I think you have no idea in what a serious situation she is. I don't mean serious, because of the difficulty to find a job; but serious because she is now actually standing at a crossroad. One road leading to perpetual misjudging of her intellectual powers and thereby to hurt pride and vanity etc. etc. The other would lead her to a knowledge of her own capacities and that *always* has good consequences. – You are the only person who now has any

The disagreement between Miss Ambrose and Wittgenstein was partly over an article 'Finitism in Mathematics', which she published in two instalments in *Mind*, of which Moore was at the time editor. These appeared in vol. 44, 1935, pp. 186–203 and 317–40. The former (April) number Wittgenstein borrowed from Trinity College Library on 1 May (his second and last entry in the Library register). The instalment there printed contains, as well as some particular acknowledgements, the general statement:

> The view presented is guided throughout by certain suggestions made by Dr. Ludwig Wittgenstein in lectures delivered in Cambridge between 1932 and 1935.

In the second instalment (whose very publication was in question in these letters but which did in fact appear) this is explicitly modified, in a particular context, as follows:

> This is a view which I understood Dr. Ludwig Wittgenstein to put forward in his lectures and which but for them would never have occurred to me. It is only in this sense that any view which I have put forward can be said to have been guided by suggestions made by him.

Wittgenstein was evidently in some measure content with this, for he did not in fact write to *Mind*.

influence on her and I wish you'ld use it for a good end! – I have given up the idea to talk to Newman. I think the right thing for me is not to have my hand in this matter any more. Whether I shall write to 'Mind' or not I don't yet know.

Yours ever

LUDWIG WITTGENSTEIN

However there was clearly also a disagreement whether Miss Ambrose was ready to submit her thesis for the Ph.D., for which Wittgenstein had been nominated as examiner, of which thesis the two articles objected to formed part. In the event she was awarded her degree in absentia in April 1938.

This contretemps caused some stir at Cambridge and also, by interrupting the dictation of "The Brown Book", perhaps contributed to changing the pattern of Wittgenstein's own work. On the whole matter see Professor Ambrose's own account in *Ludwig Wittgenstein: Philosophy and Language*, Ed. Alice Ambrose and Morris Lazerowitz, pp. 22–4.

she wrote me a letter. – Miss Ambrose herself described it to Mrs Moore in a letter of 8 February 1936, "I defended myself . . . I told him what I thought of his own conceit. I'm tired of his going about laying down the moral law . . . And yet there is a very great deal in him to love."

Newman. – The mathematician M. H. A. Newman (1897–1984), who had been appointed co-examiner of Miss Ambrose.

154.   LW – JMK

Sunday 30.6.[35.]

MY DEAR KEYNES,

I'm sorry I must trouble you with my affairs again. There are two things I want to ask you:

(a) I thought the other day when we talked in your room you were not disinclined to give me some sort of introduction to Maisky the Ambassador. I then said I thought he would not be the man who would give me the advice I wanted. But I've been told since that *if* he were inclined to give me a letter of introduction to some officials in Russia it would help me a lot. Therefore my first question is, would you be willing to give me an introduction to Maiski so as to make it possible for me to have a conversation with him, as the result of which he *might* give me an introduction?

(b) I have now more or less decided to go to Russia as a Tourist in September and see whether it is possible for me to get a suitable job there. If I find (which, I'm afraid is quite likely) that I can't find such a job, or get permission to work in Russia, then I should want to return to England and if possible study Medicine. Now when you told me that you would finance me during my medical training you did not know, I think, that I wanted to go to Russia and that I would try to get permission to practise medicine in Russia. I know that you are not in favour of my going there (and I think I understand you). Therefore I must ask you whether, under these

---

trouble you with my affairs again. – This perhaps refers to the fact that Wittgenstein in the spring of 1935 had been discussing with Keynes his plans of publishing the book on which he was then working. Keynes mentions this in a letter to Moore of 6 March 1935. Keynes expressed his willingness to contribute to the printing costs, should the publication plans meet with financial difficulties. Wittgenstein seems to have wanted his work published under the auspices of the British Academy.

Maisky. – Ivan Mikhailovitch Maisky (1884–1975), Ambassador of USSR to Great Britain 1932–43.

circumstances, you would still be prepared to help me. I don't like to ask you this question, not because I risk a "No", but because I hate asking any questions about this matter. If you reply please just write on a P.C.:

(a) No or (a) Yes, etc.

(b) No, etc.

as the case may be. I shall not think it the least unkind of you if you answer both *a* and *b* negatively.

I left your room the other day with a sad feeling. It is only too natural that you shouldn't entirely understand what makes me do what I am doing, nor how hard it is for me.

Yours ever

LUDWIG

K. 25   Briefe 222

155.   **LW – JMK**

Saturday 6.7.35.

MY DEAR KEYNES,

Thanks for your letter. To thank you for your answer to point
(a) wouldn't be the right thing, for no word of thanks would be
really adequate. – As to (b) I can't see Vinogradoff because he has
left for Moscow. He told me he was going to leave on the Saturday
after my conversation with him. In this conversation he wasn't at
all very helpful i.e. not as helpful even as *he* might have been. I'm
sure however he didn't show this when you asked him about me in
the presence of Maisky. Vinogradoff was *exceedingly careful* in our
conversation and I'm sure he has to be. He of course knew as well
as anyone that recommendations might help me but it was quite
clear that he wasn't going to help me to get any, at least none that
might carry real weight. – Now what I wanted with Maisky was
this: I wanted to see him and have a conversation with him. I know
that there is VERY little chance that I or my case could make a good
impression on him. But I think there is an off chance of this
happening. There is further a small chance of his knowing some
official at Leningrad or Moscow to whom he might introduce me.
I want to speak to officials at two institutions; one is the 'Institute
of the north' in Leningrad, the other the 'Institute of national
Minorities' in Moscow. These Institutes, as I am told, deal with
people who want to go to the 'colonies' the newly colonized parts
at the periphery of the U.S.S.R. I want to get information and
possibly help from people in these Institutes. I thought that Maisky
might recommend me to someone there. I *imagine* that such a
recommendation or introduction could be of two kinds. It may
either be purely official; in which case it could only say 'would so
and so be so kind to *see* me and listen to my questions'. For it is clear

---

Vinogradoff. – Serge Vinogradoff, Press Attaché at the Russian Embassy, was
perhaps temporarily absent: he spoke in Cambridge in January 1936.

to me that Maisky could not do anything else qua Ambassador. Or it might be an unofficial recommendation to someone he knows well and this he would only give me if I made a good impression on him, which – I *know* – is very unlikely. If what I think is sound – and God knows whether it is – then it might be useful for me to get an introduction from you to Maisky. In this introduction I don't want you to *ask* him to give me introductions, but only to allow me to have a conversation with him in order to get some information or advice. If he grants me an interview I will myself ask him whether he could give me an introduction that I am your personal friend and that you are sure that I am in no way politically dangerous (that is, if this *is* your opinion). – If you feel, either that such an introduction and consequent conversation could do me no good or if you feel uncomfortable about giving me such an intro-duction for any other reasons, whatever they may be, I will feel PERFECTLY satisfied with your not giving me an introduction.

I am sure that you partly understand my reasons for wanting to go to Russia and I admit that they are partly bad and even childish reasons but it is true also that behind all that there are deep and even good reasons.

Yours ever

LUDWIG

K. 26   *Briefe 223*

156. JMK – LW

10.7.1935

Dear Ludwig,

I enclose a letter of introduction to Maisky. I suggest that you might send this to him with a covering note asking if he could manage to spare the time to give you an interview.

I gathered from Vinogradoff that the difficulty would be that you have to receive an invitation from some Soviet organisation. If you were a qualified technician of any description of a sort likely to be useful to them, that might not be difficult. But, without some such qualification, which might very well be a medical qualification, it would be difficult.

Yours ever

JMK

Briefe 224

Keynes's letter of introduction was as follows:
Dear Monsieur Maisky,

May I venture to introduce to you Dr Ludwig Wittgenstein, a Fellow of Trinity College, Cambridge, who is anxious to find means of obtaining permission to live more or less permanently in Russia.

Dr Wittgenstein, who is a distinguished philosopher, is a very old and intimate friend of mine, and I should be extremely grateful for anything you could do for him. I must leave it to him to tell you his reasons for wanting to go to Russia. He is not a member of the Communist Party, but has strong sympathies with the way of life which he believes the new régime in Russia stands for.

I may mention that Dr Wittgenstein is an Austrian subject, though he has had long periods of residence in Cambridge both before and since the war. He has already had an interview with Mr Vinogradoff, who gave him some preliminary advice, but I gather that Mr Vinogradoff is no longer in England.

157.   **LW – JMK**

Friday
[July 1935]

DEAR KEYNES,

This is only to thank you for your introduction and to tell you that my interview with Maisky went off all right. He was definitely nice and in the end promised to send me some addresses of people in Russia of whom I might get useful information. He did not seem to think that it was utterly hopeless for me to try to get permission to settle in Russia though he too didn't think it was likely.

Yours ever

LUDWIG

K. 27   *Briefe 226*

Wittgenstein visited Russia early in September 1935. After his return to Cambridge from his year in Norway, 1936–7, he still had plans to go to Russia. See Paul Engelmann, *Letters from Ludwig Wittgenstein*, p. 58.

158.   **LW – GEM**

Postcard from Moscow with view of the Kremlin

18 September 1935

DEAR MOORE,

I shall come back to Cambridge in about two weeks. I will try to get something ready for publication. Whether successfully, God knows. I intend to stop in Cambridge for the whole academic year and to lecture. If you think it wise, please have my lectures announced.

Yours

LUDWIG WITTGENSTEIN

159. **LW – BR**

Trinity Coll[ege]
Wednesday
[Academic year 1935–1936]
[Presumably Autumn 1935]

DEAR RUSSELL,

Two years ago, or so, I promised you to send you a M.S. of mine. Now the one I'm sending you today isn't *that* M.S. I'm still pottering about with it and God knows whether I will ever publish it, or any of it. But two years ago I held some lectures in Cambridge and dictated some notes to my pupils so that they might have something to carry home with them, in their hands if not in their brains. And I had these notes duplicated. I have just now been correcting misprints and other mistakes in some of the copies and the idea came into my mind whether you might not like to have a copy. So I'm sending you one. I don't wish to suggest that you should read the lectures; but *if* you should have nothing better to do and *if* you should get some mild enjoyment out of them I would be very pleased indeed. (I think it's very difficult to understand them, as so many points are just hinted at. They were meant only

The "MS" which Wittgenstein sent to Russell must have been the so-called Blue Book. It was dictated to his class in the academic year 1933–4. The other piece of writing to which Wittgenstein refers here can hardly be anything other than a typescript of 768 pages which Wittgenstein compiled some time in 1932–3 and which was a successor to the *Philosophische Bemerkungen* of 1930. An account of this typescript was given in the Editor's Note in *Philosophische Grammatik* (Oxford: Basil Blackwell 1969) and it has been much discussed since, see for example, A. J. P. Kenny, *The Legacy of Wittgenstein* pp. 24–37, and S. Hilmy, *The Later Wittgenstein*, ch. 1. Russell's copy of the Blue Book, with some corrections and changes by the author, is now in the Russell Archives at McMaster University.

for the people who heard the lectures.) As I say, if you don't read them *it doesn't matter at all.*

Yours ever

LUDWIG WITTGENSTEIN

R. 56   *Briefe 227*

160.   **LW – BR**

Trin[ity] Coll[ege]
Sunday
[Presumably November 1935]

DEAR RUSSELL,

I'm in a slight difficulty: I gather that you're coming up to read a
paper to the Moral Sc[iences] Club on the 28ᵗʰ. Now it would be
the natural thing for me to attend the meeting and take part in the
discussion. – But: – (a) I gave up coming to the Mor[al] Sc[iences]
Cl[ub] 4 years ago; people then more or less objected to me for
talking too much in their discussions. (b) At the meeting there will
be Broad, who, I believe, objects most strongly to me. On the other
hand (c), if I am to discuss at all it will – in all likelihood – be the
only natural thing for me to say *a good deal*, i.e., to speak for a
considerable time. (d) Even if I speak a good deal I shall probably
find that it's hopeless to explain things in such a meeting.

There are therefore the following possibilities: (a) I don't come
to the meeting at all. This is obviously right, unless you *definitely*
want me to come.

(b) I could come but take no part in the discussion. This too is all
right with me, if it is what you want me to do. (c) I come and speak
up whenever you want me to, i.e., whenever you say so.

You may not quite understand my point of view. It is, roughly,
this: If I felt that I had to make a stand against something and that I
could do it with any chance of success I would do it, Broad or no
Broad. But as it is, I feel like someone who's intruding in a tea-party
in which some people don't care to have him. If, on the other hand,
you wished me to be there and to speak (in my natural way, of

---

paper to the Moral Sciences Club. – The date is presumably 28 November 1935. The
paper was "The Limits of Empiricism" which Russell subsequently, on 5 April
1936, read to the Aristotelian Society and which is published in the Society's
Proceedings.

course) then it would be as if the host wanted me to be at the tea-party, and in this case I wouldn't care whether any of the guests objected. – If I don't come to the Mor[al] Sc[iences] Club some of the members and I could still have a discussion with you the next day in my room, or just you and I.

I should be glad if you'ld write to me a line about this. (Provided that you don't think that I wrote some sort of polite nonsense or fishing for compliments; etc.) We also could decide what is the right thing to do just before the meeting, if I could see you for a minute then.

I am pleased that you're reading my M.S. But please don't think it's in any way necessary. You need neither write nor speak a review about it. I know that it isn't as good as it ought to be and, on the other hand, that it might be still worse.

Yours ever

LUDWIG WITTGENSTEIN

R. 57   *Briefe 228*

my M.S. – The so-called Blue Book, see notes to 159.

161. **LW – GEM**

Friday
[6 March 1936]

DEAR MOORE,

I'm sorry to say I can't see you today as I've got a bl. . . . cold and must stay indoors.

I hope to see you next Friday.

Yours

LUDWIG WITTGENSTEIN

Briefe 229

The dates of this and of the following letter, given by Moore, do not quite agree with Wittgenstein's pocket diary, which suggests the date of 6 March for 162.

162.   **LW – GEM**

Thursday

[19 March 1936]

DEAR MOORE,

The Thomsons want you and me to come to them tomorrow at teatime. (They live: Lavender Cottage, Storey's Way off Huntingdon Rd.) Now I don't feel very well, I may have a slight 'flu or something, so I probably shan't be able to come. But they should like to see you without me, and possibly you might play some piano duets with Mrs Thomson. So would you go there, say at 4.15 or if you can't, write them a note?

Yours

LUDWIG WITTGENSTEIN

I wish I could be there and hear you play!

M.26   *Briefe 230*

the Thomsons. – George Thomson and his wife Catherine (née Stewart) were particular friends of Wittgenstein, whom he continued to visit when George was appointed Professor of Greek at the University of Birmingham. Professor Thomson (1903–87) was, or deserved to be, equally well known for his rather Marxist accounts of ancient thought and for his sensitive translations of colloquial Irish texts.

163. **LW – GEM**

Thursday
[21 May 1936]

DEAR MOORE,

Mrs Thomson wants us, you and me, to come to tea to her tomorrow. So I shan't come to you but meet you at the Thomsons' (Lavender Cottage, 25 Storey's Way).

Yours

LUDWIG WITTGENSTEIN

Briefe 231

164.   **LW – GEM**

Tuesday
[2 June 1936]

DEAR MOORE,

I am having a social gathering of my students in my room, on Friday at 4.30. Would you mind coming? If I don't hear from you I shall expect you.

Yours

LUDWIG WITTGENSTEIN

M.28   *Briefe 232*

The gathering, no doubt, marked the ending (as it seemed) of both Wittgenstein's fellowship and his teaching activity at Cambridge.

165. **LW – GEM**

[Postcard with picture of Skjolden]

Skjolden i Sogn
Norway
Thursday
[September 1936]

DEAR MOORE,

I'm in Skjolden again and living in the little house I built for myself before the war. When I came here I was very ill but thank God I've recovered now though I'm still rather weak. My work doesn't go badly considering. I'm very much alone and very undisturbed. I think it may have been the right thing to come here. The country round me is wonderful and just now we've got fine weather. I haven't forgotten about the photos I promised to send you and Mrs. Moore but I haven't got them yet. Please remember me to Mrs. Moore and to Wisdom. I shall write to him soon.

Yours

LUDWIG WITTGENSTEIN

My house is not on the p[ost]c[ard]. It's about half an hour to row and walk from the village.

In the summer of 1936 Wittgenstein settled down in his hut in Norway. He was first working on a German version of the so-called Brown Book which he had dictated to Alice Ambrose and Francis Skinner in 1934–5. He soon abandoned this and made a fresh start which resulted in a first version of the *Philosophical Investigations*. Wittgenstein's stay in Norway lasted for nine months, interrupted only by a visit to Vienna and England round New Year 1937. See 169.

Wisdom. – John (A. J. T.) Wisdom (1904–93), Lecturer and later Professor of Philosophy in the University of Cambridge.

166. **GEM – LW**

86 Chesterton Road,
Cambridge
Sept. 30. 1936

DEAR WITTGENSTEIN,

I was glad to hear from you, and glad that your work has been going pretty well. I hope it will turn out to have been the right thing for you to go there. I remember your taking me to the site where you said you intended to build a house: I remember the sort of place it was very well. But I don't think I knew that you had actually built a house there; and perhaps you didn't, but on some other site. If I remember right, the site you took me to would be not far outside the post-card, on the right hand side, a good way up above the fiord.

My work has not been going at all well: I have not got anything finally written. I have been trying to think hard, but I find things very puzzling: there are so many different points, which I cannot fit together. I have been reading through again all of your work that I have, in the hope of getting clearer.

In other respects all has been going well with us. I met Wisdom today, for the first time since you left: he has not been back long. He was finding his mare on Empty Common. I told him I had heard from you, and that you said you would write to him soon. We had a bit of a walk and talk together, and I was very glad to see him.

I have just heard from Rhees that he has got a job in Deighton

Rhees. – Rush Rhees (1905–89), a pupil of Wittgenstein's and later the executor of his will.

Bell's book-shop. He found he could not get anything written for the Trinity Fellowship; so he is not competing. He was very distressed about it.

Yours,

G. E. MOORE.

Briefe 233

167.   **LW – GEM**

Wednesday
[October 1936]

DEAR MOORE,

I was very glad to get your letter. My house is not built on the site you mean. This map will show you where it is and why I can't get into the village without rowing; for the Mountain is much too steep for anyone to walk on it along the lake. I do believe that it

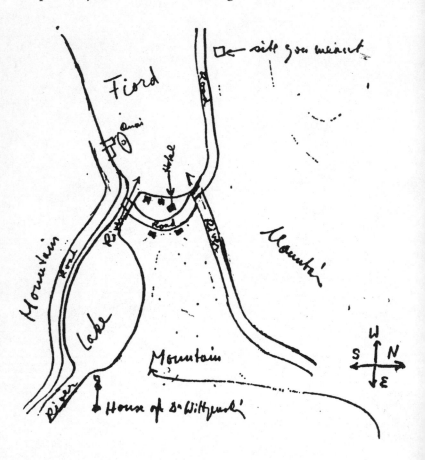

was the right thing for me to come here thank God. I can't imagine that I could have worked anywhere as I do here. It's the quiet and, perhaps, the *wonderful* scenery; I mean, its quiet seriousness.

I am sorry to hear that your work hasn't been going well, or satisfactorily. I'm sure somehow that you're doing good work, and at the same time I think I can understand why you don't get "anything finally written". That, I think, shows that what you're doing is right. I don't mean that it would be wrong however if you got anything finally written and in fact I hope you *will*. Rhees' case is, of course, quite different, but here too I can't help feeling that it's not bad, *in fact that it's good that he found himself unable to write anything*. Please, if you see him, remember me to him and tell him that I was glad to hear that he could not get anything written. That's a *good* sign. One can't drink wine while it ferments, but that it's fermenting shows that it isn't dish-water. You see, I still make beautiful similes. – Tell Rhees that I'm not glad because I'm malicious.

We have had the most wonderful weather for the last 4 weeks, though it's already getting cold. The waterfalls are entirely frozen and it's about $-3°$C. at nights. But I don't suffer from the cold as I would in England, for it's dry.

Remember me to Mrs Moore and to Hardy and Littlewood if you should see them.

Yours

LUDWIG WITTGENSTEIN

M.29   Briefe 234

Dated by Moore.

168. **LW – GEM**

Wednesday
[November 1936]

DEAR MOORE

Enclosed please find the photos. I don't know whether they are any d. . . . good, but anyhow they're easily as good as I am. One – in the Botanical garden – was taken in Dublin by Drury, the other two by Pattisson in France. The one on which I look like an old prophet was taken when I was rather ill. The one with the bridge in the background was taken while I was taking a photo myself. If you don't like them throw them away and I'll send you better ones when there will be some. I enclose a p[ost] c[ard] which shows exactly where my hut stands though it doesn't show the hut, which was built after the picture was taken. The scaffolding you see in the foreground does no longer exist and, I think, only bits of it existed when you saw it before the war.

Yours

LUDWIG WITTGENSTEIN

M.30   *Briefe 235*

Dated by Moore.

Drury. – Dr Maurice O'Connor Drury (1907–76), a close friend of Wittgenstein's at Cambridge and later in Dublin where Wittgenstein visited him in June 1936 and fairly frequently thereafter.

Pattisson. – Gilbert Pattisson also became a close friend of Wittgenstein's while an undergraduate at Cambridge and Wittgenstein always arranged to meet him on his way through London in the thirties. The two men spent a short holiday in France in July 1936.

169.   **LW – GEM**

Thursday

20 Nov. [1936]

DEAR MOORE,

I was glad to get your letter. My work isn't going badly. I don't know if I wrote to you that when I came here I began to translate into and rewrite in German the stuff I had dictated to Skinner and Miss Ambrose. When about a fortnight ago, I read through what I had done so far I found it all, or nearly all, boring and artificial. For having the English version before me had cramped my thinking. I therefore decided to start all over again and not to let my thoughts be guided by anything but themselves. – I found it difficult the first day or two but then it became easy. And so I'm writing now a new version and I hope I'm not wrong in saying that it's somewhat better than the last. – Besides this all sorts of things have been happening inside me (I mean in my mind). I won't write about them now, but when I come to Cambridge, as I intend to do for a few days about New Year, I hope to God I shall be able to talk to you about them; and I shall then want your advice and your help in some very difficult and serious matters. –

stuff I had dictated. – The so called Brown Book. Cf. comments to 164. above; Wittgenstein's German version of part of this (with an independent translation of the rest of the book) has been published as "Eine philosophische Betrachtung" in L. Wittgenstein *Schriften* 5 (Frankfurt: Suhrkamp, 1970).

new version. – This is a first version of the *Investigations* up to section 189. The manuscript, which was written in a big bound notebook Wittgenstein gave as a Christmas gift to his sister, Mrs Stonborough. She entrusted it, with other manuscripts, to Wittgenstein's friend Rudolf Koder (see 106.), whose son has recently published an account of the matter, see *Mitteilungen aus dem Brenner-Archiv* 12 (1993): 52–4.

talk to you. – When Wittgenstein visited Vienna and England round New Year 1937 he talked to several of his friends about personal matters and his inner struggles. He referred to these talks as "confessions": Cf. *Letters from Ludwig Wittgenstein*, p. 58, and Fania Pascal in *Ludwig Wittgenstein, Personal Recollections*, ed. Rush Rhees (Oxford: Blackwell, 1981), pp. 26–62

283

I was very glad to hear that Skinner came to the Mor[al] Sc[iences] Club and that he spoke. I wish it were possible for you to see him once in a while! It would do him masses of good. For he *needs* someone he can talk to decently and seriously!

If ever you see Ryle or write to him give him my love. I can quite imagine that he didn't read a good paper and also that he was nice and decent and agreeable in the discussion.

I intend to leave here for Vienna about Dec. 8th and to come to Cambridge about the 30th Dec. and to stay *about* a week.

Best wishes!

LUDWIG WITTGENSTEIN

M.31   *Briefe 236*

Skinner.–Francis Skinner who came up to Trinity in 1930 was Wittgenstein's principal friend and companion until his death in 1941. The two shared lodgings in East Rd (see 170.) when Wittgenstein was not housed in college. Skinner may be said to have given up mathematics (he had been a Wrangler and a Research Student) to live and think along Wittgenstein lines.

Ryle. – Gilbert Ryle (1900–76) had known Wittgenstein since 1929. He was during these years Student of Christ Church and later became Waynflete Professor of Metaphysical Philosophy, in the University of Oxford. He may be said to have been principally responsible for introducing "linguistic philosophy" to that university. On this occasion, 30 October 1936, he had read to the Moral Sciences Club a paper entitled "Unverifiability by me", subsequently published in *Analysis* 4, (1936–7): 1–11. Ryle was to succeed Moore as editor of *Mind*.

170.   **LW – GEM**

81 East Rd
Monday
[11 January 1937]

DEAR MOORE,

I could not leave Cambridge last week as I wished. Instead I had to go to bed on Wednesday with a 'flu. I'm out of bed again but still *very* weak. Do you think you could come and have tea with me here tomorrow? – But on second thought I find that I shall be absolutely well enough to come to you. So I'll come to you at about 5 p.m., unless I hear from you to the contrary. I *very* much want to speak to you.

Yours

LUDWIG WITTGENSTEIN

M.32   Briefe 237

171.   **LW – GEM**

Tuesday

[12 January 1937]

DEAR MOORE,

I'm sorry I didn't come to you today but I didn't feel quite well enough for it. Mrs Moore wrote to me that you too were having 'flu. I hope it was only a light attack. With me a 'flu, however short, has a long epilogue. And I'm just in the beginning of it. When I shall be well enough I'll come round and try to see you, for I'm sure you'd better stay at home for several days.

Yours

LUDWIG WITTGENSTEIN

M.33   *Briefe 238*

172.   **LW – GEM**

Skjolden i Sogn
Thursday 4.3.[1937]

DEAR MOORE,

   This is only to say that I wish to hear from you. – My work hasn't been going well since I came back here. Partly because I've been troubled about myself a lot. In the last few days I've been able to work a bit better, but still only very moderately. The days are getting longer now and that cheers me up, but I still don't see the sun from where I live. (Though in the village it shines for many hours.)

   Give my love to Wisdom and tell him, please, to write to me occasionally. Have you heard from Rhees? I suppose you haven't seen Skinner, or I would have heard it from him. Though I wish you had! –

   I enclose two stamps which might be of use to Mrs Moore. Please remember me to her. I hope to hear from you soon.

   Lots of good wishes!

Yours

LUDWIG WITTGENSTEIN

M.34   Briefe 239

173.   LW – GEM

Postcard from Ireland with view of Trinity College, Dublin

22 February 1938

DEAR MOORE,

I should be very grateful if you would let me know the result of the Council meeting regarding my MSS. My address is

36 Chelmsford Rd.,
Ranelagh, Dublin

Council meeting regarding my MSS. – Wittgenstein at about this time planned to place his papers in Trinity College Library. As regards those still in Austria, he wrote to his sister requesting that they be sent in a locked chest: Meine M.S.S. werden nämlich bis auf weiteres für niemand, außer mir und noch *einem*, in der Bibliothek zugänglich sein. [The point is that in the library my manuscripts will, until further notice, be accessible to nobody but myself and one other person].

This letter (the first page of which, with the date and the motivation of the instructions given, seems to be missing) is evidently addressed to his sister Hermine, and is now in the Brenner Archive at Innsbruck. Internal evidence (a birthday mentioned) suggests that it was written about the beginning of March, presumably in 1938. This dating is supported by a typescript list among Wittgenstein's papers which corresponds exactly with that made by his sister. It contains, however, manuscript notes possibly in Friedrich Waismann's hand. He was in contact with Wittgenstein in January and February of 1938 and it may have been planned that on his return to Vienna (which the Anschluss in fact prevented) he should see to the despatch of the manuscripts.

The "one other person" mentioned may well have been Wittgenstein's friend Skinner, see comments on 169.

At all events there must have been a prior request to Trinity College Library to house these or other manuscripts, for on 22 January 1938, T. Nicholas, the Senior Bursar, wrote to Moore saying that though the Council was "entirely willing" that Dr Wittgenstein's manuscripts should be deposited in the Library, it wished to know what the conditions about access and copyright were to be. "I am sorry," Nicholas concludes, "that he will not publish the work himself."

The Austrian papers did not arrive then, or in some cases ever. The gifts of papers to the Library after Wittgenstein's death by his literary heirs in England and by members of his family in Austria are part of another story.

I wish you'ld see Skinner one of these days.

Ever yours

LUDWIG WITTGENSTEIN

174.   **PS – LW**

King's College
Cambridge
14 March 1938

DEAR WITTGENSTEIN,

Before trying to discuss, probably in a confused way, I want to give a clear answer to your question. If as you say it is of "vital importance" for you to be able to leave Austria and return to England, there is no doubt – *you must not go to Vienna*. Whether you are a lecturer at Cambridge or not, now you would not be let out: the frontier of Austria is closed to the exit of Austrians. No doubt these restrictions will have been somewhat relaxed in a month's time. But there will be no certainty for a long time that you will be allowed to go out, and I think a considerable chance of your not being allowed out for some time. You are aware no doubt that you are now a German citizen. Your Austrian passport will certainly be withdrawn and then you will have to apply for a German passport, which may be granted if and when the Gestapo is satisfied that you deserve it.

This is the only letter of Sraffa's preserved among Wittgenstein's papers. The other Piero Sraffa (1898–1983) a brilliant though not prolific Italian economist, editor of the works of David Ricardo. Essentially a refugee from Fascism since 1926, he pursued his career in Cambridge, at first under Keynes's aegis, and was attached to King's College, but in 1939 became a Fellow of Trinity. He was not only a friend of Wittgenstein's from 1930 but one of the few whose intellectual influence Wittgenstein recognized, as may be seen from the preface to *Philosophical Investigations*.

This is the only letter of Sraffa's preserved among Wittgenstein's papers. The other side of the correspondence (mostly arrangements to meet and the like) was for long preserved by Sraffa but seems at present to be lost.

A speaking testimony to the nature of Sraffa's friendship is that he himself travelled to Austria around Easter 1938 to carry news and greetings to Wittgenstein's family and to bring back news of them. (This is known from a letter from Hermine Wittgenstein to Ludwig Hänsel in *Ludwig Hänsel – Ludwig Wittgenstein Eine Freundschaft* (Ilse Somavilla et al. Ed.) Innsbruck, Hayman, 1994, p.148.

As to the possibility of war, I do not know: it may happen at any moment, or we may have one or two more years of "peace". I really have no idea. But I should not gamble on the likelihood of six months' peace.

If however you decided in spite of all to go back to Vienna, I think: a) it would certainly increase your chance of being allowed out of Austria if you were a lecturer in Cambridge; b) there would be no difficulty in your entering England, once you are let out of Austria (of Germany, I should say); c) *before* leaving Ireland or England you should have your passport changed with a German one, at a German consulate: I suppose they will begin to do so in a very short time; and you are more likely to get the exchange effected here than in Vienna; and, if you go with a German passport, you are more likely (though not at all certain) to be let out again.

You must be careful, I think, about various things: 1) if you go to Austria, you must have made up your mind not to say that you are of Jewish descent, or they are sure to refuse you a passport; 2) you must not say that you have money in England, for when you are there they could compel you to hand it over to the Reichsbank; 3) if you are approached, in Dublin or Cambridge, by the German Consulate, for registration, or change of passport, be careful how you answer, for a rash word might prevent you ever going back to Vienna; 4) take great care how you write home, stick to purely personal affairs, for letters are certainly censored.

If you have made up your mind, you should apply at once for Irish citizenship – perhaps your period of residence in England will be counted for that purpose: do it before your Austrian passport is taken away from you, it is probably easier as an Austrian than as a German.

In the present circumstances I should not have qualms about British nationality if that is the only one which you can acquire without waiting for another ten years' residence: also you have friends in England who could help you to get it: and certainly a Cambridge job would enable you to get it quickly.

I shall be in Cambridge till Friday: afterwards letters will be forwarded to me in Italy, so take care what you say, that you may be writing for the Italian censor.

My telephone is 3675: you will find me available before noon and in the evening after 10.

Yours

PIERO SRAFFA

Excuse this confused letter.

175.   **LW – JMK**

81 East Rd.
Cambridge
18.3.38

MY DEAR KEYNES,

I am so sorry to have to trouble you with my own affairs at a time when you yourself are not too well. I want however to describe to you my present situation and ask you whether you can by any chance, in some way not too difficult for you, give me some advice or help. You know that by the annexation of Austria by Germany I have become a German citizen and, by the German laws, a German Jew (as three of my grandparents were baptised only as adults). The same, of course, applies to my brother and sisters (not to their children, *they* count as Aryans). As my people in Vienna are almost all retiring and very respected people who have always felt and behaved patriotically it is, on the whole, unlikely that they are at present in any *danger*. I have not yet heard from them since the invasion and there hasn't yet been time as they would wait in any case with giving me news until things had settled down a bit. I wrote to them a week ago saying that if they needed me I would come home any time. But I *believe* that they aren't going to call me and also that I couldn't at present do anything for them, except possibly cheering them up a little. – If however I went to Vienna now the consequences would be

a) that my passport, being an Austrian one, would be taken away from me and b) that, in all likelihood, *no* passport would be given

---

not too well. – Keynes had been seriously ill with heart trouble since 1937.

baptised only as adults. – And hence undeniably Jewish (though in the event one of them was classified as Aryan).

to me; as passports, except in very special cases, are not, I gather, issued to German Jews. I could therefore c) not leave Austria again and d) never again get a job.

My people, who were rich before the war, are still wealthyish and will probably, even when a lot will be taken away from them, still have enough money to keep me (and they would *gladly* do so) but I needn't say this would be the last thing that I'ld wish to happen.

I also must say that the idea of becoming (or being) a German citizen, even apart from all the nasty consequences, is APPALLING to me. (This may be foolish, but it just is so.)

For all these reasons I have now decided to try 1) to get a University job at Cambridge, 2) to acquire British citizenship.

The thought of acquiring British citizenship had *occurred* to me before; but I have always rejected it on the ground: that I do not wish to become a sham-Englishman (I think you will understand what I mean). The situation has however entirely changed for me now. For now I have to choose between two new nationalities, one of which deprives me of *everything*, while the other, at least, would allow me to work in a country in which I have spent on and off the greater part of my adult life, have made my greatest friends and have done my best work.

Now if I wish to try to become naturalised here I'm afraid I have to make haste; one of the reasons being that (as Sraffa pointed out to me) it would be easier as long as I hold an Austrian passport. And this I might have to give up before so very long.

As to getting a job at Cambridge you may remember that I was an assistant faculty lecturer for 5 years, and that the regulations don't allow one to hold this job for more than 5 years. When my 5 years had expired the faculty allowed me to go on lecturing as before and they went on paying me as before. Now it is for *this* that I shall apply, for there is no other job vacant. I had, in fact, thought of doing so anyway; though not now, but perhaps next autumn. But it would be important now for me to get a job *as quickly as possible*; for a) it would help me in becoming naturalised and b) if I failed in this and *had* to become a German I would have more chance to be allowed out of Austria again on visiting my people if I had a JOB in England.

I have talked all this over with Sraffa yesterday. He is leaving today or tomorrow for Italy and I came here in a hurry from Dublin to see him and talk with him. He thought the right thing for me is to see a solicitor about becoming naturalized, one who is an expert in this kind of thing. Sraffa thought that you might possibly be able to tell me the right person or give me some sort of advice about the matter, or also about applying for a University job.

I want to add that I'm in no sort of financial difficulties. I shall have about 300 or 400 £ and can therefore easily hold out for another year or so

Well, this is all. Forgive me for making you read this *long* letter; if indeed you ever get to this line.

I hope I may see you again before so *very* long. *Whatever* you may think about me or my problems I am

Yours ever

LUDWIG

P.S. If my people wrote to me now that they wanted me at home I would, of course have to go. But, as I said, this is most unlikely.

Briefe 242

a solicitor. – To judge from Wittgenstein's pocket diary Keynes seems to have suggested F.A.S. Gwatkin of McKenna & Co., with whom Wittgenstein had appointments on 11 April and 30 June 1938. The desired certificate of naturalization was issued by the Home Office on 5 April of the following year and Wittgenstein took the Oath of Allegiance on 12 April 1939.

176. **LW – GEM**

[April 1938]

DEAR MOORE,

In case you see any pupils on or before Monday who might be interested in my classes, would you mind telling them that I'll have the first meeting on Monday (25ᵗʰ) at 5 p.m.? We shall meet in Taylor's rooms in Trinity.

LUDWIG WITTGENSTEIN

Briefe 243

Taylor. – James Taylor (1914–46), a Canadian reading a second undergraduate course at Trinity. He was a pupil and friend of Wittgenstein's, subsequently studied at Berkeley and was killed when just about to take up a university post in Australia. Some letters of his to Wittgenstein are preserved.

177.   **LW – GEM**

81 East Rd
Tuesday [26 April 1938]

DEAR MOORE,

I find that I shall have to be in Paris on Thursday (day after tomorrow) so my Friday discussion is off. Would you please be so kind [as] to let your pupils know this, and also that I shall lecture on Monday next, D.v.

Yours

LUDWIG WITTGENSTEIN

Wittgenstein had wired his sister, Mrs Stonborough, WISH TO SEE YOU ON YOUR RETURN JOURNEY PARIS OR SOUTHAMPTON WIRE CAMBRIDGE LUDWIG (she would be going back to Vienna from New York) and he did indeed spend 28–30 April in Paris, clearly in connexion with the family business described in comments on 179.

178.   **JMK – LW**

Dr. Ludwig Wittgenstein,   August 30th, 1938
81 East Road,
Cambridge.

MY DEAR LUDWIG

I am glad to get your letter about Alister. In truth, it is more important that he should be getting on as well as you say he is than that his Fellowship should be continued. As you know, I am rather out of touch. But my impression is that the question of the Fellowship has been practically settled and that there is no chance of its renewal. If he had obtained a University lectureship, it might make a difference. But, in the circumstances, it would be a very unusual thing to continue him further. A continuation from 3 years to 6, which is what was previously in question, is quite a different thing from the prolongation beyond 6 years.

I rather think, however, that the loss of his Fellowship will not mean that he will leave Cambridge. I am not speaking of this out of knowledge, but I think he has some resources from his parents and will continue much as before. I have, of course, scarcely seen him lately, since I have been away. I will let you know, but, as I say, my belief is that the matter is virtually settled.

This letter, an answer to a now lost one from Wittgenstein, is printed from the carbon copy retained in the Keynes Papers. The original was presumably dated from London: see notes on 175 for the reason for Keynes's absence from Cambridge.

Alister. – A. G. D. Watson (1908–82), scholar and from 1933 fellow of King's, was an Apostle and a member of both Keynes's and Wittgenstein's circles, particularly liked for his personal qualities. He was distinctly left-wing in his views. He published on "Mathematics and its foundations" in *Mind* 47 (1940) but during and after the war turned to work (for the Admiralty) on radio communication, then sonar, then oceanography.

Very glad to hear that you are near publishing. I should feel perfectly certain that the Press would take the book as soon as they asked any competent person's advice about it.

I am now vastly better. But I still have bad days. But the important point is that the depressions are not so long or so deep as they used to be. I hope to be quite a bit in residence next term.

Yours ever,

JMK

---

the Press. – Cambridge University Press, to whom Wittgenstein offered what is now part I of *Philosophical Investigations* at about this time. In Wittgenstein's notebooks (MS 117) a preface to it is dated to the same month as this letter. See G. H. v. W.'s "*The Origin and Composition of the Investigations*" in his *Wittgenstein*, pp. 120–1.

179. **LW – GEM**

81 East Rd.
Cambridge
19.10.38.

DEAR MOORE,

I am still not at all well. I am bodily very weak and shaky, and feel incapable of thinking properly about any subject. I cannot therefore start lecturing now, and I don't know whether I shall regain sufficient strength in the next 3 weeks, say, to do so. What the cause of my condition is I don't know for certain, but I believe it is the recent 'flu and the great nervous strain of the last month or two. (My people in Vienna are in great trouble.)

I wonder whether it had not better be announced in the Reporter that I can't lecture for the present and until further notice.

Would you mind letting me know what you think best, or just *do* what you think best?

Good wishes.

Yours

LUDWIG WITTGENSTEIN

M.37   Briefe 245

My people in Vienna. – See 174. During 1938 an attempt to obtain Yugoslav citizenship had even led to a brief but very alarming spell of custody in prison for two of his sisters and a nephew-in-law. (Forged passports had been passed off on them.) During the year that followed Wittgenstein was on several occasions involved in negotiations with the Nazi authorities (and indeed also within the family) which led to a compromise – essentially the conferring of mixed-race status in return for the repatriation of some part of the family property held outside Austria.

180.   **LW – GEM**

81 East Rd.
20.10.38.

DEAR MOORE,
    I had a note from Ewing today saying that I have been appointed
a member of the Mor[al] Sc[iences] faculty. Could you tell me what
exactly this means? Didn't I belong to the faculty before, and what
has changed, now I do belong to it? Do I have new duties, or new
rights? If you would let me have a line explaining this I should be
grateful. Good wishes!

                              Yours

                    LUDWIG WITTGENSTEIN

P.S. I have seen the programme of the Mor[al] Sc[iences] Cl[ub]. I
think it's *awful*.

M.38   Briefe 246

Wittgenstein's Faculty Assistant Lectureship had expired in 1935 and since then
relatively small sums had been found to pay for lectures when he gave them. (The
Board noted that nothing could be promised after 1938–9: if not elected Professor
he might have had no income at all.) His inclusion with the normal list of lecturers
re-appointed members of the faculty (a matter of some few voting and speaking
rights) had no financial implications but may have been intended to assist his
application for a certificate of naturalization (see no. 174 and comments) or more
generally to mark him as not simply one of the emigré scholars given a temporary
home at Cambridge.

Moral Sciences faculty. – The traditional name of what has, since 1969, been called
the Faculty of Philosophy at Cambridge. A. C. Ewing was secretary of the Board.

Programme of the Moral Sciences club. –It included Braithwaite, Ewing, Ryle, Wisdom
and Sir Arthur Eddington, see T. Redpath, *Ludwig Wittgenstein*, pp.78–9.

181. **LW – GEM**

[Postcard from, and with a view of, Hastings]

25 November 1938 [postmark]

DEAR MOORE,

We have been staying at 3 Pelham Crescent for ten days and have found it *very* satisfactory. I'm feeling better. I'll be back in Cambridge Monday. The weather is moderate.

Good wishes!

LUDWIG WITTGENSTEIN

Best wishes. F. Skinner

very satisfactory. – This is probably an instance of Wittgenstein's mockery of commercial and advertising language.

I'm feeling better. – See 179.

182.   **LW – GEM**

81 East Rd
Cambridge
5.12.38.

DEAR MOORE,

I shall arrange times with my students at 3 p.m. on Wednesday Jan.
18ᵗʰ in Wisdom's room at *Trinity*

I should like to see you again some time this week if you don't
mind. Would Friday at 4 or 5 be all right?

Yours

LUDWIG WITTGENSTEIN

Briefe 247

Wisdom. – See comments on 165.

183.   **LW – JMK**

81, East Rd
Cambridge
1.2.39.

DEAR KEYNES,

I went round to King's College last night with the M.S. but was
told that you had gone to London; so I took it back again and shall
keep it till Friday unless you want it before then. I want to use the
two days to look a little through the translation and perhaps correct
some of the worst mistakes. I haven't yet had time to do this (queer
as this may sound). My translator did about half of the first volume
and then had to leave for America where his father died some
weeks ago. I'll also give you the German text – in case it's any use
to you. Not that I think that it's worth your while looking at it, or
at the translation; but as you wish to see it of course you'll get it.
(Moore has read most of the German text and might possibly be
able to give some information about it.) I'm afraid there's *only one*
copy of the English in existence and only one *corrected* copy of the
German; you'll get these two copies.

Thanks ever so much for taking all this trouble (in what I believe
to be a lost cause).

Yours ever

LUDWIG

K.28   Briefe 248

M.S. – A translation into English of the beginning of the then existing version of
the Investigations. A typescript of this exists and is numbered 226 in G. H. v. W.'s
catalogue.

lost cause. – Wittgenstein had applied for the professorship of philosophy which was
to become vacant after Moore's retirement. Keynes was one of the Electors to the
Chair.

184.   **LW – GEM**

81, East Rd.
Cambridge
2.2.39.

DEAR MOORE,

I had a p[ost] c[ard] on Wednesday from Keynes saying that he would like to see the English version of my book, or whatever is ready of it. I needn't say the whole thing is absurd as he couldn't even make head or tail of it if it were translated very well. But as a matter of fact the translation is pretty awful as I saw today when I tried to go through it in order to correct it before giving it to Keynes. Though I worked quite hard on it the whole day with Smythies we only did 12 pages, because masses of it had to be altered. Tomorrow I must go on with it because tomorrow night Keynes ought to get it. So I'm afraid I shan't be able to come to you in the afternoon. I have written to Keynes that you have read the first half of my first volume and could give him some information about it; for obviously you must be able to get more out of reading the original than Keynes could get out of a bad translation *and in a hurry*. So I *hope* he'll ask you to give him your opinion. By the way,

Cf. 183., 185., 186.

first half of my first volume. – This will have been roughly the first 188 sections of *Philosophical Investigations* (in German), which Wittgenstein proposed to send also to G. H. v. W. later in 1939. It corresponds to 220 in the catalogue just mentioned. The second volume was to deal with the Philosophy of Mathematics.

Smythies. – A particularly favoured pupil of Wittgenstein's from 1937 onwards. Sometimes he was the only one allowed to take notes during Wittgenstein's lectures. Like Skinner (see 169.) he gave up the normal paths of preferment in order to live and think in a Wittgensteinian way.

please don't mention to *anyone* that I don't think highly of the translation. Rhees did his very best and the stuff is damn difficult to translate.

I hope to see you soon. Best wishes!

Yours

LUDWIG WITTGENSTEIN

M.40   *Briefe 249*

185.   **LW – JMK**

81, East Rd
Cambridge
3.2.39.

MY DEAR KEYNES,

When yesterday I began to look through the English translation of my book I saw that it was a good deal worse than I had expected, so correcting it seemed almost hopeless. But I went through it nevertheless, as far as I could get in these two days, and corrected it almost word for word, as you will see when you look at the English M.S. I couldn't do more than about 20 pages in this way. If you can read a little German I should try to read the German text. The whole thing seems even more of a farce now than it did a few days ago.

Good wishes!

Yours ever

LUDWIG

K.29   *Briefe 250*

186. **LW – JMK**

81, East Rd
Cambridge
8.2.39.

Dear Keynes,

Thanks for your kind notes. Yes, the translation is pretty awful, and yet the man who did it is an *excellent* man. Only he's not a born translator, and nothing's more difficult to translate than colloquial (non-technical) prose.

Yours ever

Ludwig

K.30   *Briefe 251*

187.   **LW – JMK**

81, East Rd
Cambridge
11.2.39.

MY DEAR KEYNES,

Thanks for the telegram, and thanks for all the trouble you've gone to. I hope to God that you haven't made a mistake. I know, it's up to me to prove that you haven't. Well, I *hope* I'll be a decent prof.

Thanks again

Yours ever

LUDWIG

K.31   *Briefe 252*

telegram. – Evidently a telegram of congratulation on the occasion of Wittgenstein's election to the professorship on 11 February 1939.

81, East Rd
Cambridge
19.4.39.

DEAR MOORE,

When I talked to you on Monday and last week I thought that I had to start lecturing today, and only yesterday I found out that I wouldn't have to lecture before next Monday. As this gives me another 5 days to collect my thoughts I feel it increases my chance of being able to lecture, and I think, therefore, it might be better if you said nothing about the matter at the Mor[al] Science[s] Board meeting. (If however you think you ought to that's different.)

Yours

LUDWIG WITTGENSTEIN

Briefe 254

189. **LW – GEM**

DEAR MOORE,

I had a letter from Malcolm the other day in which, among other things, he told me about a book which is being written about you & in which you too, so he says, are going to write an article. Forgive me, please, for saying that I read all this with a good deal of concern. I fear that you may now be walking at the edge of that cliff at the bottom of which I see lots of scientists & philosophers lying dead, Russell amongst others. My whole object in writing you was to say: *may a good spirit be with you* & keep you from getting dizzy & falling down.

I wish you'ld do me a favour. Take the poems of Conrad Ferdinand Meyer out of some library (he was a Swiss Poet in the last century) & read a poem "Die Vestalin". It's quite short. Please

Moore, who had retired from his chair at Cambridge, was at this time Visiting Professor in Princeton.

Malcolm. – Norman Malcolm (1911–90), an American pupil of Moore's and Wittgenstein's, who had at this point returned to work for his Ph.D. at Harvard.

a book. – Clearly *The Philosophy of G. E. Moore*, in the Library of Living Philosophers edited by Paul Schilpp. (Evanston and Chicago: Northwestern University, 1942). Malcolm's article is entitled, "Moore and Ordinary Language".

"Die Vestalin" ["*The Vestal* "]. – See 190. where the true title is given. The poem is printed overleaf, with a translation on p. 313

read it more than once. I hope you will like it & I hope it will tell you exactly what I want to say.

Please remember me to Mrs Moore. I wish you *lots* of good luck.

Yours

LUDWIG WITTGENSTEIN

Briefe 255

German text of the poem referred to:

Auf das Feuer mit dem goldnen Strahle
Heftet sich in tiefer Mitternacht
Schlummerlos das Auge der Vestale,
Die der Göttin ewig Licht bewacht.

Wenn sie schlummerte, wenn sie entschliefe,
Wenn erstürbe die versäumte Glut,
Eingesargt in Gruft und Grabestiefe
Würde sie, wo Staub und Moder ruht.

Eine Flamme zittert mir im Busen,
Lodert warm zu jeder Zeit und Frist,
Die, entzündet durch den Hauch der Musen,
Ihnen ein beständig Opfer ist.

Und ich hüte sie mit heil'ger Scheue,
Daß sie brenne rein und ungekränkt;
Denn ich weiß, es wird der ungetreue
Wächter lebend in die Gruft versenkt.

190.   **LW – GEM**

Trinity College
Cambridge
17.6.41

DEAR MOORE,

Thanks for your letter. Forgive if I have an entirely ungrounded fear. – I was a fool to give you a wrong title: the poem is called «Das heilige Feuer» & it begins with the words «Auf das Feuer . . .» . I'm sorry I caused you unnecessary trouble in looking for it.

Tim, as you know, has come to my classes this year & perhaps wrongly, I thought I saw an improvement in his thinking towards the end; he seemed to me to have become more lively & to get hold of the method – touch wood! (I'ld rather you kept this entirely to yourself.)

"Das heilige Feuer" / "The Sacred Fire"

(English Translation)

> On the fire with its golden rays
> In the deepest hours of the night
> Unsleepingly the Vestal bends her gaze,
> To guard the goddess's eternal light.
>
> Should she slumber, should she drop to sleep,
> Should the neglected embers fade and die,
> In coffin-vault must she be buried deep,
> Alone with dust and foul decay to lie.
>
> Within my breast another flame does shine,
> It leaps up warm at every tide and turn,
> A standing offering at the Muses' shrine:
> By their breath kindled, for them does it burn.
>
> And close I tend it, with a holy dread,
> Pure and unsullied seek its light to save,
> Knowing, that, who this wardship has betrayed,
> Will be sent down into a living grave.

Tim. – Moore's son Timothy, who was an undergraduate at Cambridge at the time.

About 6 weeks ago I suddenly – for no reason I can imagine – began to be able to write again. Quite possibly this will only last for a very short time; but it feels good while it lasts & has made a great deal of difference to me.

My very best wishes!

Yours

LUDWIG WITTGENSTEIN

Briefe 256

191.   **LW – GEM**

Trinity Coll[ege]
Friday
[October 1944]

DEAR MOORE,

I should like to tell you how glad I am that you read us a paper
yesterday. It seems to me that the most important point was the
"absurdity" of the assertion "There is a fire in this room and I don't
believe there is." To call this, as I think you did, "an absurdity for
psychological reasons" seems to me to be wrong, or *highly* misleading.
(If I ask someone "Is there a fire in the next room?" and he answers
"I believe there is" I can't say: "Don't be irrelevant. I asked you

Dated by Moore

The paper was called "Certainty" and read at the meeting of the Moral Sciences
Club on 26 October. The paper was not identical with the one with the same title
in *Philosophical Papers* (London and New York: Allen and Unwin, 1959), since the
nearest that paper comes to the point that Wittgenstein praises is to say (p. 238):
    "I feel certain that p" does not entail that p is true (although by saying that I
    feel certain that p, I do imply that p is true).
However, in the manuscript from which the publication is taken, which was
originally written in ink, evidently in 1941 for delivery as the Howison Lecture in
the University of California, there are a number of alternative words, phrases, and
whole pages in pencil, partly designed to accommodate a different form of delivery.
Thus the ink has Moore "standing" (a lecture) while the pencil tolerates 'sitting'.
Everything indicates that it was the version emended in pencil that Moore read to
the Club in 1944; and there on pp. 16–17 he says:
    "It is certain that p but I don't know that p" is certainly not self-contradictory,
    though it is a perfectly absurd thing to say of myself. The reason why it is
    absurd for me to say it of myself is the same as the reason why it would be
    absurd to say "Dogs bark but I don't know that they do" or "Dogs bark but
    I don't believe that they do". What is asserted by saying these two things is
    something which might well be true: there is no contradiction in it. But it
    would be quite absurd for anyone to say either of them, because though what
    he would be asserting would be something which might quite well be true,
    yet by asserting that dogs bark, he implies, though he does not assert and
    though it does not follow from what he does assert, in the one case that he
    knows that dogs bark and in the other that he doesn't believe they don't.

about the fire, not about your state of mind!'') But what I wanted
to say was this. Pointing out that "absurdity" which is in fact
something *similar* to a contradiction, though it isn't one, is so
important that I *hope you'll publish* your paper. By the way, don't be
shocked at my saying it's something "similar" to a contradiction.
This means roughly: it plays a similar role in logic. You have said
something about the *logic* of assertion. Viz.: It makes sense to say
"Let's suppose: p is the case and I don't believe that p is the case",

An earlier, incomplete draft of the lecture (on American paper and so presumably
also from 1941) contains a fairly long discussion of the difference between "I know
for certain that p", which is certainly contradicted by "not-p", and "I feel certain
that p", which is not contradicted by "not-p", but certainly can't be said alongside
"not-p".

That Moore published the original (ink-written) version only, if it requires
explanation, may be attributed to the implicit obligation he was under to publish
the actual Howison Lecture, unless indeed it is due to the unresolved dispute over
the present problem. In Moore's *Selected Writings* (London and New York:
Routledge, 1993), pp. 171–96, the editor Thomas Baldwin has published much of
the 1944 version – its new conclusion, for example – but not the details relevant to
us.

The change of example indicated by Wittgenstein's letter (from "Dogs bark", as
in the pencilled version, to "There is a fire in this room" – of greater actuality
perhaps in a college context – and the suggestion that the absurdity was such for
psychological reasons (of which there is no trace in this particular paper) may have
been generated by the occasion and the discussion (but see below).

The paradox itself (in one form or another) was much discussed in *Analysis*
before the war ("this old problem", Austin with slight exaggeration called it in
1940). Moore's first reference to it in print is in his own Schilpp volume (see notes
to 189.) as part of a (very effective) reply to C. L. Stevenson, but Margaret
Macdonald reported in 1936 (*Aristotelian Society Supplementary, vol* xvii, p. 30) that
Moore had pointed out in lectures that 'you cannot say without absurdity . . . "He
has toothache but I'm not sure whether he has".' There have been many discussions of the problem and its history: for recent ones see Joachim Schulte, *Experience
and Expression* pp. 135ff. and Jane Heal, *Mind*, January 1994.

Wittgenstein opened a discussion on "Moore's Paradox" in the Moral Sciences
Club on 25 October 1945 and Moore a further one entitled "P but I do not believe
P" on 29 November of the same year. According to the minutes of the former
meeting Wittgenstein maintained that the problem raised by this utterance was not
to be solved by regarding it as a piece of inconsistent behaviour; nor could it be
said simply that it must be a lie, for even if it was a lie the absurdity remained.

We should rather consider the asymmetry of psychological expressions such
as "know", "believe" and so on, i.e. the asymmetry between their use in the
first person present and in other persons and tenses or in supposition.

whereas it makes *no* sense to assert "p is the case and I don't believe that p is the case". This *assertion* has to be ruled out and *is* ruled out by "common sense", just as a contradiction is. And this just shows that logic isn't as simple as logicians think it is. In particular: that contradiction isn't the *unique* thing people think it is. It isn't the *only* logically inadmissible form and it is, under certain circumstances, admissible. And to show this seems to me the chief merit of your paper. In a word it seems to me that you've made a *discovery*, and that you should publish it.

I hope to see you privately some day.

Yours sincerely

L. WITTGENSTEIN

M.42   Briefe 257

The text (or the notes, rather) from which Moore read at the latter meeting must be what Dr Baldwin (Moore's *Selected Writings*, pp. 207ff.) has printed as "Moore's Paradox". Moore followed the line indicated in his Schilpp volume (and no doubt had done so a year earlier). The implication that when I assert p, I do not believe that not-p, is a factual matter: people do not usually lie. Perhaps this may be regarded as a psychological law, thus explaining Wittgenstein's comment in the letter we are considering.

Moore's notes reveal (op. cit. 211) that Wittgenstein had also discussed the absurdity of saying "Possibly it isn't raining, but as a matter of fact it is" (also a theme discussed in the 1930's). He was aware, therefore, that the problem did not arise simply from peculiarities of 'psychological verbs'.

I hope to see you privately some day. – The familiar intercourse of the two men had been interrupted (though it was now to be resumed) by Moore's absence in America followed by Wittgenstein's war work and his eight month's stay at Swansea, which had just ended when this letter was written.

192.   **LW – GEM**

Trin[ity] Coll[ege]
Monday
[November 1944]

DEAR MOORE,

I was sorry to hear in the Moral Sc[iences] Club on Saturday that you were resigning your Chairmanship. It wasn't really necessary to resign it as I could always have deputized for you, whenever you didn't feel inclined or able to come. – I was, as you can imagine, elected chairman, after your letter had been read to the Club. I *hope* this doesn't mean that you aren't going to come to the meetings when your health will again permit it (and some moderately interesting person reads a paper). I should very much like to see you before long if it's all right with you.

Yours

L. WITTGENSTEIN

M.43   *Briefe* 258

Dated by Moore.

Moore had been Chairman (a distinct office from that of President) since 1912, when indeed Wittgenstein had proposed him for the post (see *Young Ludwig*, p. 143). For Wittgenstein's own fluctuating relations with the Club, see 160. above: he had, however, resumed attending its meetings from at latest February 1939 and, after taking up his professorship, quite often took the chair, no doubt usually in Moore's absence, but also, naturally enough when Moore was speaking (see notes on 191.) Wittgenstein was twice (in 1941 and 1943) elected Chairman for the ensuing year. There seems to have been a certain fluidity in all the Club's formal arrangements, as is not unusual with such societies.

193. LW – GEM

Trinity Coll[ege]
Sunday
22 July 1945

DEAR MOORE,

I'm sorry I can't come on Tuesday, but I can and shall on Friday, and I'm looking forward to it. – Looking through a copy of the stuff I gave you I see that there are a good many *nasty* misprints, *i.e.* such as suggest a wrong sense. If I have an opportunity I'll correct them.

Yours

L. WITTGENSTEIN

M.45   *Briefe 259*

Dated by Moore.

stuff I gave you. – Refers presumably to a collection of remarks (*Bemerkungen*) which Wittgenstein used for the final version of the first part of the *Investigations*.

194.   **LW – GEM**

[Date unknown]

DEAR MOORE,

This copy is lousy, but it's all I can get. Probably you have the "Studien" already, then just throw these away. My favourites are No 4 and 5.

5 must be played very *crisply* and with a *serious* expression, *not* as though it were meant, in some way, to be witty.

Yours

L. WITTGENSTEIN

P.S. The marmalade is grand and not at all *bitter*.

M.44   Briefe 260

The date of this letter is not known but there is evidence that it belongs in this place in the series.

The pieces of music for the piano referred to were Schumann's "Studien für den Pedal-Flügel", op. 56. of which Mr Timothy Moore still has the score Wittgenstein procured, edited by Clara Schumann. She (who gave piano lessons to Wittgenstein's aunt) herself liked no. 4 best: Mendelssohn much admired no. 5 when she played it to him.

195.   **GEM – LW**

86, Chesterton Road,
Cambridge
Aug. 5/45

DEAR WITTGENSTEIN,

Tim has been told that he will have to work over-time every day this week, because of the harvest. This will make him probably too late and in any case too tired to play duets in the evening; so I am afraid we must put off playing Bruckner's VIIth to you till after you come back.

I thought the Schubert Quintet quite as wonderful as you had said; but I need to hear it many more times. It seemed to me very different from the Schubert works I know – to differ from them in the same direction in which the late Beethoven works differ from the early ones.

Yours ever

G. E. MOORE

Briefe 261

the harvest – Timothy Moore's war work was on the land.

until you come back. – Wittgenstein was to spend the rest of August and the whole of September in Swansea. From a letter to his sister Helene it seems that the Bruckner was played for him in March 1946.

the Schubert Quintet. – Schubert's String Quintet in C major, op. posth. 163 (=D.956), which Wittgenstein thought one of the greatest of works of music.

196.   **LW – GEM**

Trin[ity] Coll[ege]
Tuesday
[7(?) August 1945]

DEAR MOORE,

   Thanks for your letter. I'm sorry I shan't hear the Bruckner now.
Poor Tim! – I think I understand your remark about the Schubert
and I feel something I could express in the same words. I believe it's
something like this, that the Quintet has a *fantastic* kind of greatness.
Is this what you'd say? By the way, it was played *by far* better than
I had expected.
So long! Good wishes!

Yours

L. WITTGENSTEIN

M.46   *Briefe 262*

197.   **LW – GEM**

Trinity College
Cambridge
Thursday
[Probably October 1946]

DEAR MOORE,

I was sorry I was not allowed to see you today. Mrs Moore wrote to me, could I come next Tuesday, instead. Now I'm free on Tuesday afternoon and, as you know, should like to see you, not for any particular reason, but in an ordinary friendly way. But I am sure you'll understand that, – under the peculiar circumstances, – I should like to know whether what Mrs Moore wrote to me was an honest to God invitation for me to come and see you on Tuesday, or whether it was a kind of hint that I'd better not try to see you. If it was the latter, please don't hesitate to say so. I will not be hurt *in the slightest*, for I know that queer things happen in this world. It's one of the few things I've really learnt in my life. So please, if that's how it is, just write on a p[ost] c[ard] something like "Don't come". I enclose a card in case you haven't got one. I'll understand everything. Good luck and good wishes!

Yours

LUDWIG WITTGENSTEIN

M.47   Briefe 263

not allowed to see you. – This seems to refer to an occasion on which Mrs Moore turned Wittgenstein away at the door, on the grounds that the doctors did not want Moore (who had had a stroke) to excite himself in discussion. Norman Malcolm, *Memoir*, pp. 56–7 has a similar story about a time-limit set on visits: he describes how Wittgenstein was rather displeased and felt that Moore should be allowed "to die with his boots on", if it so turned out. Mrs Moore, in conversation, confirmed an actual exclusion on one occasion, maintaining, however, that Moore himself did not feel equal to the visit.

198.   **LW – GEM**

Trin[ity] Coll[ege]
Camb[ridge]
14.11.46.

DEAR MOORE,

I don't believe for a moment that you'll want to come to the Moral Sc[iences] Club tonight (I'm giving a talk, roughly, on what I believe philosophy is, or what the method of philosophy is) – but I want to say that if you *should* turn up for the paper, or the discussion, the club, and particularly I, would be *honoured*.

Yours sincerely

L. WITTGENSTEIN

M.49   Briefe 265

---

a talk on . . . what the method of philosophy is. – The minutes of the meeting show that this was a reply to the talk, entitled "Methods in Philosophy", given on 26 October by Dr K. R. Popper (Sir Karl, 1902–94), which occasioned much controversy then, and indeed since. See Popper's "Intellectual Autobiography" in *The Philosophy of Karl Popper*, in the Library of Living Philosophers, ed. Paul Schilpp (LaSalle, IL 1974), pp. 97–9 and I. Grattan-Guinness, in *russell* 12.1 (1992) pp. 6–18. According to the minutes, Wittgenstein's talk made use of a favourite quotation from Hertz illustrating how philosophy might proceed not by giving explicit answers but by showing that the question was a muddled one.

199.   **LW – GEM**

Trinity College
Cambridge
3.12.46.

DEAR MOORE,

As far as I can see now I will be in London on Thursday afternoon
and unable to see you. Would it be all right if I called on you in case
I were here after all? If you're otherwise engaged then, it doesn't
matter and I'll just go again. If, as is most likely, I shan't be back on
Thursday afternoon, could I see you Thursday week? – Price at the
last Mor[al] Sc[iences] Cl[ub] meeting was *by far* better than Austin
had been. Price was willing to discuss important points. Unfortunately (I believe) Russell was there and most disagreeable. Glib and
superficial, though, as always, *astonishingly* quick. I left at about

Price. – H. H. Price (1899–1984) Wykeham Professor of Logic in the University of
Oxford. The minutes of the club show that on 29 November 1946, with Wittgenstein in the chair, Price spoke on "Universals and Resemblances", which is also the
title of the first chapter of his *Thinking and Experience* (London: Hutchinson, 1953).

Austin. – J. L. Austin (1911–60) at this time Fellow of Magdalen College, later
White's Professor of Moral Philosophy at the University of Oxford. In his case the
minutes record a paper on "Nondescription" delivered on 31 October 1946, also
with Wittgenstein in the chair. They make it clear that Austin's point of departure
was the occurrence of ceremonial or contractual uses of verbs in the first person ('I
name this ship the Queen Elizabeth'', and the like), where the temptation to regard
the utterance as true or false should (according to Austin) be resisted. The minutes
record that "A not very successful attempt was made to separate philosophical from
linguistic considerations", and any who remember Austin will believe this to be
accurate. Austin developed these ideas later in "Performative Utterances" (reprinted in his *Philosophical Papers*, Oxford, 1961) and in *How to Do Things with
Words* (Oxford, 1962). (These publications were both posthumous.)

10.30 and felt exceedingly happy when I was out in the street and away from the atmosphere of the M[oral] Sc[iences] Cl[ub].

So long!

Yours

L. WITTGENSTEIN

M.51   *Briefe 267*

200.   **LW – GEM**

[Trinity College, Cambridge]

Wednesday
5.2.47

DEAR MOORE,

I'm having a cold now, or rather, a sore throat. It isn't bad at all
but I very much want to get rid of it by the end of the week and I
think I'd better stay at home. So I shan't see you tomorrow. If
I don't hear from you, and nothing unexpected happens, I'll come
Thursday next week.

I hope you're well again and keeping that way in spite of this bl. –
weather.

So long!

LUDWIG WITTGENSTEIN

Briefe 268

---

weather. – The winter of 1946–7 was thought exceptionally cold; and England
shared a fuel crisis with much of Europe.

201. **LW – GEM**

[Trinity College, Cambridge]
18.2.47.

DEAR MOORE,

I think I'd better not come and see you this Thursday. I'm in good health, but teaching philosophy almost every day seems to exhaust me a good deal and it might be better if I avoid a serious talk on Thursday. You know, of course, I'd *like* to come, for I enjoy talking with you, and I don't really know if it's worth saving my strength for teaching people most of whom can't learn anything anyway. If you let me I'll come to you next week or the week after.

Yours ever

LUDWIG WITTGENSTEIN

M.53   *Briefe 269*

202.   **LW – GEM**

> [Trinity College, Cambridge]
> Wednesday
> [1947]

DEAR MOORE,

I'm sorry to say, I'm in bed again; this time with something that looks like a gastric 'flu. So tomorrow's off again. An evil star or something seems to preside over our meetings.

I hope to see you before long, star or no star.

> Yours
>
> LUDWIG WITTGENSTEIN

Briefe 270

203. **LW – GEM**

[Trinity College, Cambridge]
Sunday
[November 1947]

DEAR MOORE,

This is only to say that I've found the missing M.S.S. Miss Anscombe had not just *one* copy, as I believed, and I found part of a M.S. in my own possession, and together and with the bit you have the three copies are complete. I needn't say I'm glad.

I also wish to say that I enjoyed VERY much seeing you these last 5 weeks. I think, in a way, more than I used to. I wish you lots of good luck!

Yours

L. WITTGENSTEIN

P.S. I shall give Drury your good wishes. You didn't actually tell me to, but I know it's all right with you.

M.55   Briefe 271

dated by Moore

In October 1947 Wittgenstein had resigned the professorship. The resignation became effective from 31 December. The Michaelmas Term he spent at Cambridge on a ("sabbatical") leave of absence.

M.S.S. – Refers to the typescript of the first part of the *Investigations*.

Miss Anscombe.– G. E. M. Anscombe, at the time a pupil, later a literary heir, editor, and translator of Wittgenstein's and also one of his successors as Professor of Philosophy at Cambridge.

Drury.– See 168.

204. **LW – GEM**

Ross's Hotel
Parkgate Street
Dublin, Eire
16.12.48.

DEAR MOORE,

The enclosed card is to wish you as much happiness and as little unhappiness as possible. But I'm also writing you this note: for two reasons. I had a letter and Christmas card from Malcolm, and he says that he hasn't yet heard from you. When I read this I thought of your telling me that you'd write to him; that was in October in your room when I mentioned the fact that he had complained to me about not hearing from you. And at the same time I thought of something else you promised me then, i.e., putting it into your will that my typescripts, now in your possession, should, after your death, go to my executors, or to me if I should then be alive. – This letter is to remind you of both matters, in case you have forgotten. You are in a position to give a *great* deal of pleasure (in the first case) and to avert a *great* deal of distress (in the second) by comparatively simple means.

Rhees is coming here for 10 days next week. I am well and working pretty hard. May you be well, too!

Malcolm. – Norman Malcolm, an American pupil of both Moore and Wittgenstein, gave an account of his friendship with the latter in his *Memoir.*

typescripts. – At the death of Wittgenstein in 1951 Moore had in his possession only the typescript of the *Philosophische Bemerkungen* which Wittgenstein had given him some time in the 1930s. Moore shortly after gave it to Wittgenstein's Literary Executors.

Forgive me this lengthy letter.

Yours

LUDWIG WITTGENSTEIN

P.S. I know it's a lot to ask it – but if you could write me a line I'd be *very* glad. The above address is my address.

M.56   *Briefe 272*

205.   **LW – GEM**

Ross's Hotel
Parkgate Street
Dublin
31.12.48.

DEAR MOORE,

Thanks for your letter and for having fulfilled both promises. My executors are *Rhees* and *Burnaby of Trinity*.
I wish you all good luck!

Yours

L. WITTGENSTEIN

Rhees leaves me tomorrow. He sends his love and respects, and so does Drury. I can still work fairly well though not as I did a month ago.

M.57   *Briefe 273*

Burnaby. – The Rev. John Burnaby (1891–1978), Fellow of Trinity College, lecturer and later Regius Professor of Divinity at Cambridge.

In his final will, dated Oxford, 29 January 1951, Wittgenstein appointed Rhees alone as his executor and Anscombe, Rhees and von Wright as his Literary Executors.

List of Works Cited

A. Works Cited in the Letters

Bibliographical details for works cited in the Letters themselves are given only when both relevant and clearly implied.

Bosanquet, B. 1911: *Logic* (2nd edition), Oxford: Clarendon Press.

Dostoevsky, F., *The Brothers Karamazov*.

Frege, Gottlob I. 1893; II. 1903: *Grundgesetze der Arithmetik*, Jena: H. Pohle.

Goethe, J. W. von, *Faust, Iphigenie*.

James, William, 1902 etc.: *Varieties of Religious Experience*, London: Longman Green.

Johnson, W. E., part i 1921, ii 1922, iii 1924: *Logic*, Cambridge: Cambridge University Press.

Keynes, J.M. 1919: *The Economic Consequences of the Peace*, London: Macmillan.

—— 1921; *A Revision of the Treaty*, London: Macmillan.

—— 1921; *A Treatise on Probability*, London: Macmillan.

—— 1923: *A Tract on Monetary Reform*, London: Macmillan.

—— 1925: *A Short View of Russia*, London, L.& V Woolf.

Lessing, Gotthold Ephraim, *Religiöse Streitschriften*.

Lichtenberg, B. C. 1879: *Ausgewählte Schriften* (ed. Eugen Reichel) Leipzig: Philipp Reclam.

Meyer, Conrad Ferdinand, *Gedichte*, "Das heilige Feuer".

Moore, G. E. 1903: *Principia Ethica*, Cambridge: Cambridge University Press.

— — 1906: "On the Nature and Reality of the Objects of Perception", in *Proceedings of the Aristotelian Society*, n.s. vol. 6, pp. 68–127.

Mörike, Eduard, *Gedichte*.

Ogden, C. K. (with I. A. Richards) 1st edition 1923: *The Meaning of Meaning*, London: Kegan Paul.

Ramsey, F.P. 1925: "The Foundations of Mathematics" in *Proceedings of the London Mathematical Society*, series 2, vol. 125, part 5, pp. 338–84.

Ritchie, A. D. 1923: *Scientific Method*, London: Kegan Paul.

[Russell, Elizabeth (Beauchamp) Countess] 1899 etc.: *Elizabeth and her German Garden*, London: Macmillan.

Russell, Bertrand 1st edition 1910: *Philosophical Essays*, London: Longman Green.

— — 1st edition 1914: *Our Knowledge of the External World*, London: Allen & Unwin, Chicago: Open Court.

— — 1st edition 1918: *Mysticism and Logic*, London: Longman Green.

— — 1st edition 1919: *Introduction to Mathematical Philosophy*, London: Allen & Unwin.

— — 1923: *The A. B. C. of Atoms*, London: Kegan Paul.

— — (with Dora Russell) 1923: *The Prospects of Industrial Civilization*, London: Allen & Unwin.

— — (with A. N. Whitehead) *I* 1910; *II* 1912, *III* 1913: *Principia Mathematica*, Cambridge: Cambridge University Press.

Schlick, Moritz, 1st edition 1918, 2nd edition 1925: *Allgemeine Erkenntnislehre*, Berlin: Springer.

Tolstoy, L., *Chadschi Murad (Hadji Murat)*.

Weininger, Otto, 1906 etc: *Sex and Character*, London: Heinemann.

Wittgenstein, Ludwig 1922, 1931: *Tractatus Logico-Philosophicus*, London: Kegan Paul, Routledge & Kegan Paul.

B. Works Cited in the Notes

Ambrose A. and M. Lazerowitz (eds) 1972: *Ludwig Wittgenstein: Philosophy and Language*, London.

Austin, J. L. 1961: *Philosophical Papers*, Oxford: Oxford University Press.

—— 1962: *How to Do Things with Words*, Oxford; Oxford University Press.

Clark, R. 1975: *Life of Bertrand Russell*. London: Cape and Weidenfeld & Nicolson.

Copi I. M. and R. M. Beard (eds) 1966: *Essays on Wittgenstein's Tractatus*. London: Routledge & Kegan Paul, New York: Macmillan.

Engelmann, P. 1967: *Letters from Ludwig Wittgenstein with a Memoir*, ed. by B. F. McGuinness. Oxford: Basil Blackwell.

Frege, Gottlob 1984: *Collected Papers*, Oxford: Blackwell.

Harrod, R. F. 1951: *The Life of John Maynard Keynes*. London: Macmillan.

Hilmy, S. 1987: *The Later Wittgenstein*. Oxford: Basil Blackwell.

Kenny, A. J. P. 1984: *The Legacy of Wittgenstein*. Oxford and New York: Blackwell.

Levy, P. 1979: *Moore*, London: Weidenfeld & Nicolson.

Malcolm, N. 1984: *Memoir*, Oxford: Oxford University Press.

McGuinness, B. F. 1990: *Young Ludwig*. London: Duckworth, Berkeley, CA: University of California Press, and London: Penguin Books, 1990

Menger, K. 1994: *Reminiscences of the Vienna Circle*. Dordrecht: Reidel.

Moore, G. E. 1993: *Selected Writings*, ed. T. Baldwin, London: Routledge.

[Pinsent, D. H.] 1991: *A Portrait of Wittgenstein as a Young Man, From the Diary of David Hume Pinsent 1912–1914*. Ed. by G. H. von Wright. With an introduction by Anne Pinsent Keynes. Oxford: Basil Blackwell.

Price, H. H. 1953: *Thinking and Experience*, London: Hutchinson.

Ramsey, F. P. 1931: *The Foundations of Mathematics*, ed. R. B. Braithwaite, London: Kegan Paul.

—— 1978, *Foundations*, ed. D. H. Mellor, London: Routledge.

—— 1988: *Collected Papers* ed. D. H. Mellor, Cambridge: Cambridge University Press.

Redpath, Theodore 1990: *Ludwig Wittgenstein, A Student's Memoir*, London: Duckworth.

Rhees R. 1981: *L. Wittgenstein, Personal Recollections*. Oxford: Basil Blackwell.

Russell B. 1968: *Autobiography*. London: Allen & Unwin.

Russell's Collected Papers: Theory of Knowledge, ed. Elizabeth Ramsden Eames and Kenneth Blackwell, London, Boston, and Sydney: George Allen & Unwin, 1984

Ryan A. 1988: *Russell, A Political Life*. London: Allen Lane.

Schilpp P. A. (ed.) 1942: *The Philosophy of G. E. Moore*, in the Library of Living Philosophers. Evanston and Chicago: Northwestern University.

Schilpp P. A. (ed.) 1974: *The Philosophy of Karl Popper*, in the Library of Living Philosophers, LaSalle IL: Open Court.

Schulte J. 1993: *Experience and Expression*. Oxford: Oxford University Press.

Skidelsky, R. vol. 1, 1983; vol 2 1992: *John Maynard Keynes*. London: Macmillan.

Somavilla, Ilse, Anton Unterkircher and Christian Paul Berger (eds) 1994: *Ludwig Hänsel–Ludwig Wittgenstein, Eine Freundschaft*, Innsbruck: Haymon.

von Wright, G. H. 1982: *Wittgenstein*. Oxford: Basil Blackwell.

Waismann, F. 1979: *Wittgenstein and the Vienna Circle*. Oxford: Basil Blackwell.

Wijdeveld P. 1994: *Ludwig Wittgenstein, Architect*. London: Thames and Hudson.

Wittgenstein, Ludwig 1953: *Philosophical Investigations*, ed. G. E. M. Anscombe and R. Rhees, Oxford: Blackwell.

—— 1958: *The Blue and Brown Books*, ed. R. Rhees, Oxford: Blackwell.

Wittgenstein, Ludwig 1964: *Philosophische Bemerkungen*, ed. R. Rhees, Oxford: Blackwell.

—— 1970: "Eine philosophische Betrachtung", ed. R. Rhees, in *Schriften 5*, Frankfurt: Suhrkamp.

—— 1993: *Philosophical Occasions*, ed. James C. Klagge and Alfred Nordmann, Indianapolis and Cambridge: Hackett

—— 1969: *Briefe an Ludwig von Ficker*, ed. G. H. von Wright in co-operation with W. Methlagl, Salzburg: Otto Müller Verlag.

—— 1st edition 1961, 2nd edition 1979: *Notebooks 1914–1916*. Oxford: Basil Blackwell.

—— 1971: *Prototractatus*, ed. B. F. McGuinness, T. Nyberg, and G. H. von Wright, London: Routledge.

Index of Letters

FORMAT: no./description/date/previous publication information*

1/LW–BR/ [probably June 1912]/R.1/Briefe 1
2/LW–BR/22.6.12/R.2/Briefe 2
3/LW–BR/1.7.12/R.3/Briefe 3
4/LW–BR/ [Summer 1912]/R.4/Briefe 4
5/LW–BR/16.8.12/R.5/Briefe 5
6/LW–BR/ [Summer 1912]R.6/Briefe 7
7/LW–BR/26.12.12/R.7/Briefe 8
8/LW–JMK/3.1.13/K.1/Briefe 9
9/LW–BR/6.1.13/R.8/Briefe 10
10/LW–BR/Jan. 1913/R.9/Briefe 11
11/LW–BR/21.1.13/R.10/Briefe 12
12/LW–JMK/ [1913] /Briefe 13
13/LW–BR/25.3.13/R.11/Briefe 14

* R.n., K.n., M.n., Briefe n indicate the number assigned in *Letters to Russell, Keynes and Moore* and *Briefe* respectively. Six letters from Ramsey and one from Keynes were published in L. Wittgenstein, *Letters to C. K. Ogden* (Oxford: Blackwell and London: Routledge, 1975) as is here indicated by Ogden. p. n. The letters from and to Russell previously published in the periodical *russell* (see "Introduction" above) are indicated by "New Corr." followed by the reference there assigned ("BR–LW1" or the like).

86/BR–LW/19.3.1920/New Corr. BR–LW7
87/LW–BR/9.4.1920/R.46/Briefe 127
88/LW–BR/6.5.1920/R.47/Briefe 129
89/BR–LW/1.7.1920/New Corr. BR–LW18
90/LW–BR/7.7.1920/R.48/Briefe 133
91/LW–BR/10.7.1920/R.49/Briefe 134
92/LW–BR/6.8.1920/R.50/Briefe 136
93/LW–BR/20.9.1920/R.51/Briefe 138
94/LW–BR/20.9.1920/New Corr. BR–LW19
95/BR–LW/3.6.1921/New Corr. BR–LW20
96/LW–BR/23.10.1921/R.52/Briefe 147
97/BR–LW/5.11.1921/New Corr. BR–LW21
98/LW–BR/28.11.1921/R.53/Briefe 148
99/BR–LW/24.12.1921/New Corr. BR–LW22
100/BR–LW/7.2.1922/New Corr. BR–LW23
101/LW–BR/ [1922] /New Corr. BR–LW24
102/BR–LW/ [before 25.7.1922] /New Corr. 25 BR–LW
103/LW–BR/ [Nov/Dec 1922] /New Corr. 26 BR–LW
104/LW–BR/7.4.1923/New Corr. BR–LW27
105/LW–JMK/ [1923) /K10/Briefe 154
106/LW–FPR/ [1923]
107/FPR–LW/15.10.1923/ Ogden p. 79
108/FPR–LW/11.11.1923/ Ogden p. 80
109/FPR–LW/27.12.1923/ Ogden p. 82
110/FPR–LW/20.2.1924/ Ogden p. 83
111/FPR–JMK/24.3.1924/ Ogden p. 117
112/JMk-LW/29.3.1924/Ogden p. 116
113FPR–LW/ [Spring 1924] /Briefe 164
114/FPR–LW/ [Spring 1924] /Briefe 165
115/LW–JMK/4.7.1924/K.11/Briefe 166
116/FPR–LW/15.9.1924/*Ogden* p. 86
117/FPR–LW/22.[9].1924/Briefe 168
118/JMK–LW/27.12.1924/Briefe 169
119/LW–JMK/8.7.1925/Briefe 176/K12
120/LW–JMK/ [July/Aug. 1925] /K.13/Briefe 177
121/LW–JMK/7.8.1925/K.14/Briefe 178

343

Index